Contemporary

Scrimshaw

By Eva Halat

Schiffer Publishing Ltd
4880 Lower Valley Road, Atglen, Pa 19310

Other Schiffer Books on Related Subjects

Scrimshaw Techniques. Jim Stevens. ISBN: 9780764328312. $29.95
Advanced Scrimshaw Techniques. Jim Stevens. ISBN: 9780764330179. $14.99
Nautical Antiques. W.D. Ball. ISBN: 0887406025. $39.95
Scrimshaw: The Whaler's Legacy. Martha Lawrence. ISBN: 0887404553. $69.95

Schiffer Books are available at special discounts for bulk purchases for sales promotions or premiums. Special editions, including personalized covers, corporate imprints, and excerpts can be created in large quantities for special needs. For more information contact the publisher:

Published by Schiffer Publishing Ltd.
4880 Lower Valley Road
Atglen, PA 19310
Phone: (610) 593-1777; Fax: (610) 593-2002
E-mail: Info@schifferbooks.com

For the largest selection of fine reference books on this and related subjects, please visit our web site at **www.schifferbooks.com**
We are always looking for people to write books on new and related subjects. If you have an idea for a book please contact us at the above address.

This book may be purchased from the publisher.
Include $5.00 for shipping.
Please try your bookstore first.
You may write for a free catalog.

In Europe, Schiffer books are distributed by
Bushwood Books
6 Marksbury Ave.
Kew Gardens
Surrey TW9 4JF England
Phone: 44 (0) 20 8392-8585; Fax: 44 (0) 20 8392-9876
E-mail: info@bushwoodbooks.co.uk
Website: www.bushwoodbooks.co.uk
Free postage in the U.K., Europe; air mail at cost.

Library of Congress Control Number: 2008930145

Type set in Dauphin/ITC Eras

ISBN: 978-0-7643-3049-0
Printed in China

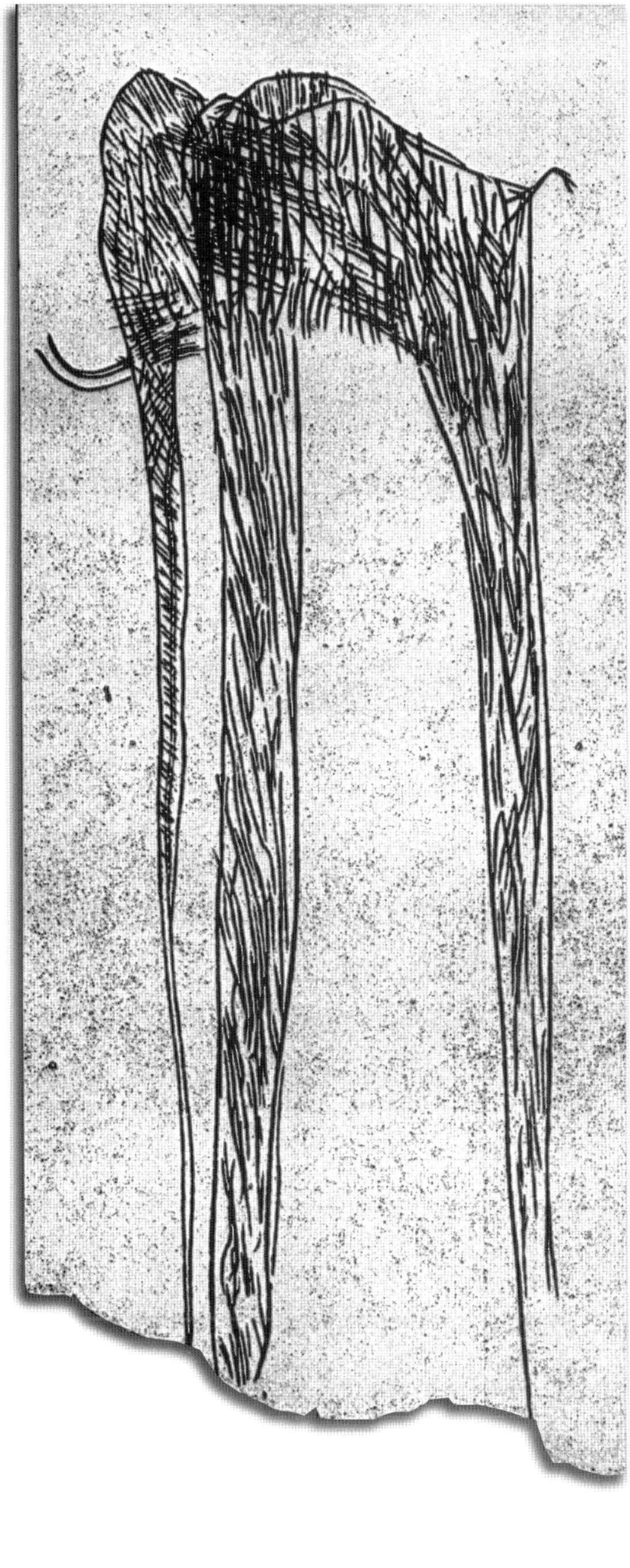

This tracing [1:1] of a mammoth figure engraved on a mammoth tusk is one of the first "scrimshaws" by our ancestors. The tusk was discovered in 1965 near the village of Bereliyach in Yakutsk, northern Russia.
Based on comparisons with other discoveries in the region and radiocarbon dating, it has an estimated age of 12,240 years.
The mammoth was probably scratched into the ivory with a piece of flint. The surface of the ivory is brownish-yellow, and the scratches have been colored a deep, dark brown by the high iron oxide content of the local water.
This is the second known discovery of an engraved Stone Age figure of a mammoth in Russia, and also the first Stone Age discovery known from above the Arctic Circle.

Source: O.N. Bader, V.E. Flint: Engraving on a mammoth tusk from Berelyach, in: The Mammoth Fauna of the Russian Plain and East Siberia, published by the Zoological Institute 72, Leningrad, 1977. p. 68-72.

I wish to express my heartfelt thanks to all those who have helped make this book a success. Horst Heinle, Stefan Steigerwald, Wolf Borger, Werner Schirmer, Ken Fredericks, and Bob Hergert for making information and materials available to me; Michael Staubach for providing contacts and for making it possible to obtain photographs of pieces from his scrimshaw collection; Christiane Koerner and Sergej Winter for their willingness to prepare a special illustration and for their German copy editing; Helmut Voss for the wonderful microscopes; Robert Dohrenwend for the helpful information on powderhorns and the translation; all the artists for permission to publish their works; Angelika, who at the beginning, when the book was more an idea than a reality, wanted to publish it right away; my husband Eddy, who was so patient and understanding while I sat for months late at night in front of the computer; and not least of all those who have patiently waited for this long anticipated book.

Contemporary Scrimshaw

Eva Halat

Preface

"I'll write a book about scrimshaw!"
At some point I was no longer able to get this idea out of my mind. Whenever I presented scrimshaw techniques at exhibitions and knife shows, I was often asked about introductory literature, and this strengthened my resolve to put my ideas on paper.

I was introduced to scrimshaw in 1993, when I first saw this marvelous art at a knife maker's convention. I was fascinated by the detailed, precise, delicate work and startled by the high prices. Like a lot of people, I had no idea how much time and effort it took to produce such scrimshaw. At the time, I could see little difference between good and not so good scrimshaw, but I was certain that I had to try it at least once. I had been working as an artist for my whole life, and this technique was a new challenge to me.

I ordered a scrimshaw kit from the United States, and after my first efforts on a polymer, an ivory-colored plastic, were behind me, I was able to work on my first knife. I had to fit a scene with an Indian shooting a bow, a flying eagle, and a bear onto an inlay about two by three centimeters. By this time, I knew that there were a number of ways to work the material. I had begun with a scalpel, so this time I tried my luck with the burin that came with the kit. I now know that this tool was much too unstable and quite useless for good scrimshaw work, but it probably wouldn't have made any difference if I'd used a better tool. When I look back and compare what I did then with what I am doing now, it shows that you shouldn't let your very first attempts discourage you.

Luckily and quite by accident, I got my hands on a fantastic book by Bob Engnath, "The Second Scrimshaw Connection" (1985). This is virtually a Bible of scrimshaw. In it, Bob Engnath provides a great deal of valuable information about scrimshaw in the United States and Hawaii. He devotes a great deal of space to a long instructional chapter, and the book has an enormous number of black-and-white illustrations of scrimshaw. Without "censorship", Bob included almost everyone who considered himself a scrimshander and wanted his work presented. This let me train my eyes to detect the difference between good and bad scrimshaw. Unfortunately, this book is out of print.

Step by step, I learned, especially from talking with my colleagues and listening to knife makers, who generally have a good eye for scrimshaw. I was constantly aware that there was really very little information available in print on contemporary scrimshaw. So I wrote a book about scrimshaw.

Naturally it was more work than I had thought at first. When I started, it was only going to be a small book showing people how to do scrimshaw, but then I came to feel that scrimshaw's interesting history and other important aspects also belonged in the book. These things give the scrimshander a deeper respect for his work and the observer a different feeling for the art. Besides, it is very useful to study works by various artists. These ideas led to the development of the fantastic gallery section.

The scrimshaw artists whose works are presented in this book were given considerable freedom to determine the amount of detail to be included in the descriptions of their careers and techniques. As a result, the biographies vary a lot in length. I found that most scrimshanders already had artistic training or experience before they began to do scrimshaw. And in addition, being an artist myself, I believe that getting an insight into the sometimes unusual career of an artist, enables one to relate a little better to his art.

The instructional section is primarily for the beginner, but the experienced scrimshander may also find a number of interesting new ideas and tips there, since each scrimshander has his own way of doing things and his own individual style.

I hope that you will find the contents enjoyable both to read and to look at.

Eva Halat

Scrimshaw by Eva Halat
on mammoth ivory, ca. 1:1

Photo by Halat

Foreword

Germany, 1983. A conversation at a knife show.
"I'd like to get some scrimshaw done on the handle of this knife."
Short silence.
"You'd like what?"
"Scrimshaw! I saw something like that last year in America, in a knife collector's catalog. It was a hunting knife with an ivory handle, beautifully decorated with an Indian head. It was almost as detailed as a photograph. And something like that is what I want."
"But how do they do it? How do you do scrimshaw?"
"Well, as far as I know, sailors and whalers in the old days used to put artistic decorations on whale teeth and bones, by cutting and engraving them with simple needles and knives. They rubbed soot into the engravings to make them visible. In the 20th century, artists refined these old techniques, and now modern scrimshaw is capable of producing knife handles like the one I saw."
Once again there was a long silence. I thought about it for a minute.
"Okay. I'll get some photos and books on this rare art, and I'll learn how to do it."

And I started off, devoting myself to a search for scrimshaw, a search that rapidly became a passion and that has now taken a good twenty years of my life.
"Scrimshaw" has a great feeling of mystery. It's a word that catches your imagination, and people want to know more about it. So, what is "scrimshaw"?

Scrimshaw is associated with adventure in foreign lands and with the romance of the sea. Sometimes it evokes a certain nostalgia. Wonder and pride are part of it, but there is also something there that is basic to our humanity. It speaks to something deep in our souls. If you look it up in the dictionary, you will find; "Scrimshaw. v. i. & t. Naut. To do any neat small mechanical job; specif. to ornament, as shells, ivory, etc. by engraving." But that's not really all it is. There is a lot more to it. Scrimshaw isn't just an artistic handicraft. It is redolent of sorcery and magic. It binds and dazzles, bringing both artist and observer under its spell.

But what is its hidden secret? Is it in the process of making it? Is it the eternal conflict between "hunter and hunted" that it expresses?

Prehistoric shaman-artists first gave it shape on the teeth, horns, and bones of animals killed in the hunt. They drew the animals, immersing themselves in the souls of their prey. In the process, the artist and the animal merged and became one. The pictures took strength to draw and gave strength back to the artist. The animal "lived" again in the picture and in the mind of the person seeing it. This closed an eternal circle, art as cult, rooted deeply in man's past.

In her book, *Contemporary Scrimshaw*, the artist Eva Halat has managed to find the trail to the secrets of this art and has cast light on some of its many aspects. She leads you through its history and technique to contemporary artists presented in an impressive selection of photographs. And it is here that the reader will discover the fascination and magic of scrimshaw.

Now, I want to invite you to go on a journey through this wonderful book and into the fascinating world of scrimshaw waiting for your discovery.

Sincerely,
Richard "Ritchi" Maier

Scrimshaw on mammoth ivory by "Ritchi" Maier. ca. 1:1

Contents

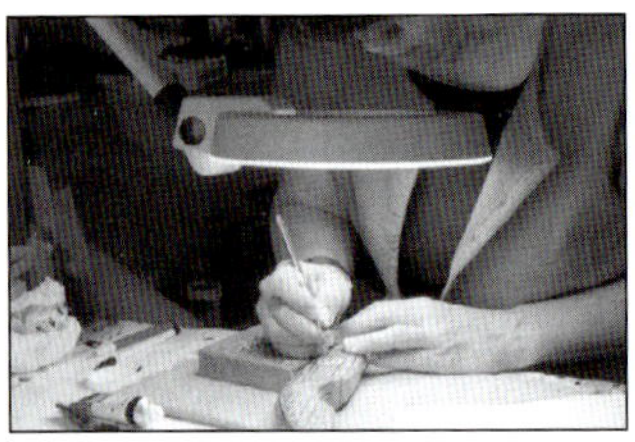

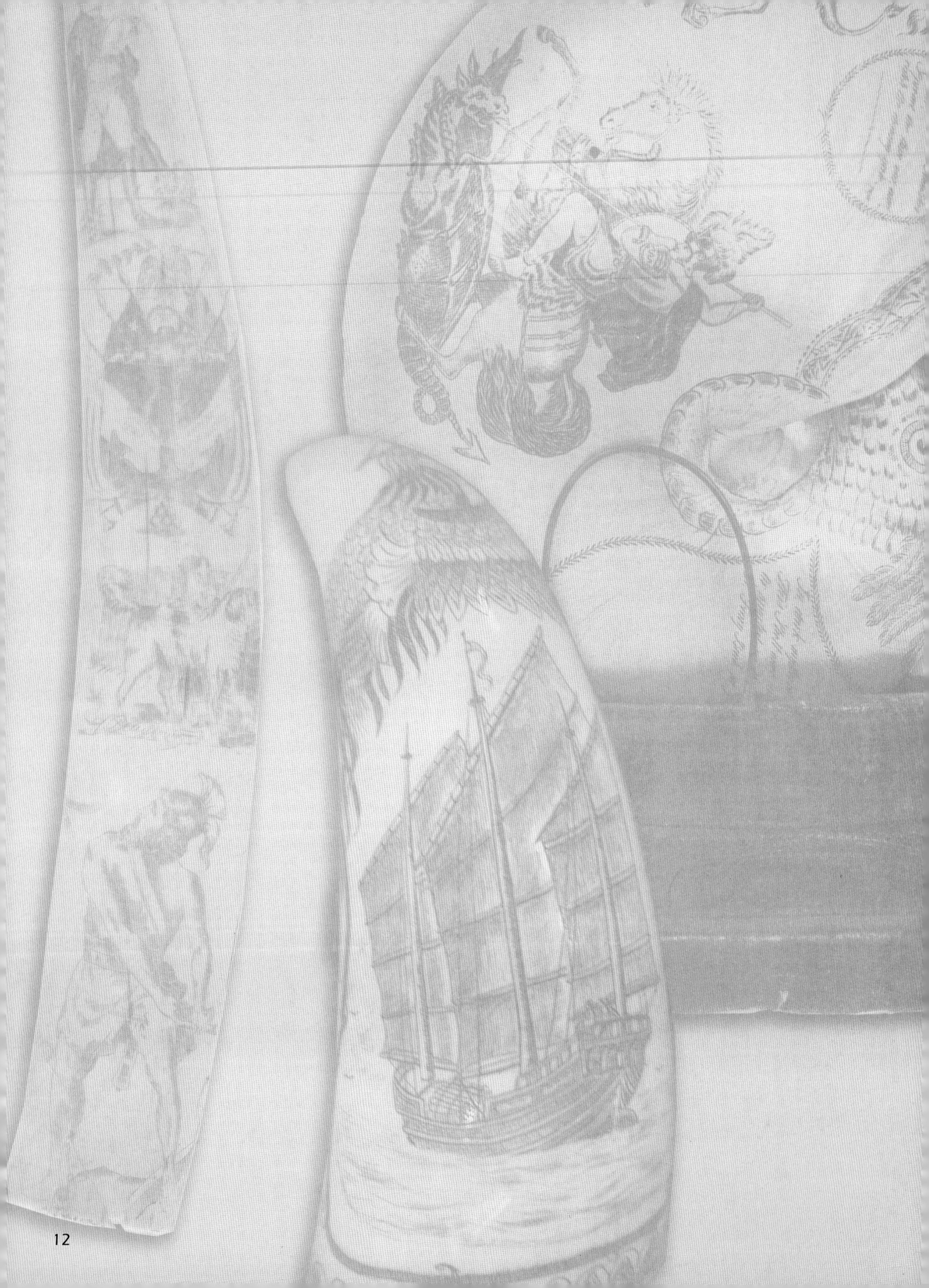

History

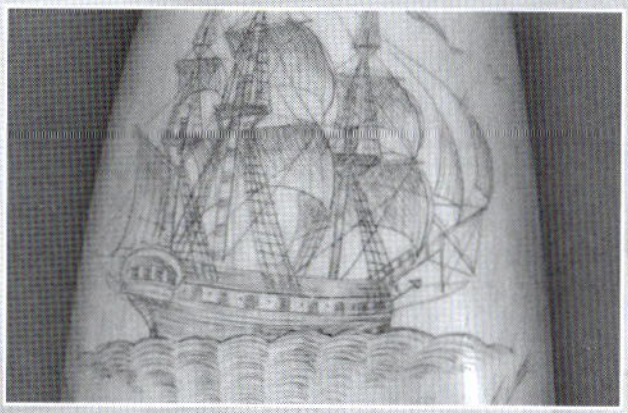

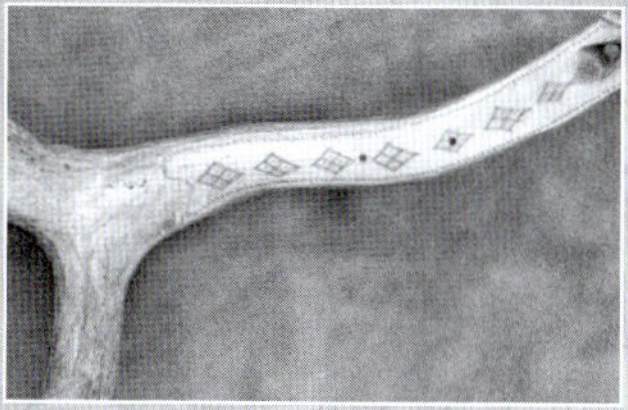

ebone
For people who appreciate scrimshaw
1988
Published by Rappahannock Design, Inc.
HIGHLIGHTS

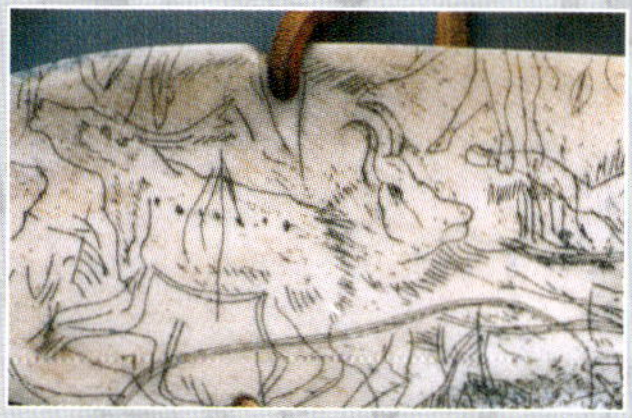

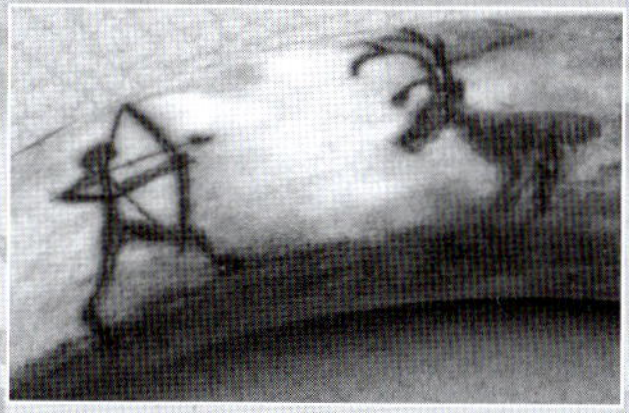

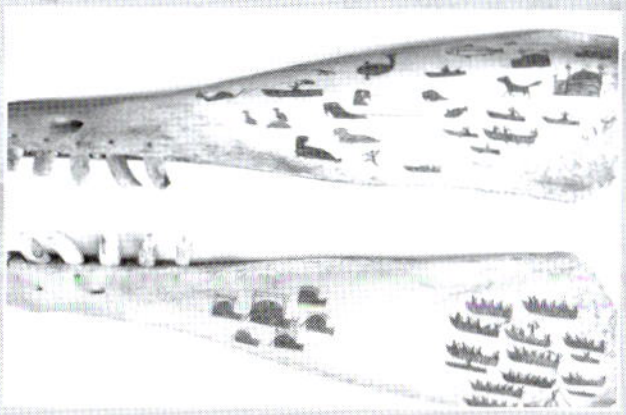

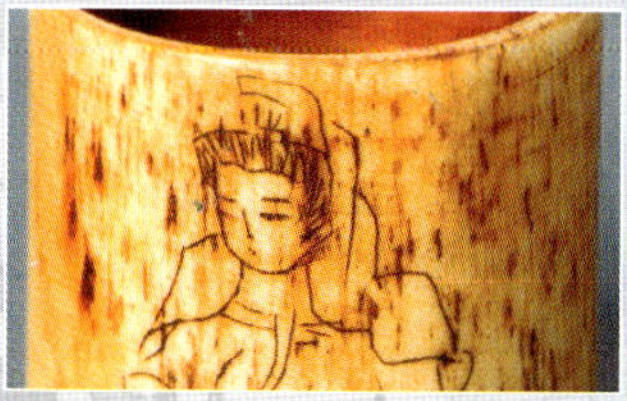

Scrimshaw techniques create miniature works of art on expensive natural material, art with a uniquely warm aura. Extraordinary patience and love go into each piece. The dexterity and gifts of the artist combined with the slow-growing material, a material that may be a marvelous antique or fossil treasure itself, gives the finished work soul and value that are easily felt but very hard to price.

In our fast-moving world, time seems to stand still when we pause to quietly examine such a gem, reflecting on the age of a mammoth tooth and the vast time it was entombed in ice, or on the life of the animal that slowly grew the ivory we use. We now know that these natural resources are not renewable in any quantity and that we have to protect the few animals that supply the ivory we use today. The tiny supply of available fossil ivory already demands very high prices. Anyone who works with such materials must be aware of their value and use them with proper respect.

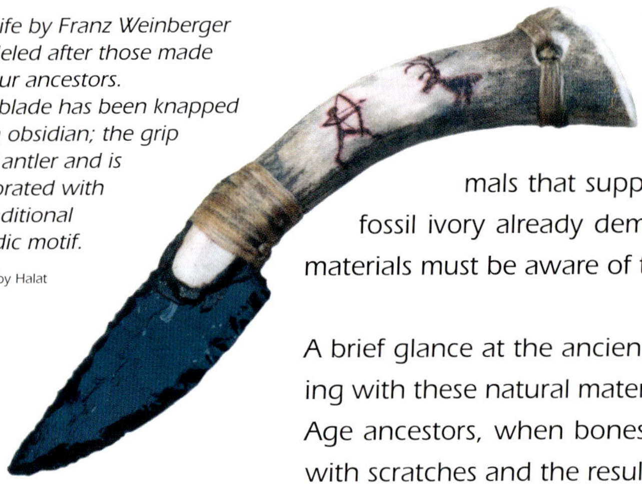

A knife by Franz Weinberger modeled after those made by our ancestors. The blade has been knapped from obsidian; the grip is of antler and is decorated with a traditional Nordic motif.

Photo by Halat

A brief glance at the ancient history of scrimshaw reveals a long tradition of working with these natural materials, a tradition that goes all the way back to our Stone Age ancestors, when bones, teeth, and other parts of an animal were decorated with scratches and the resulting patterns sometimes colored.

In every Northern culture, objects for daily use were made of ivory and bone and decorated with traditional motifs and patterns. Discoveries dating from the Dorset Culture (ca. 1000 – 2000 years ago) in the Canadian Arctic were decorated with relatively simple incised patterns. In time, the original inhabitants of that region developed more delicate techniques of carving and decorating natural materials. From about 1000 AD, the Thule peoples wandered east from the region of Alaska along the coast, living in part by whaling and bringing along their delicately decorated tools, figures, and amulets of engraved ivory, bone, stone or wood.

Bracer for archery made of bone with incised Stone Age motifs. Work by Werner Schirmer.

During the Little Ice Age (1600 – 1850), native whaling in the Arctic decreased greatly or was even abandoned. The Eskimos could maintain their usual life-style and whaling practices only in the warmer parts of Greenland, southern Baffin Island, and Labrador, which surrounded the ice-free waters of Baffin Bay.

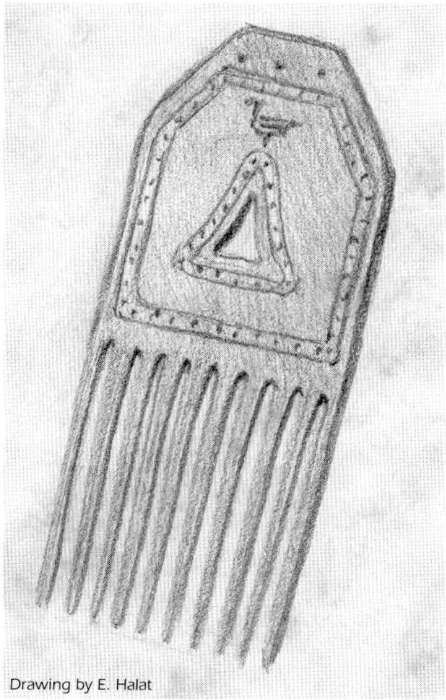

The Thule people decorated their objects in the same style as this ivory comb.

In these regions, from the 18th century on, contact was increasingly frequent between the Eskimos and the whaling fleets from Europe. This was the first time that scrimming American and European whalers encountered the similar art of the whaling Eskimos, not yet considered scrimshaw. The degree to which Eskimos and whalers influenced each other in the development of their scrimshaw technique must be left largely to our imagination.

Whaling also has a very long history in Europe. A whaling scene scratched in stone was discovered in Sweden with an estimated age of about 3500 years. Even before the period of American colonialization, European whalers had used parts of the baleen whale to make small works of art. A casket from 1631 with its sides made from baleen is one of the earliest objects known to be made of whalebone. It was made in the Dutch whaling fleet operating at that time in the North Atlantic and around Greenland. Baleen and whalebone were used then to create art work during the whalers' spare time.

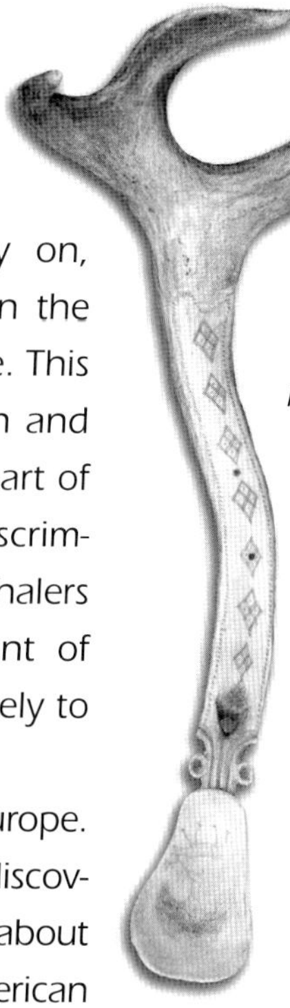

This spoon of reindeer antler, a tourist souvenir from Scandinavia, is a very fine example of the type of simple traditional pattern with which the northern peoples decorated objects of daily use.

Photo by Halat

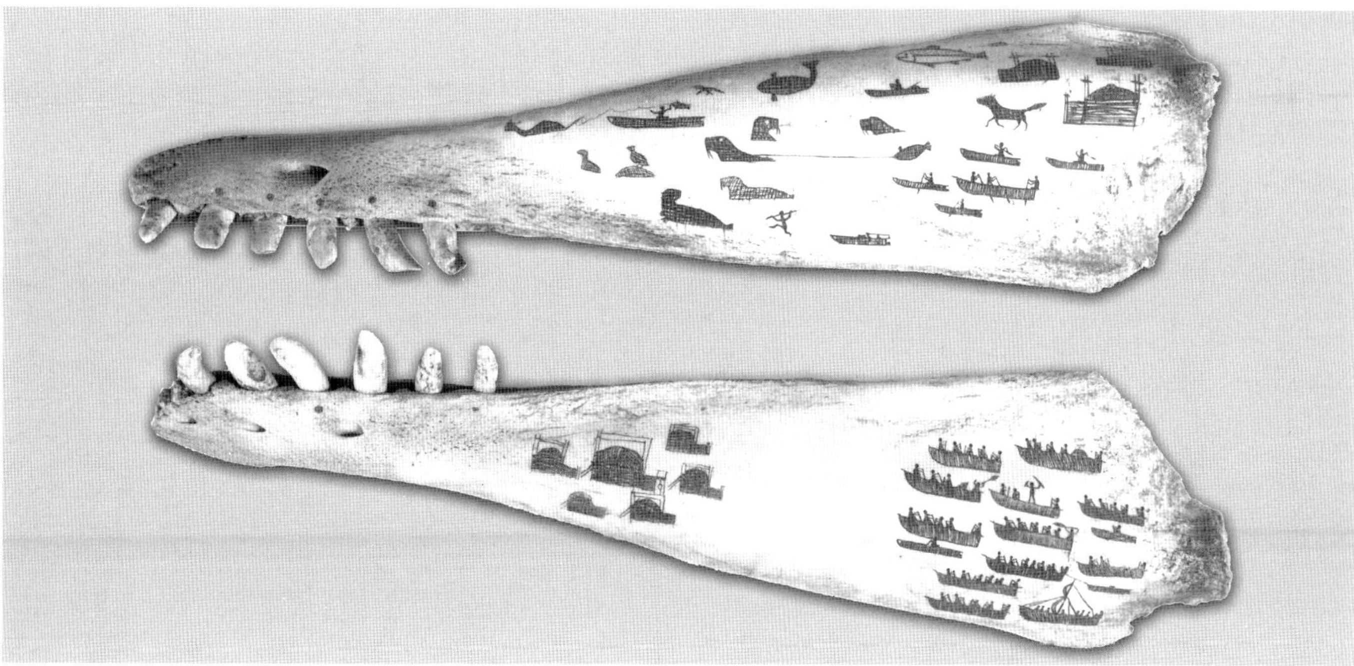

Above: A pair of Beluga whale jawbones from the area of St. Michael's, Alaska, around 1860 – 75. They are decorated in the traditional old Eskimo style and show hunters attacking walrus, fish, kayaks, igloos with fish drying on lines, and a large number of umiaks, which the Eskimos used for travel on the open sea.

Presumably, the work was done after contact with whaling ships, for such small jawbones were not traditionally used for this purpose among the Eskimos. (Illustration provided by kind permission of the Hull City Museum, Hull, England).

An engraved bone thumb ring of the type used by Asiatic archers and an ivory netsuke figure, shown front and back. The engraved line pattern can be easily seen. Photos by Halat

Northern peoples were not alone in working ivory, bone, and horn in this way; this art is to be found all around the world.

Lid from an old Chinese compass. Reproduction with an inlay of artificial ivory.

Traditional Japanese netsuke, small carved figures of ivory, horn, or wood with holes for cords, are desirable collectors pieces. Since Japanese clothing lacked pockets, the cords were used to fasten pouches and small boxes to kimono sashes. Many of these small ivory figures are also provided with delicately cut patterns and texture. There is a very long tradition of using ivory for delicate carving in Asia, and today Japan is one of the major consumers of the fossil ivory available from Russian sources.

In the Pacific, the Maori carved figures from sperm whale teeth and decorated them with scratched patterns; in the Fiji Islands, these teeth were strung into chains. These native peoples were not whalers and were limited to using these very coveted teeth from stranded whales. Later, after American and European whalers arrived in these islands, there was a long period when sperm whale teeth were prized trading goods among the islanders and whalers.

Northern Russia also has a long tradition of decorating and carving ivory. Ivory articles were in daily use in Archangelsk, Pomorye. During the 17th and 18th centuries, the local populations of Kholmogory (in Pomorye) and the neighboring villages were more occupied with the production of objects from walrus tusks, fossil ivory, and reindeer bone than with agriculture. The carvers of Kholmogory were artists in carving, engraving, and painting, and they developed special tools for this work.

Below: A reindeer bone carving in traditional Russian style.

Drawing by Halat

By the end of the 17th century, carvers from Kholmogory were to be found working in Moscow along with local artists. In 1711, the workshops were moved to St. Petersburg. In this cultural center, the traditional style merged with the baroque and the rococo. At the end of the 18th and the beginning of the 19th century, there was a thriving trade in ivory objects such as jewel and tobacco boxes, toilet articles, candlesticks, and other items, which spread far beyond the borders of Russia. Russian ivory art is still being produced today. The style reflects Russian folklore, and it is very different from the style of Western scrimshanders and whalers.

In Africa today we can find artistic scrimshaw on eggs from ostrich farms, although mainly for the tourist trade. In general, this "egg scrimshaw" is a great deal cruder than most of today's scrimshaw work. Scrimshaw in the "modern" style only managed to find its way to South Africa in the last twenty years.

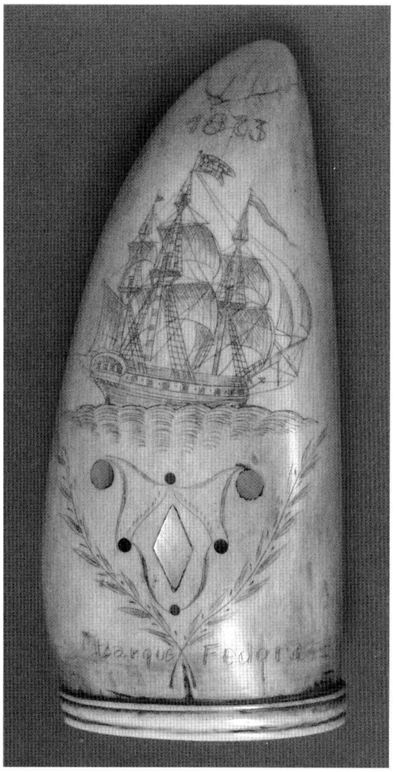

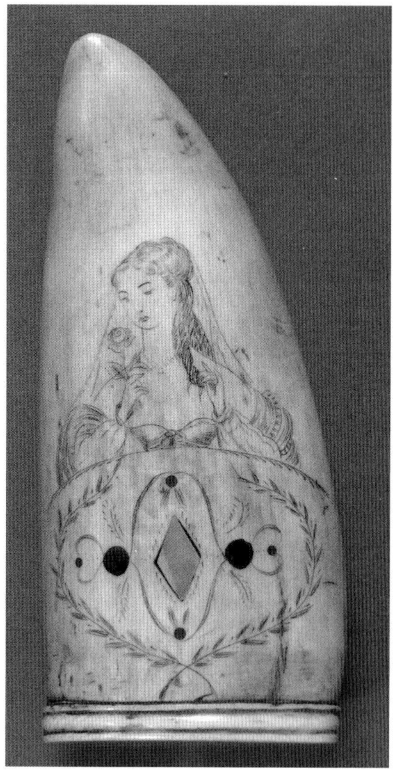

The "Barque Fedora", an antique work on a sperm whale tooth with unusual inlays of mother-of-pearl. (private collection)

The modern concept of "scrimshaw" has only been around for about 200 years, and its history clearly began among American and European whalers during the early part of that period.

We do not have a very clear idea of the origin of the word "scrimshaw". One possible explanation is that it comes from the word "skrimshank", a derivation which is to be found in British dictionaries today. Skrimshank is defined as "to shirk or avoid duty; or an idle man". For example, some books mention a log entry by a New Bedford whaling captain, who wrote, "An idle head is the workshop of the devil. Employed scrimshon." This explanation seems plausible when you remember that scrimshaw could only be done during idle periods, in order to keep boredom at bay. More than one seaman must have discovered a love for art in this activity and preferred working on his scrimshaw to avoid the hard and dangerous work of whaling or the stinking work of "trying out".
A different explanation comes from a dictionary of English dialects dating from 1898. There the word "scrimption" along with "scrimt(i)on" and "scrimshin" is mentioned to describe a tiny piece or starvation wages. And "scrimp" means "to be sparing and frugal, to try and make ends meet". So perhaps "scrimshaw" comes from the practice on whaling ships of letting the crew have those parts of the whale with no commercial value.

In any case, before 1712, there were no whale teeth for the kind of scrimshaw that became so famous as the "Eastern Scrimshaw of the Whalermen". Early whalers stayed fairly close to the coast in relatively shallow water where only baleen whales, whales without teeth, were to be found. Some carving and engraving was done on the baleen, a hard, gray-green, horn-like material. This material, well suited for corset stays because of its flexibility, was also called whalebone by the whalers. Real whale bones, especially the jawbones, were also used for art work.

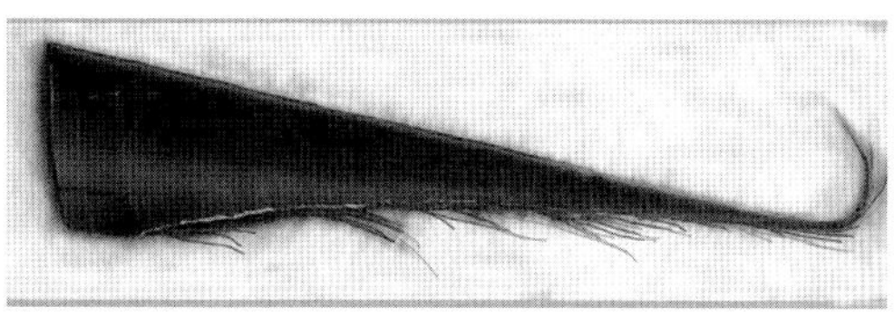

Baleen, a horn-like, fibrous material in the upper jaw of baleen whales, with which they filter plankton, small fish, and krill out of the sea.

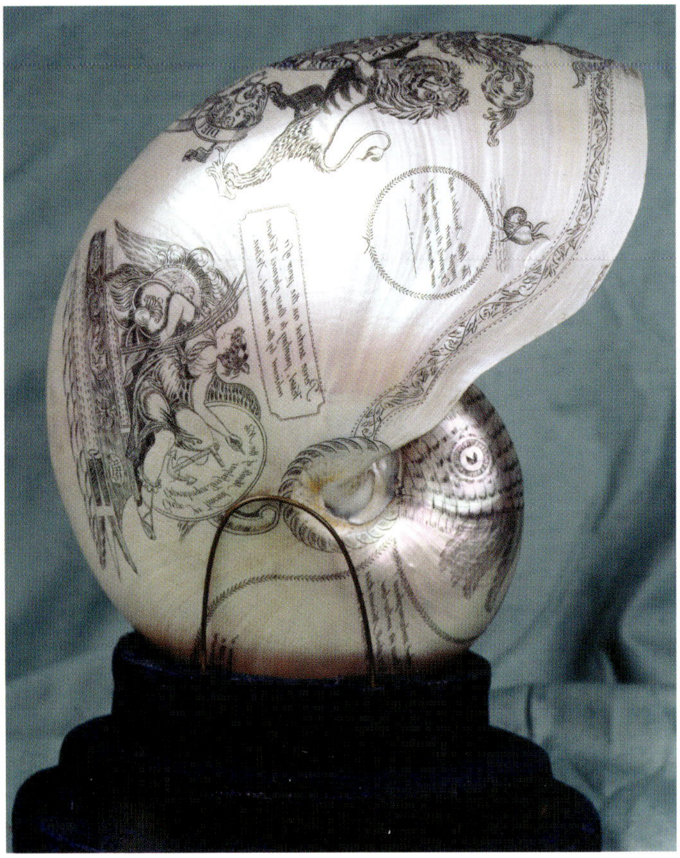

A very beautiful piece of work on a mother-of-pearl surface. A nautilus shell with scrimshaw work by C.H. Wood. The work was produced in the middle of the 19th century. Little is known about the artist himself, who did a great deal of scrimshaw work on mother-of-pearl. (Picture provided with the kind permission of the Hull Maritime Museum, Hull, England.)

However, in 1712, a small ship sailing from Nantucket to the whaling grounds was blown off course into deep water by strong winds. Suddenly the little ship found itself surrounded by a large number of whales - sperm whales, not baleen whales! The first sperm whale was taken, and they discovered it had spermaceti, valuable sperm oil for lamps, and... teeth!

The sperm whale lives in deeper waters farther from the mainland, so voyages naturally had to be longer. In time, larger whaling ships were built to enable the whales to be processed at sea and the oil rendered on board. Earlier, when ships were smaller and voyages shorter, whales had been brought back to land and processed there. However, by the end of the 18th century, this new kind of whaling from large ships far out at sea became the rule and voyages were made around Cape Horn and out into the Pacific Ocean. Voyages of two to three years were not uncommon. The longest known was that of the ship *Nile* out of New London. It lasted from 1858 to 1869!

Whaling ships had a larger crew for whaling than was really necessary to sail the ship. Twenty- four or twenty-five men was the minimum crew on a ship that could be easily handled by six to eight seamen. So there were periods during a voyage when there was little or nothing to do, and the empty periods waiting for wind or whale could be filled with the production of scrimshaw. (The famous book and the film Moby Dick give a very good idea of these empty periods.)

From cabin boy to captain, everyone scrimmed. The surface of the tooth was first smoothed with a file or rasp. The "old-time" scrimshanders used sharkskin to give the tooth surface a fine sanding, and then used ash or pumice stone for the final polish. Usually a mixture of soot and oil was used to give the scrimshaw color.

They produced the oddest things, often as gifts for family or for the girl back home The sailors expressed their dreams of home in their work, making sewing tools, combs, jewelry, and even richly decorated corset stays from whalebone. Many of them "drew" scenes of daily life aboard ship or "wrote" short verses about drinking, nostalgia, or love. The favorite themes, however, were always ships and whaling scenes.

In his foreword to W. Gilkerson's book, *The Scrimshander*, Karl Kortum, Director of the San Francisco Maritime Museum, gives a good description of what scrimshaw meant to the sailors: "The old scrimshaw was an escape from the sea - from too much sea - back towards the land."

By the middle of the 19th century, the American whaling fleet had extended its range to the Azore Islands. Whales could be taken close to the islands there and

were generally processed ashore. The remains were thrown back into the sea, along with many sperm whale teeth. Even today, divers search anchorages in the Azores for these valuable teeth, which they sell to the local scrimshanders, many of whom still produce scrimshaw in the old way.
At the beginning of the twentieth century, whaling was slowly dying. Kerosene offered an economical replacement for whale oil and provided better light than the older whale oil "sparklers." Ships lost at sea to storm or an attack by an angry whale were no longer being replaced. Many of the veteran whalers had lost their lives, and many others found better paid, less smelly, and safer berths on other ships, where they would not have to put up with such long separations from their families. In 1924, a hurricane dashed the last ship of a once proud whaling fleet on the rocks of Buzzards Bay, only twenty-four hours after the start of its voyage.

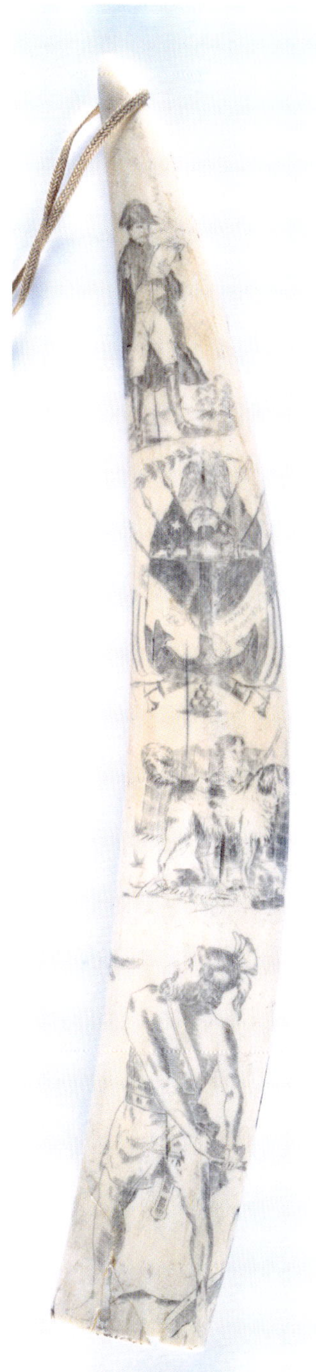

Antique scrimshaw from France on a walrus tusk, signed by F. Beaudoin. Napoleon is scrimmed on it, along with other subjects. (From the Tizard Collection of the Maritime Museum, Hull, England. With the kind permission of the museum.)

Whaling died out, but the art to which it gave birth lived on. Scrimshaw entered a new era, but controversy arose about its definition. Many people believed that the only true scrimshaw was that made by whalers on whaling ships, and they excluded any themes that didn't concern whaling. Sea serpents, mermaids, and other fabulous creatures of the deep were regarded as borderline cases. Some very odd definitions appeared, for example that work done by a retired whaler could be considered scrimshaw only if the work had been done in the 19th century.

Scrimshaw also reached Hawaii during the whaling period. It was rediscovered there in the 1950s and '60s as a type of folk art thanks to increasing tourism and the movie industry. Because of this increased demand, a great deal of work was produced in Asia (Hong Kong, Taiwan, the Philippines) and imported. These mass-produced copies of the old whaling themes were frequently sold as cheap tourist souvenirs.

Even then, there were serious collectors of antique scrimshaw art. The best known collector was President John F. Kennedy, and his collection led to an increasing acceptance of this art. In 1964, Clare Barnes wrote the first book on scrimshaw entitled "John F. Kennedy, Scrimshaw Collector". It became well-known among artists and collectors and was reprinted in 1969.

The real change in the scrimshaw scene, however, didn't occur until the '70s. A whaling museum was built on Maui in 1968 with a restored whaling ship, a reconstructed sperm whale skeleton, many whaling tools, and naturally, genuine, antique scrimshaw. Most of the items displayed had been obtained at auction on the East Coast of the United States. This attention paid to scrimshaw by a museum led to increased collector interest.

Although scrimshaw was being produced once again, the art seemed condemned to death by the Marine Mammals Act of 1972 and the Species Protection Law of 1973. But because the raw material had become so expensive, the old pieces were no longer producible and were getting harder to find, so demand from scrimshaw enthusiasts increased for good new or antique pieces. Still, people were not immediately ready to switch to other materials, so the Species Protection Law of 1973 caused scrimshaw to take a step backward. Scrimshaw was still supposed to be done only on whale teeth!

Unfortunately, because of this increasing demand for antique scrimshaw, it became profitable to counterfeit scrimshaw (fakeshaw) from the whaling era. The production of fakes is not difficult; there are no technical problems, and a faker does not have to attribute his work to any known artist, since most of the old work was never signed or dated.

Perhaps these restrictions on the ivory trade also helped cause a rebirth of the art of scrimshaw. Because of the increasing rarity and value of the raw material, the quality of the art work improved, acquiring a value comparable to that of expensive ivory.

In 1972, one of the best known works on old scrimshaw, Norman Flayderman's "Scrimshaw and Scrimshanders, Whales and Whalermen" appeared. It provided a good overview of antique scrimshaw and displayed recent work. It was a good reference for the collector and, for the first time, established standards for evaluating scrimshaw. This was followed in 1975 by another book, *The Scrimshander*, by W. Gilkerson. Other materials such as hippopotamus, elephant, and walrus ivory were mentioned in this book. The book also introduced a few new subjects to go along with the nautical themes, such as land animals, mountain scenes, fantasy subjects, and other atypical pictures. Other books by Gilkerson appeared in 1978 and 1979 and helped to further popularize scrimshaw.

"Mack Truck", a recent work by Bob Hergert that in no way corresponds to the themes of the old whaler's scrimshaw. Mastodon ivory, 3.5 x 7 cm.

With increasing public interest, scrimshaw changed, and dry land subjects were scrimmed, country scenes, wildlife, western scenes, fantasy themes anything was now possible. The technique had remained the same in principle, but it had been refined. The new scrimshander had vastly better working conditions than his predecessor, who had to work in poor light on a pitching and tossing whaling ship. Today scrimshanders work in good light, under magnifiers, with much more precise tools. Most of them are artists who already know how to draw and paint, and they have inexhaustible access to reference materials and art books. Many are professional artists who produce their works for galleries and collectors. There is a much greater selection of materials, as well. Today, scrimshaw has been done on almost every possible material: elephant ivory, fossil walrus ivory, black and white horn, antler, bone, micarta, ceramics, warthog and hippopotamus teeth, and naturally, most often on fossilized ivory from mammoth tusks.

A letter by scrimshaw artist and collector Rick Jager in Gilkerson's 1975 book gives a good glimpse of the changes in the scrimshaw scene and at the artist's related problems with materials and identity. The letter is a thank-you note to Gilkerson, who had sent Jager a medium-sized sperm whale tooth after the latter had expressed his indignation at the horribly high price for sperm whale teeth that he had bought from a sailor's widow: 450 dollars for 12 medium-sized whale teeth. Earlier, in 1961, he had had to pay a dealer from Europe only 3 dollars per (large) tooth.
Jager gave free rein to his unbounded pleasure of the gift and luxuriated in the memory of the wonderful knocking sound that the whale tooth made when the unopened package was shaken.
Jager is a scrimshander of the old school, and he earnestly asked Gilkerson to limit himself to nautical themes in his scrimming: *"...I hope that you will abandon the fantasy themes you sometimes put in your scrimshaw. I hope that you will abandon them altogether and just be a scrimshaw purist. There is no place for any fantasy on whale teeth, particularly now that they are so scarce. It dismays me somewhat, for the subjects in whaling are endless and wonderful... ships in storms, in calms, whale barks caught in the polar ice, rounding the Horn in a gale, trying out the oil, attacking the whale, attacked by the whale, the girl back home, shields with eagles, anchors, the American flag... The possibilities are endless! Therefore when I read a year or so ago about a guy somewhere scrimshawing Rocky Mountain big horns and Winnie-the-Pooh on whale teeth, it made me want to throw up."*
Certainly the traditional scrimshander at that time felt that the tradition and honor of his art was under attack. He also felt, as Rick Jager expressed in his letter, *"...that I've secretly hated the Winnie-the-Pooh guy for demeaning the great and honorable fraternity of the real, honest-to-gosh New Bedford, Nantucket, Sag Harbour scrimshanders of the Present Day..."*

But it would have been a genuine tragedy if scrimshaw had come to an end with whaling. It is asking too much of scrimshaw artists who never had anything to do with either whaling or sailing to limit themselves to those subjects. Besides, "new" materials such as mammoth ivory or horn have no connection with the sea.

At the beginning of the '70s, there were comprehensive scrimshaw studios in Bellingham on the West Coast and in Nantucket on the East Coast, where a number of artists worked together. Scrimshaw jewelry was produced by hand at the Alaska Silver and Ivory Company (ASI) in Bellingham, a workshop for commercial scrimshaw art. More than twenty artists were employed there during its most active period. When the ASI ceased production in 1980 for economic reasons, some of the former artists formed independent studios, but these studios no longer exist today.

Bellingham became known for the new, delicate style of scrimshaw developed there. Today we speak of the "Bellingham" or "West Coast" style or of the "Bellingham School". Even the selection of themes was different from the older, conventional scrimshaw: mountain landscapes, bears, bighorn sheep, leopards, birds, Native Americans, etc., but of course, they also scrimmed the "old" subjects as well. It was more pleasant working in a studio than alone at home. You could take a break from the demands of work and relax for a moment to talk, exchange experiences, and solve problems together. Certainly this factor played a role in the development of first-class work and extremely advanced and precise technique. The use of color was also perfected in the Bellingham studios. Customers marveled at the exquisite, beautifully-colored scrimshaw artistry produced there and placed orders for it. Representatives from galleries and collectors came to pick up commissioned pieces and to see new work.

Bear fishing for salmon. A colored scrimshaw by Matt Stothart, who formerly worked as a scrimshander at ASI in Bellingham.

It is still possible to find a fine selection of scrimshaw by numerous artists at galleries in the traditional scrimshaw regions on the East and West Coasts of the United States, in Hawaii, and in the Azores. The pieces range from cheap, mass-produced stuff, standard reproductions of antique scrimshaw, to first-class, original work by famous scrimshaw artists.

A small, bi-monthly publication, called *Whalebone*, devoted exclusively to scrimshaw and carving, appeared in January 1988, published by Rappahannock Design, Inc. in Fairfax, VA. It introduced artists and their work, provided working tips, gave dates, and included addresses and other items of interest. For example, the July 1989 edition first mentioned the United States government's declaration of a moratorium, the temporary suspension of all imports of elephant ivory, effective from July 9, 1989. The one hundred and two countries belonging to the Convention of International Trade in Endangered Species (CITES) were then debating whether trade in elephant ivory should be prohibited permanently.

Today, however, there is still no internationally valid law regulating traffic in ivory of any kind. The different laws in different countries concerning the use of and trade in ivory are often similar, but vary in detail. Every country, and even each type of ivory, has its own rules. In the United States, trade (both import and export) in elephant ivory is prohibited. The material now being worked on comes from "old stock" that was legally imported years ago. Also in the United States, other types of ivory require export licenses before they may be exported.

Commerce in sperm whale and walrus teeth is a very complex subject, because the law treats these teeth differently according to their age and date of registration. Even the Eskimos must satisfy certain conditions with respect to the possession, trade, and preparation of walrus ivory.

In the appendix to this book, you will find more exact information on this subject, along with current addresses and Internet sites for the responsible officials in various countries, from whom you can get more precise information concerning specific cases.

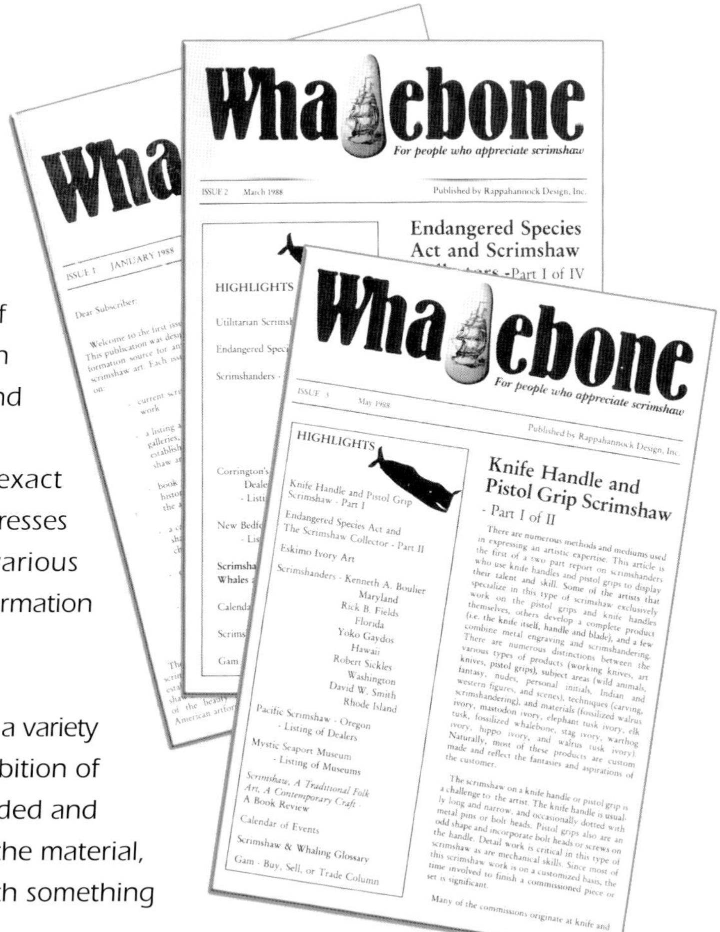

Scrimshaw has often been declared dead as an art for a variety of reasons, such as the end of whaling or the prohibition of various ivory materials, but each time it has rebounded and improved in quality. The rarer and more expensive the material, the greater the demand on the artist to adorn it with something at least as valuable.

The historical description provided above is mainly concerned with whaler's scrimshaw and its contemporary development. This is certainly the best-known kind of scrimshaw, especially in those countries where whaling contributed so much to its development. However, knifemakers and collectors have also made considerable contributions to the international renaissance of this art.

For a long time, there has been a considerable gap between the scrimshaw produced by "display art" artists, mostly those who have been pure scrimshanders for a considerable period, and utility work produced by those who scrim on knife grips, belt buckles, and other articles intended for use. Scrimshaw work on utility items was not as well respected as pieces by scrimshanders who had reputations as artists and whose scrimshaw was considered "real" art. These artists are often represented by galleries and the prices their art fetches reflects the quality of the work and the reputation of the artist.

There was a general belief that scrimshaw on knife grips had to be cut much deeper and not as delicately as "real art", otherwise it would not stand up under hard use. Supposedly there could be no real art on such an object, only craftsmanship. Now, however, this belief has changed. Both artists who have long been active as scrimshanders in the knife-making world and others who are newly established scrim their finest works on knife grips. The knife is no longer considered merely an object for real use, but in some cases rather as a work of art in every sense of the word: something best kept behind the glass of a display case.

Another historical variant of scrimshaw is the work done on powder horns made of cow horn. Cow horn can be cut or ornamented with engraving technique just like various kinds of ivory. Earlier, this ornamentation was called "engraving", not scrimshaw. "Scrimshaw" was supposedly a purely maritime expression and for that reason not applied to the decorations on powder horns. Indeed, engravings on antique powder horns are cruder and deeper than contemporary scrimshaw, but in style and technique they are entirely equivalent to whaler's scrimshaw.

Cow horns have been used as black powder containers for centuries, and European colonists brought the first powder horns with them to America. Not all were made of cow horn, tortoise shell and antler were used as well. In time, the colonists came to use cow horn as a means for protecting and carrying a wide variety of things, for example rum, water, salt and pepper, snuff, tinder, and fat. The American colonists made a lot of other things out of horn, such as cups, spoons, combs, knife grips, ink bottles, and even windowpanes for lanterns. Horns were also used as signal horns and for carrying messages. However, they were most popularly used as powder horns. The material is tough, waterproof, lightweight, and not flammable, so it makes an ideal container for black powder.

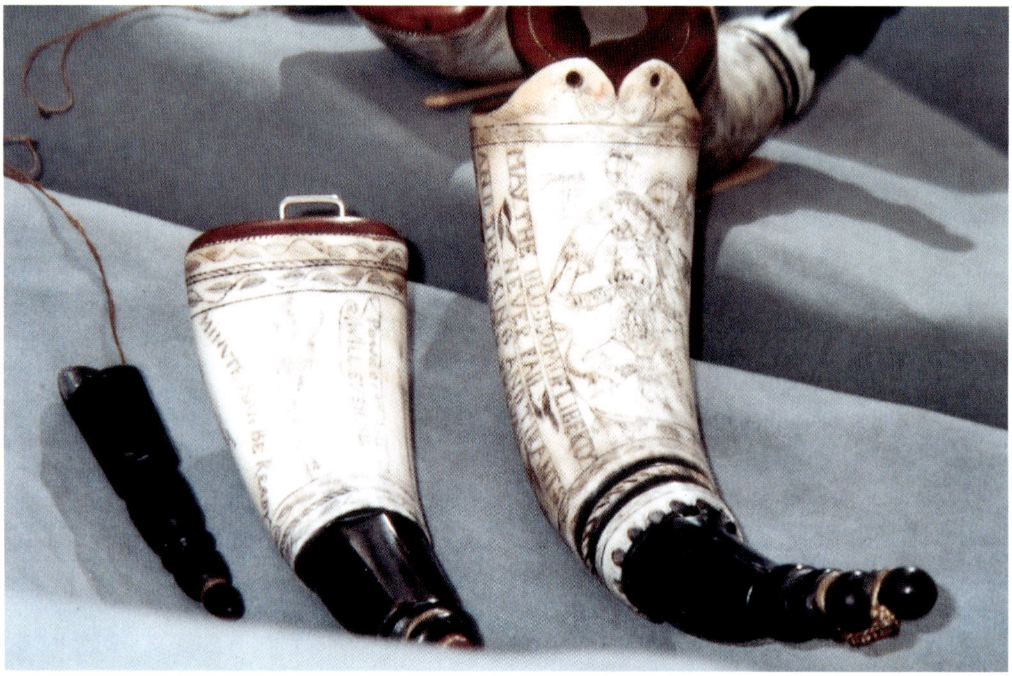

Two examples of powderhorns by Wolfgang Fubel. Picture taken in front of a mirror to make the rear side visible.

To make a powder horn, first a piece is sawn from each end of the cow horn, and the horn is then boiled in a mixture of potash and water. The large end is closed with a beautiful wooden plug or lid, and a hole is bored in the smaller, pointed end and supplied with a wooden stopper. Small quantities of black powder were poured from the small end into a powder measure for loading a gun from the muzzle. The powder horn was carried on a shoulder strap along the side of the body with the pointed end forward. The curve of the horn fits against the side of the body. Most horns were from 33 to 45 cm long.

Most decorated powder horns come from the period of the American Revolution and were used as long as powder and shot had to be carried separately. Collectors are especially avid for "Golden Age" horns, which come from the period approximately between 1753 and 1784. These horns exhibit extremely high-quality craftsmanship on the wooden ends. The horns were often colored in warm yellow-orange tones,

Detail of a map horn made by Gary Fiedler.

and, naturally, they were engraved. Many powder horns have quite deep engravings, but others were decorated with very delicate scenes and themes.

Just like sailors, soldiers and hunters engraved their powder horns with subjects from their daily life: forts, silhouettes of towns, animals, ships, soldiers, Native Americans, vines, poems, and the names of the horns' owners. The maps engraved on many horns were also very useful. These map powder horns were made especially for British officers in London by professional engravers, who copied existing maps to scale on the horns. For example, there is a powder horn that shows the route along the Hudson River to Lake Champlain and one that shows the route from the Hudson Valley to Lake Ontario by way of the Mohawk River, including the positions of the most important forts.

Even today, there are artists and hobbyists who make powder horns for black pow-

Materials

Ivory from elephants, walrus, warthogs, and hippopotami, fossil ivory, horn, antler, mother-of-pearl, bone, tagus nuts, ostrich eggs, micarta, polymers, and ceramics are all materials that can be used for scrimshaw.

Of course, the most beautiful and valuable scrimshaw is found on equally beautiful and valuable natural materials. It takes a long time for these natural materials to grow, and during that time they acquire their own history and soul. Somehow, this aura can be felt, and it can never be imitated by any rapidly produced artificial material.

If you use ivory, you must pay close attention to the legal restrictions on its purchase and use. There is a difference between trade in recent ivory, which is strictly regulated or forbidden, and in ivory that was imported and stored before the import restrictions went into effect. This latter ivory comes from so-called "old stock".

"Antique" ivory is defined in the United States as ivory from before 1872. This means that it must be at least 100 years older than the import prohibition of 1972. Then there is the category of "fossil" ivory. Legally, "fossil" simply means that the ivory is old; it has nothing to do with the process of mineralization. It may refer to "fossil" walrus teeth, which lay buried in the ground or under ice for only 300 years, and also to mammoth ivory, which is several thousand years old. Each country also has its own regulations concerning the import and possession of fossil ivory.

The interested reader can find information on current laws and regulations at the addresses and Internet sites listed in the appendix.

Elephant Ivory

Elephant ivory is a superb surface for scrimshaw, and it is a pity that a responsibly regulated, worldwide trade in ivory is not possible. Elephant tusks cannot be sold because of trade restrictions. Tusks are sometimes stockpiled in African national parks, although the money that their sale would bring is urgently needed to pay park employees and expenses.

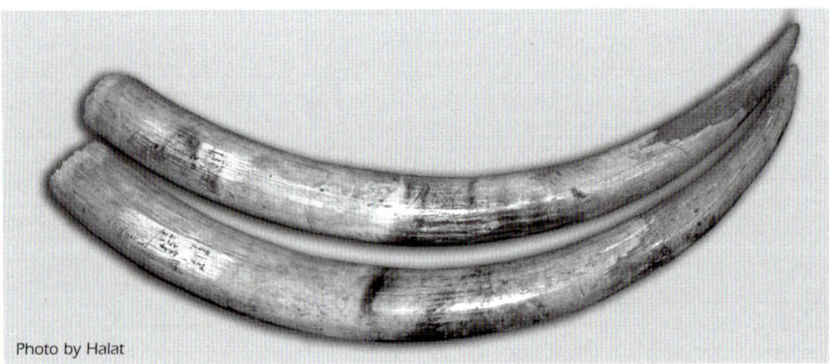

Left: A pair of elephant tusks. Right: Shown in this picture are the hollow, inside conically tapered ends of such tusks.

African elephant ivory from old stock is again available for sale in Germany under certain conditions, but trade in Indian elephant ivory is universally prohibited. Those animals are on the endangered species list. African elephant tusks are more conical in shape from the base to the tip than those of Indian elephants, whose tusks have an almost constant diameter and are significantly smaller. The ivory itself, however, is virtually identical.

The inner structure of ivory is comparable to that of wood, with annual layers laid down in rings, just as in a tree trunk. The outer layer, "rind", or "bark" is about 0.5 cm thick, and the material becomes somewhat harder toward the tip. There is a difference between elephant ivory from East Africa and that from West Africa. Ivory from veldt elephants in South and East Africa is called "milkbone" because of its milky-white appearance when fresh. However, this ivory turns yellow faster than the "glassbone" ivory from forest elephants in West Africa. Glassbone, when cut thinly, is slightly translucent and harder than milkbone.

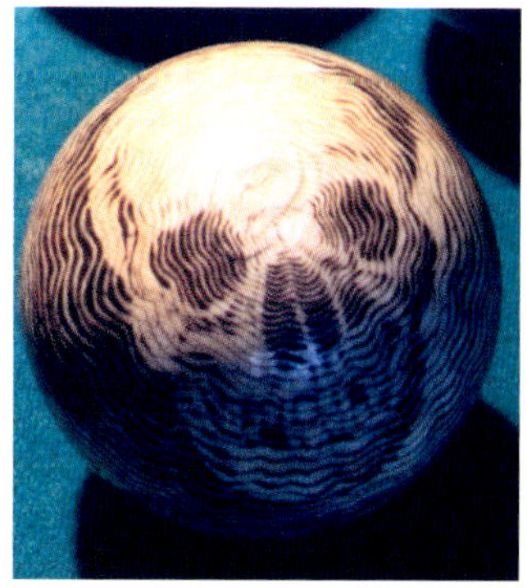

This old billiard ball scrimmed with a skull has strongly contrasting wavy lines on its round surface.
The artist, Bob Hergert, made interesting use of the natural cracks around the "pole" in his design.

Scrimshaw artists also happily use old piano keys or billiard balls. Piano keys provide small, thin plates that make fine pendants or inlays. Billiard balls are predestined to be made into world globes. An old billiard ball with fine cracks around its "pole" (to continue with the world globe analogy) and often with visible Schreger lines in the "tropics" has a beautiful antique appearance. Scrimshaw artists have made many marvelous "old" globes and other objects from billiard balls. Moreover, it is quite a challenge for a scrimshander to scrim all around a round ball. I have read that you can cut a billiard ball into sections to get round ivory plates, but I think that this is a terrible idea. It is almost a sacrilege. Flat ivory is cheaper than a well-preserved billiard ball. A ball was turned out of a massive piece of ivory, and it is impossible to justify the material lost in the turning process. It is better to cut slices from raw or flat stock. Besides, the old balls have been stored for a long time, and you can be sure that the material is well seasoned and will not crack as easily as fresh ivory.

Mammoth Ivory

Mammoth ivory is fossil ivory. Fortunately, there are no trade restrictions on it, and it can be used as a replacement for elephant ivory. Mammoth ivory varies in hardness depending on the condition of the material; it can be softer or even a little harder than elephant ivory. This fossil material often displays very beautiful coloration ranging from all possible tints of brown through blue and gray shading into reddish colors. The coloration comes from minerals that permeated the ivory during the long period it lay in the ground. Mammoth ivory from soil strata closer to the surface of the ground is usually softer and darker and of lower quality, because it has been exposed to much greater variations in annual temperature and to the freezing and thawing cycle close to the surface. However, because these processes allow much greater mobility for various minerals, which diffuse into the ivory while it is in the ground, this ivory has the most beautiful coloration. Mammoth ivory, which can be obtained from the permafrost layer only during the summer months, is more apt to produce larger, whiter pieces in good condition.

Photo by Halat

Partly polished pieces of "bark" from mammoth ivory.

We believe that mammoths and mastodons lived in the northern regions until about 10,000 years ago, and we can tell whether complete tusks came from mammoths or mastodons. Mammoth tusks weight up to 300 kg and have a corkscrew "C" shape.

Tusks from mastodons are shorter, with a smaller diameter, weigh no more than 150 kg, and are more slightly curved. However, once the material has been cut up, you can no longer tell which species it came from. In general, both are called "mammoth ivory".

These tusks are found in large quantities during the construction of roads and pipelines and while prospecting for gold, which today requires the movement of great amounts of earth. Tusks are also found by ivory dealers and prospectors specifically seeking them.

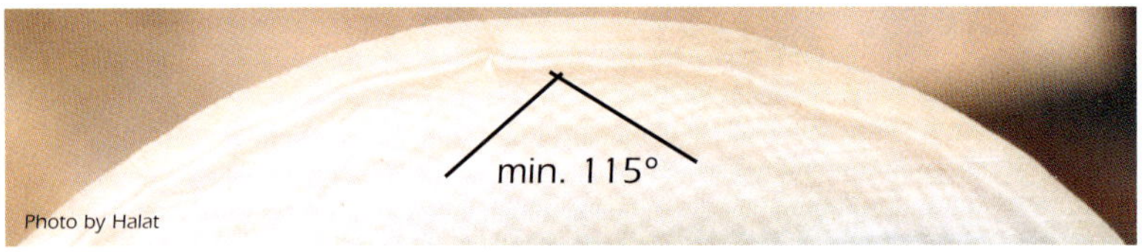

Cross-section of an elephant tusk...

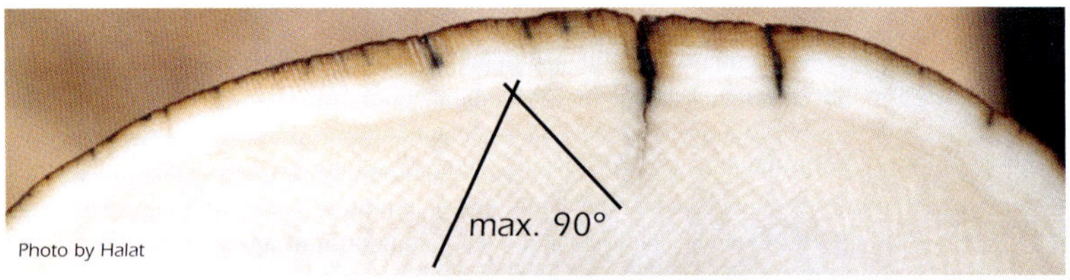

... and of a mammoth tusk with visible Schreger lines.

There is one significant characteristic that instantly allows you to tell mammoth ivory from elephant ivory. The Schreger lines, which are visible in a cross-section of the tusk, cross at a flat angle of at least 115° in an elephant tusk. However, that angle is never more than 90° in a mammoth tusk. This angle should be measured near the "bark" layer, where it is most easily seen.

Another method for differentiating the two kinds of ivory is to expose the material to ultraviolet light. Mammoth ivory accumulates iron phosphate during its long period in the ground, and it fluoresces strongly under ultraviolet light, even when this isn't apparent to the naked eye.

Mammoth ivory is easiest to recognize when it has retained the outer "bark" layer. Although elephant ivory can also have beautiful brownish gold and brown exterior colors and show cracks and indentations, it is never as coarse or deeply cracked, and the colors are never as intense as in mammoth ivory.

Sperm Whale Teeth

Sperm whale teeth are a fine surface for scrimshaw, but they are very seldom obtainable and are subject to strict import-export regulations or even outright prohibition. Sperm whale teeth have an unmistakable shape, and they can hardly be mistaken for any other kind of ivory, because normally the whole tooth is used in its natural shape. Of course there are replicas or artificial whale teeth, but anyone who has held a real whale tooth in his hands and had a chance to examine it carefully will almost always be able to tell a replica tooth from a genuine unworked tooth. (See also the chapter on fakeshaw.)

Generally, the teeth are between 10 and 20 cm long, but they can reach a length of 25 cm. Only the lower part is hollow. Killer whale teeth have the same shape as sperm whale teeth, but they are smaller and much harder. Both kinds have an outer surface of cementum, but the hard tooth enamel is only sometimes present at the tip.

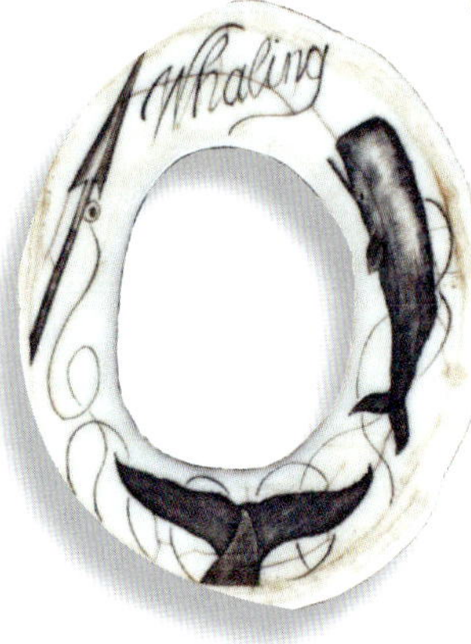

A plate from a whale tooth with the individual layers easily seen in cross-section. The hole in the middle is the root canal, which tapers toward the top. The tooth is solid at the tip. The scrimshaw is by Ritchi Maier.

Walrus Tusk

Tusks from Pacific walrus can grow up to a meter long. The tip of the tusk has an outer layer of hard dental enamel, but this is worn off while the animal is still young. Walrus ivory is superb material for scrimshaw, but commerce in walrus ivory is strictly regulated.

The thick end of the tusk has an irregular oval cross-section. The interior of the tusk has a lightly darker core that looks like marble and is clearly separate from the thick cementum layer. This "marbling" is normally visible on the upper end of the tusk because of wear on the outer layer. This is a good characteristic for identifying whole, uncut walrus tusk or even worked material.

Cross-section of a walrus tusk with the marble-like core. The tusk with the dark brown surface layer is antique.

Once in a while, you can find beautiful fossil walrus ivory for sale. Sometimes it may have been part of an object in daily use, such as a sled runner or a weight for fishnets, but even then, some countries may have strict trade restrictions. In Alaska, only the natives are permitted to search for fossil walrus ivory.

A whole hippopotamus tooth (28 cm) in front with a piece of walrus tusk (49 cm) behind it.

Hippopotamus Teeth

The hippopotamus has two upper and two lower teeth, one in each corner of its jaw, that are larger than the other teeth. The two lower teeth are the biggest. They are triangular in cross section, strongly curved, and as much as three-quarters of their length may be covered with tooth enamel. The upper teeth have a round to oval cross-section and an indentation running down the inside of the curve. Hippopotamus teeth are very hard, and the outer layer of enamel must be removed before they can be scrimmed. Generally, the cementum is also lost during this process, because it is very thin on hippopotamus teeth. Scrimshaw on this material is very demanding, and because of its hardness and corresponding brittleness, the same work requires a great deal more time than if it is done on mammoth ivory.

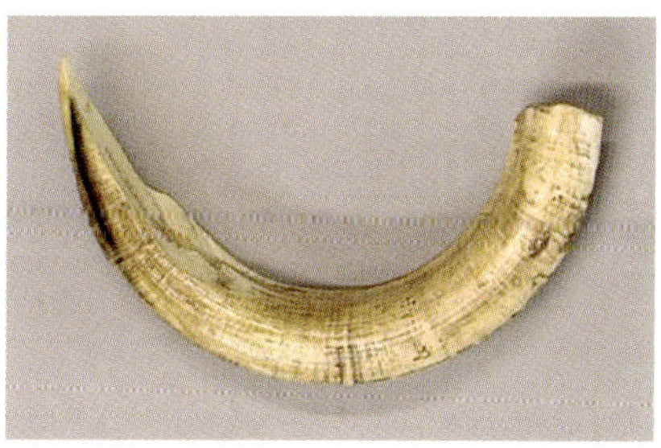

A curved hippo tusk from the lower jaw.

Wart Hog Tusks

Wart hog tusks are very suitable for scrimshaw. I was very pleasantly surprised the first time that I scrimmed such a tooth for a knife handle. The surface was soft and the needle could engrave even the finest details without great pressure. But the teeth can vary in their workability, depending on how heavily the surface, that is the dental enamel, has been worn away. The outer layer is somewhat harder and more brittle.

Wart hog teeth in unworked condition. The place where the tooth grew out of the jaw is readily apparent.

Unfortunately, wart hog teeth are fairly small, about 10-18 cm in length and strongly curved. But even that has its compensations, and with a little creativity they can be adapted to some beautiful themes. The cross-section of these teeth resembles a rectangle with heavily rounded corners. The exterior hard layer and the dark color must be removed before you start scrimming. Often cream-colored streaks are left, which can be very attractive on knife handles. There are still adequate supplies of these teeth, and fortunately you may still legally buy and work on them.

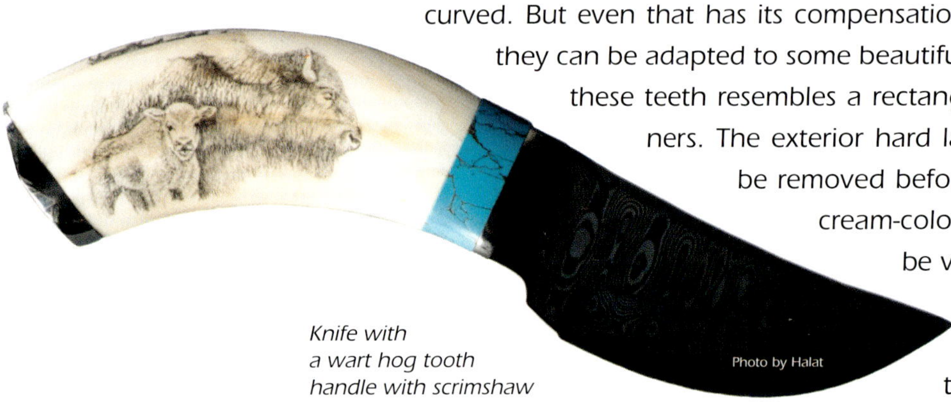

Knife with a wart hog tooth handle with scrimshaw by Eva Halat.

Cow and Water Buffalo Horn

Earlier, cow horn was often made into many useful objects, but the idea of scrimshaw or "engraving" it is most often associated with powder horns. Cow horns come in a variety of colors, from very light, almost white, to dark brown. To select an unprepared horn for its color, it is best to examine the inside, where you can more easily see the true color of the horn. Raw cow horn, obtained from a farmer or a slaughterhouse, looks coarse and rough on the outside, and the true color can be seen only after you have rasped, sanded, and polished it. Fresh horns, direct from the cow's head, have to be stored for several months to dry before use. You can also buy polished horns from hobby shops, medieval fairs, or from catalogs for buckskinners and black powder enthusiasts.

An entire water buffalo horn and a piece of the upper part of a horn where the material is no longer hollow. The white piece is polished cow horn, which is also suitable for scrimshaw.

Water buffalo horn is black and is only suitable for "negative" work. It is something of a challenge, because you have to think differently and do things in the opposite way from how you would when scrimming on a white surface. The black lines are scrimmed when you do black scrimshaw on a light background, but for black buffalo horn, those are exactly the places that must be left unworked. This requires some mental acrobatics.

Cow or buffalo horn is so soft that it feels as if your needle has suddenly become sharper. When you go back to ivory after scrimming a piece of horn, you have to get used to the "hard" material once again.

The horn fibers that make up cow horn are parallel and run lengthwise, and this can be annoying. When drawing a line, they can direct your needle in a direction you don't want it to go. That can be avoided by cutting the horn at a slight diagonal to the direction of the fibers.

Horn must be worked very carefully. If it gets too hot while you're working on it or if it dries out while stored, it has a tendency to separate into individual layers. When the surface of the horn is properly polished, it becomes very resistant to moisture and heat. Horn structure is a scaly laminate (similar to hooves or hair, etc.). When subjected to alternate warming and cooling, the horn structure expands and contracts and the scales or laminates separate and allow moisture to penetrate more easily. The surface becomes coarse and cracked. In order to avoid this, the outer layer of the horn is brought to a state of so-called "fluidity" while polishing. That means that after the surface layer is heated under the light pressure of polishing, it becomes denser to the point where it "fuses together". Some experience is required to do this properly, because you must be careful not to heat the surface too much. It is best to make a couple of preliminary attempts on test pieces first to get a feel for the right pressure and temperature. If you use a special high-performance wax especially suited for horn (obtainable from companies that make and supply abrasives), you will get optimum protection for the surface of the horn.

Antler

The thin layer of horn under the rough but beautiful outer layer of antler is also suitable for scrimshaw. Antler varies in quality, depending on the species that grew it. The antler of the European red deer has a very porous interior, and when this inner core is uncovered during the removal of the rough outer layer, the surface is worthless for scrimshaw. The open pores hold the color; without it, the background will turn gray.

Sambar stag antler comes from India and is very much sought after by knife makers for knife handles, because it is of uniform density. However, the Sambar stag is on the endangered species list, so this material is now very hard to get.

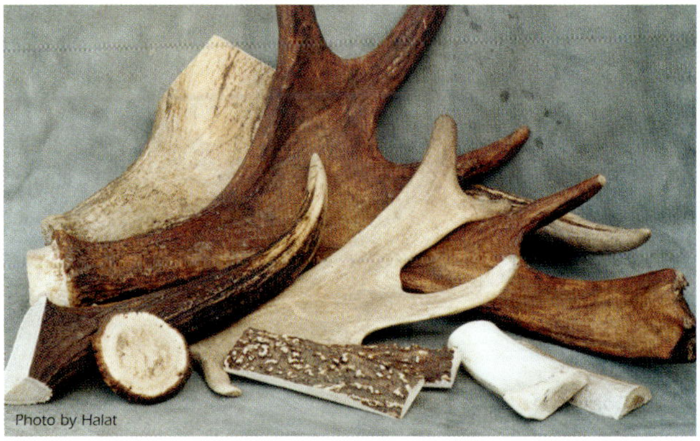

Various kinds of antlers.

I was pleasantly surprised when I sawed through some moose antler that a friend brought back from Russia. It is wonderfully dense almost all the way to the center, and it has a beautiful creamy white color. Unfortunately, this special kind of moose antler is hard to get. Although trade in this material is not prohibited and every year enough antlers are shed to fill demand, Russian officials can still be quite arbitrary about allowing its export. Some dealers who sell antler keep Russian moose antlers in stock, and moose antler from Canada and other countries with very cold winters should possess the same good properties. Reindeer or caribou antler also has very beautiful, broad surfaces for scrimshaw work. The antler of each species has its own characteristics, and each is worth trying, as my experience with Russian moose antler has shown.

You can also do very delicate work on antler, as can be seen in this piece by Dorinel Stoica.

The rosettes, the base pieces of antler, are also suitable for scrimshaw and carving. The material there is uniformly dense for a short distance and beautiful bolo ties or belt buckles can be made from the rosettes.

Bone

Although bone is certainly not the very best material for scrimshaw, it is the easiest to get. It polishes nicely and has a color similar to ivory, but there are always small pores in bone that will hold the coloring agent when a scrimshaw piece is being colored. Moreover, bone is brittle, and it is harder to scrim delicate work on bone than on ivory. Whether the scrimshander will use bone depends on his theme and the style that he wishes to use.

An ordinary boiled soup bone (marrowbone) and a piece of polished camel bone.

Beginners often start out on beef bones, although in my opinion polymer is more suitable. You need experience to get satisfactory results from bone.

Bone requires a little more preparation than other materials before you can use it for scrimshaw. If bits of meat still adhere to the bone, it must be boiled in water for several hours until completely clean. Then the bone has to be bleached with hydrogen peroxide (obtainable at any pharmacy). You let it sit in the solution for a couple of days until it is white. Then it has to be rinsed and thoroughly dried. The porous interior tissue will still contain fat, and eventually this fat can diffuse out to the surface of the bone, staining it. This porous tissue must be removed with a router or chisel. Marrowbones, (soup bones) are the most suitable, because the interior is already clean and hollow after boiling. Camel bone is very good bone. It is much more compact and dense than the bones of our domestic cattle and offers a good surface for scrimshaw. The camel bones obtainable commercially are usually already washed and bleached.

You can also use whalebone, but this is very hard to get, and the small pores must be filled after polishing with superglue, for example, until you obtain an acceptable surface for scrimshaw.

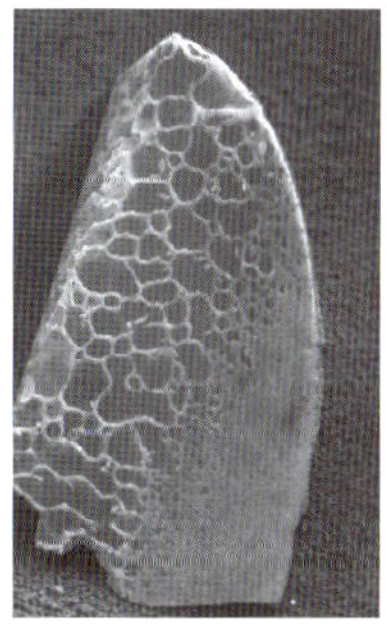

Scrimshaw on a belt buckle of whale rib and a piece in cross-section.

This hunting scene by Roberto Brucci on a knife by Ramon shows the fine detail that can be scrimmed on camel bone.

Tagua Nut

The tagua nut or vegetable ivory is the fruit of the ivory palm, which grows to a height of 10 meters in the tropical regions of South America. Most tagua nuts are exported from Colombia.

The interior of an unripe tagua nut contains a sweet, milky, edible fluid, but this fluid solidifies by the time the nut ripens and falls from the tree. Tagua nuts have a diameter of four to six centimeters. Before they are sold, these nuts are hardened for a few hours at a temperature of about 150 degrees Celsius.

The nut consists of dense cellulose material that is somewhat softer than ivory and can be easily scrimmed. It resembles animal ivory in color and can be used for either carving or scrimshaw. It is solid all the way through, but the drying process always leaves cracks of varying size in the middle

Ivory carvers have used tagua nuts for more than 200 years to make netsuke, chessmen, boxes, and other small

Tagua nuts are usually sold with the rough brown "skin". The left nut has already been polished.

decorative objects. Unfortunately, carvings of tagua nut are fraudulently sold as expensive ivory art.

Vegetable ivory was an important commercial item before artificial materials took its place. All around the world, companies made a variety of articles from it, especially buttons. Because of current restrictions on the use of ivory, the tagua nut has again acquired commercial value.

Mother-of-Pearl

Mother-of-pearl is an unusual surface for scrimshaw, and there are hardly any scrimshanders who use it. The shimmering gleam that makes the material so desirable is a disadvantage, since it diminishes the black and white effect of the scrimshaw. If it has to be scrimmed, I believe that the shimmering mother-of-pearl is better suited for "drawing" work with strong contrasts. Milky mother-of-pearl, which is actually a less valuable material, makes a quieter background for scrimshaw.

Mother-of-pearl can be obtained in plates of different size and thickness and in a variety of colors.

It is extremely important to wear a good dust mask when working with mother-of-pearl. The dust from mother-of-pearl is very poisonous, and it accumulates in the respiratory tract. Supposedly, mother-of-pearl is best worked with a diamond needle, but I find that I do very well working it with my usual steel needle.

Narwhal Tusk

Really, I mention narwhal tusk just in passing. The material also comes from a protected species. Narwhal tusk is so rare and expensive that it is very seldom that anyone will scrim it, especially since you want to preserve the characteristic counterclockwise surface twist. Male (rarely the female) narwhals develop the tusk from the left tooth in the upper jaw and it grows straight through the upper lip. The tusk can be up to 2.30 m long.

Two pieces of narwhal tooth sawn into grip scales and a cross-section.

The Vikings brought narwhal tusks to Europe in the 12th century, long before the animal itself was generally known, and there were some really strange ideas about where the tusks came from. Earlier seafarers called the narwhal a "unicorn", and perhaps this is the origin of belief in that legendary creature.

By the 19th century, the narwhal was hunted mainly for its tusk.

Artificial Materials

Various artificial materials also provide suitable surfaces for scrimshaw. Micarta™ is often used for knife handles, but only paper Micarta™ offers really good scrimming possibilities. All other types of Micarta™ have too coarse a texture and cannot be polished smooth enough for scrimshaw. Their surfaces become a "smeared" gray when the color is applied. Micarta™ is available in a variety of colors, and black Micarta™ is suitable for "negative" images.

Corian™, made by Dupont, is an artificial material that is uniformly dense and not porous. It is available in many colors and the surface is easily polished. Corian™ is heat-sensitive, as are many other artificial materials, and you have to be careful when working with it, but it is suitable for scrimshaw.

A sperm whale tooth of polymer with two small sheets of polymer in front.
On the right, two pieces of white Corian™ and a piece of light brown paper Micarta™.

Polymer is used to produce replicas of antique scrimshaw for museums. The scrimshaw kit that I purchased at the beginning of my career as a scrimshander contained a variety of plates and an artificial sperm whale tooth of this material. Polymer has a color similar to ivory. It is easily worked and very good for practice, but it is really no fun to scrim a complex subject on it.

Because of the shortage of genuine whale teeth, enthusiasts of antique scrimshaw may find it especially interesting to attempt subjects in the style of the old whalers on polymer. Perhaps future generations of scrimshanders will have to use these artificial materials much more often when they wish to scrim.

Rocks and Minerals

Scrimshaw can even be done on stone. I have seen work scratched on jade, but naturally it didn't have the delicacy of "real" scrimshaw.

Just a short time ago, I was told that Kurt Wolter, a former scrimshander from upper Michigan (now living in Virginia) had often scrimmed on a mineral called datolite (CaBSio4(0H)), calcium boron silicate hydroxide. Datolite comes in a variety of colors, but it can also be entirely colorless. Apparently, when white and sawn into sections, it is very suitable for fine scrimshaw. In the United States, this mineral is found in the region of Lake Superior. In Europe, it is found in Norway, Russia, and the Black Forest in southern Germany.

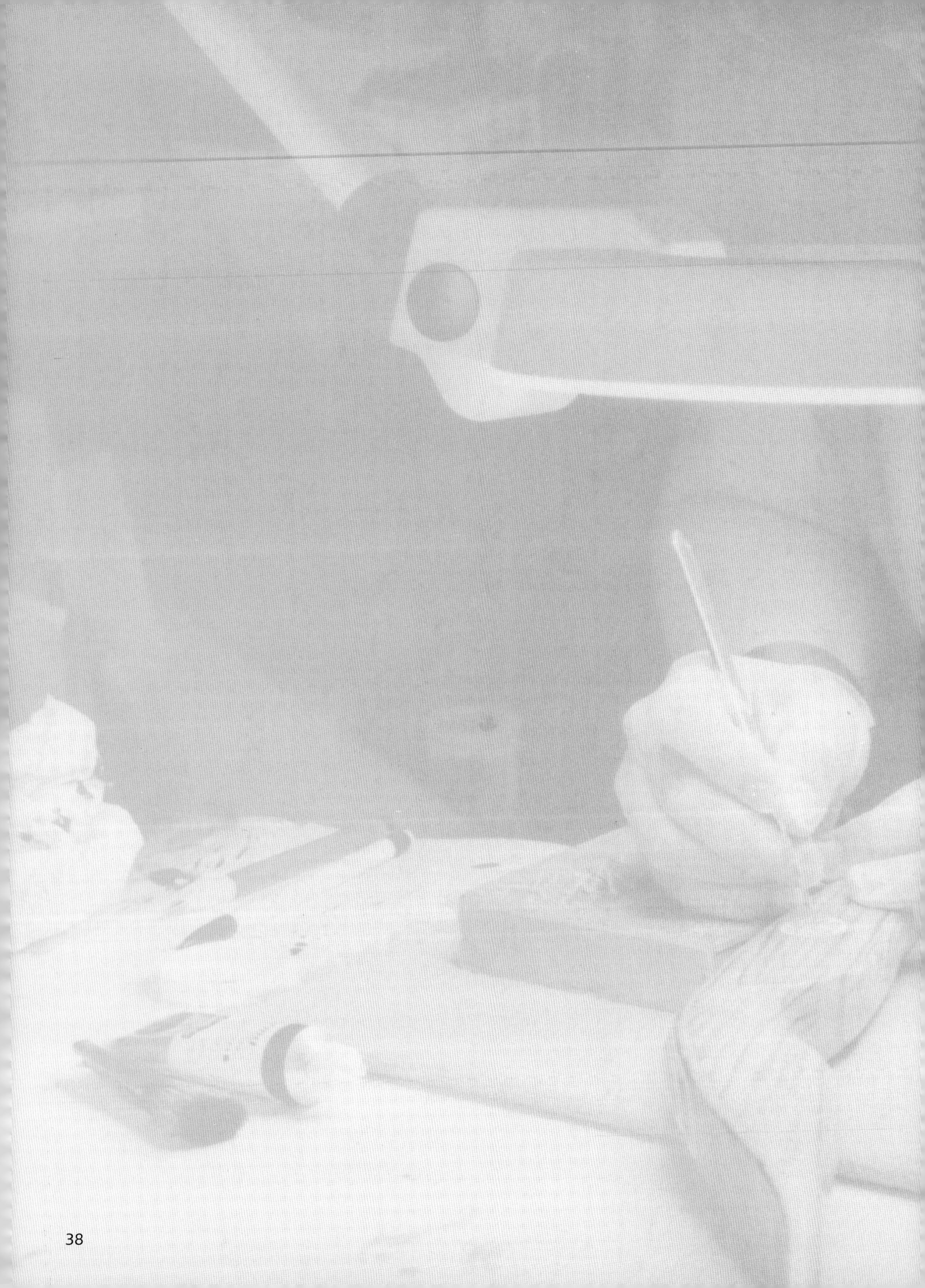

A Technical Overview

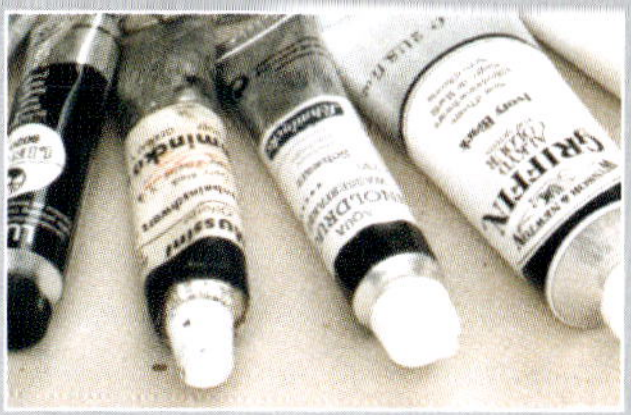

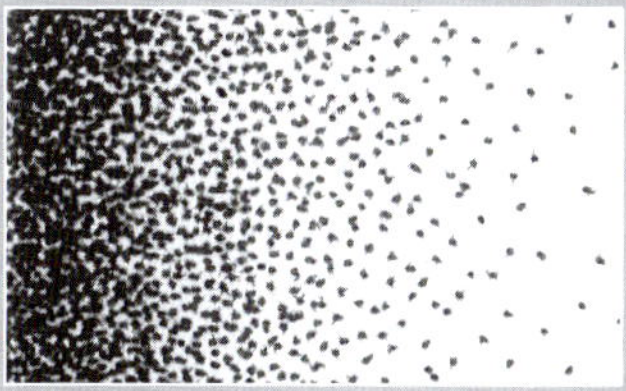

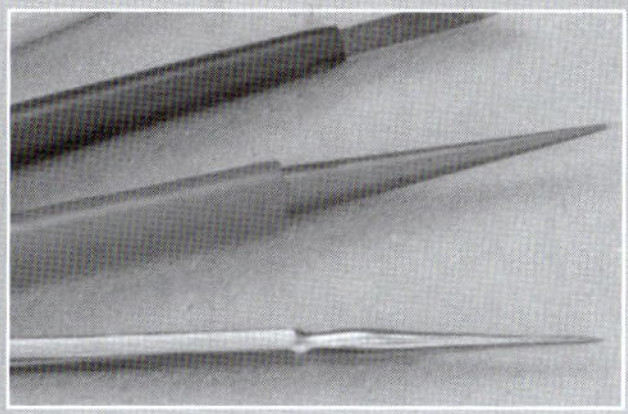

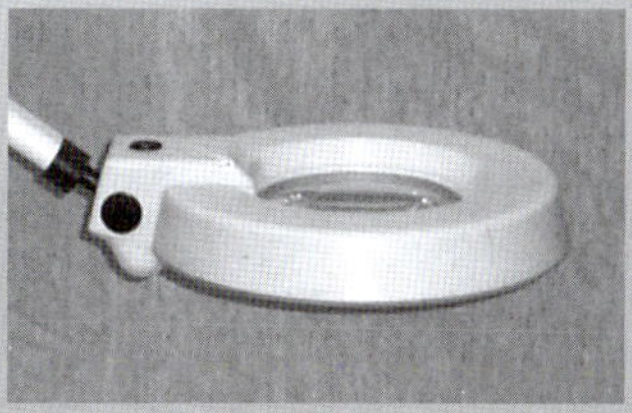

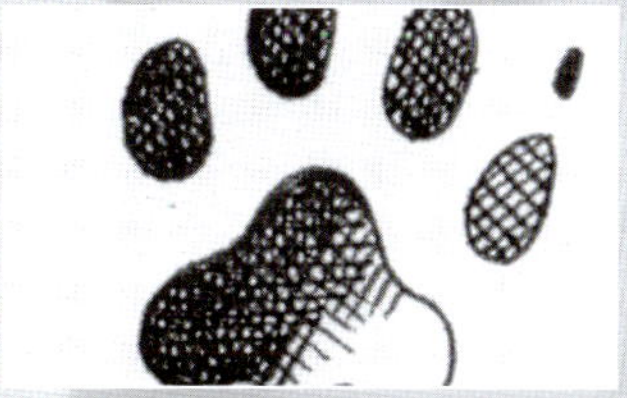

A Technical Overview

Whenever I am asked how to do scrimshaw, the explanation I give sounds quite simple: "First, you put a mirror-smooth polish on the material; then, using a magnifier, you scratch a design into its surface with a sharp needle; after that, you rub a coloring agent over the surface; and then finally, wipe the color away with a cloth. The color will remain in the grooves where the material has been worked."

Of course this description of the technique is very simple in principle, but to make a good piece of scrimshaw or even a pencil sketch, you really need a great deal more. I can explain some of the things involved, such as tools, treatment of materials, tips for transferring designs, and a variety of "engraving" techniques. However, patience, a willingness to practice, and the artistic part - drawing skill, development of your own style, and self-criticism - are things you have to provide yourself.

Tools

The first thing to describe are the various tools a scrimshander uses, and the scrimshander's most important tool is always a **"needle"** of hard steel.

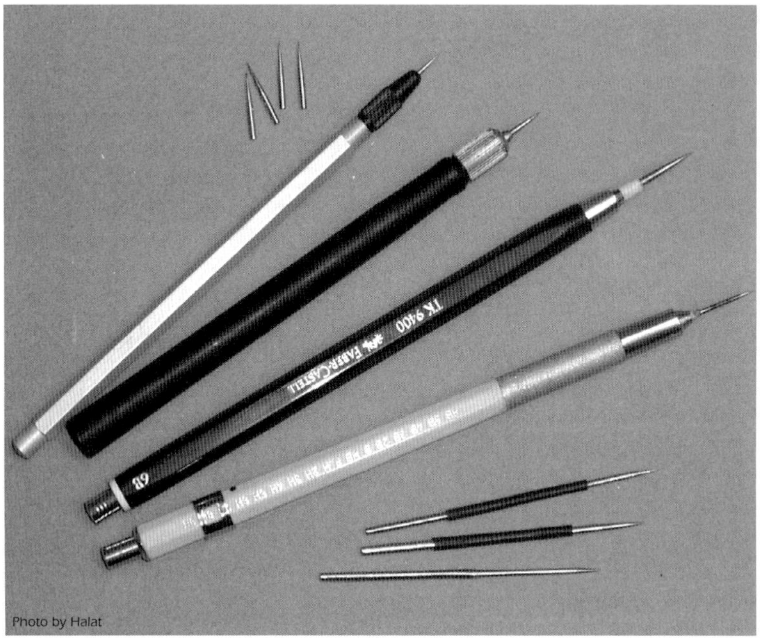

Photo by Halat

These are my preferred tools. The small needles on top are replaceable needles for a scribing tool, inserted in two different holders. The needles below are especially made for scrimshaw by Matthias Hassel (see appendix). They fit in place of leads in mechanical pencils. The black rubber material that gives the needle a perfect fit in the holder is removable when resharpening shortens the needle.

Scrimshanders who do very delicate and precise work will use only stippling to portray their subject, and for this purpose they will use needles. If you prefer, you may want to use a number of different scalpel blades as well, to give more life to your scrimshaw

For example, **etching needles**, the steel needles for copper engraving plates, can be used for scrimming. They are available in many different models of varying quality. A number have **holders** with exchangeable inserts, available with a variety of points in different shapes. You can also find holders for leads (in our case needles) of various diameters in well-stocked artist supply shops or catalogs.

I once found a really good etching needle by chance in an artists' supply shop. It has a fine point, and because it is made of massive, thick steel, it fits well in the hand, which makes stippling easier. Its disadvantage is that it is difficult to sharpen, since the conical point gets wider the more it is used.

Very useful are **scribing tools** used to engrave metals. They are available in a number of versions, either as a complete tool or as a holder with replaceable needles, which is what I used.

You can also scrim with **diamond-pointed** needles, but most materials are so soft that a steel needle works just as well. Diamond needles are designed for use on metal, but they can give very good results on mother-of-pearl and other hard materials. A diamond point is not as narrow or pointed as a metal needle. The choice to use a diamond needle instead of steel depends on the material you have to scrim. I have no experience in the use of diamond points.

I believe that you should try a variety of different tools and then use the tool that works best for you. There are no limits to inventiveness, and in any case, I know only very few tools that can be purchased ready-made specifically for scrimshaw. For a long time, my favorite tool was a large, old, sewing needle, perhaps originally made for sailmaking or for upholstery. It is about 2.5 mm thick and 16 cm long and made of good, hard, old steel. As a holder, I first used a simple ballpoint pen with the insides removed. I stuck a piece of cork or rubber on the end of the needle to keep it in place inside the holder, and that worked well at first.

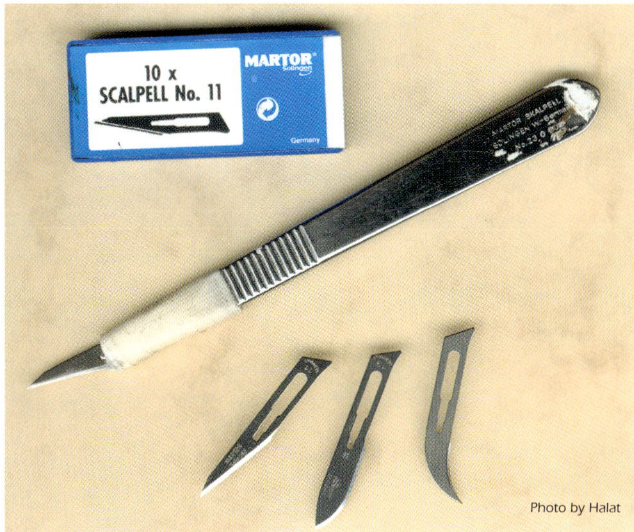

Scalpel holder and blades. You should wrap the narrow grip up toward the blade to prevent cutting a finger when you have to hold it close to the point for very precise work.

Scalpel blades are also good scrimshaw tools. You can get interchangeable blades in a variety of shapes that can be changed to scrim different shapes and textures. The blades shouldn't be so long that they flex from side to side. The holders and blades by Martor™ (Germany) or X-acto™ (United States) are very good. Mostly, I use the pointed blade. This blade shape is especially useful for hair, feathers, water, straight lines, and letters. The rounded blade is best for corrections, because the curve allows it to be used for scraping, and the hooked blade also has its uses in scrimshaw, although it doesn't look as if it would.

There are also **machines** that can be useful. Unfortunately, I have not had the opportunity to try one myself, but I believe that a machine would make the work easier, because your hand won't cramp so easily while scrimming. I have seen a variety of devices on the Internet, and Bob Engnath presents simple plans for a "scrimshaw machine" for stippling in his *Scrimshaw Connection II*. A commercially available tool is the compressed-air-driven "Turbocarver" (see the Website Appendix), and one scrimshaw artist who used it was honest enough to admit that he had.

There are very few scrimshanders who would brag about using machines to help them. Quite the contrary. Many scrimshaw artists deliberately emphasize that their work is done entirely by hand without the use of machines. This is certainly evident when you examine their work under magnification. Scrimshaw work that has been done with the help of a machine often has extremely uniform texture or script.

I don't believe that any machine can replace artistic skill. If the scrimshander doesn't know where and how to place his point, the machine isn't going to help him. Technical skill alone doesn't produce art. Only a suitable blend of excellent artistic technique, an eye for the essential, creative potential, and the ability to criticize your own work will allow an artist to eventually achieve mastery and to create outstanding work.

Magnification

A good **magnifying device** is the most expensive tool that a scrimshaw artist has to buy, but it is essential. Cheap magnifiers have inferior lenses that distort what you're looking at, and you can get dizzy or sick from looking through them too long.
In any case, if you intend to "stick with it", you should get a device for professionals with good optics and at least double magnification; the kind used by goldsmiths is a good example. Around the lens of such a magnifier is a light that illuminates only the working surface. The size of the lens is also important. It has to be large enough so that you can comfortably look through it with both eyes.

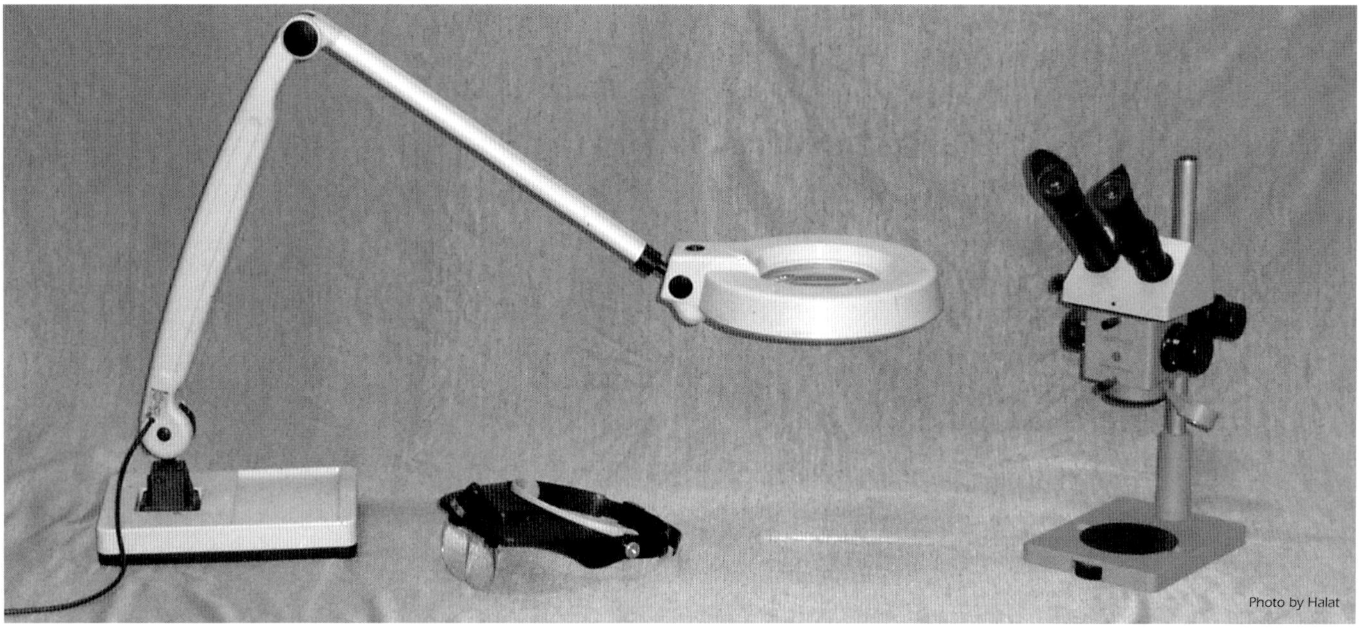

The magnifier I use, a head band magnifier and a stereo microscope. There are different models on the market.

If you work under a magnifier or microscope without built-in lighting, you will need a small supplementary light source that can be set up close to your work and that will cast its light diagonally from above. This angle helps to make the scrimmed grooves more visible on the white material. As long as no coloring agent has been applied, when you shine the light on your work the polished surface will reflect it, but the worked or scrimmed surfaces will look darker and stand out. Be careful to use a **cold light source**, such as neon lamps or LEDs, so that the heat of the lamp doesn't dry out and crack the material.

There are also **head band magnifiers** that are worn on a band around the forehead and that may come with replacement lenses of different magnifications. These magnifiers are cheaper than the larger illuminated ones, but even here you can find obvious differences in quality.

Very precise scrimmers work under **stereo microscopes**, the absolute ne plus ultra. These devices often have adjustable magnification that allows you to zoom in and work at increasingly greater magnification. You can then rapidly zoom back out for an overview of the entire work. If you want to work with scrimshaw in color, such a microscope is virtually a necessity.

At the moment, I work with several magnification devices. Generally I begin by laying out the larger subjects under two-and-a-half magnification. I also scrim the first fine lines and reference points at that magnification, because this magnifying glass gives me the best overview of the entire surface. It lets me keep a good eye on the development of the entire picture as it's being scrimmed.

Depending on the size of the subject, or when I have to work on very fine detail, I go a step further and use a stereo microscope with adjustable magnification. I always work with one when I'm doing colored scrimshaw.

The prices for these devices are reasonable, given the quality of the optics. When you purchase a stereo microscope it is important to get one that will give you enough room between the optics and the working surface to work on your scrimshaw.

Coloring Agents

There is a wide choice of coloring agents. Oil paints, printer's ink, linoleum print ink, waterproof India ink, acrylic paint, alkyd paint, and airbrush paints can all be used to give color to scrimshaw.

Waterproof India ink and **oil paints** have traditionally been used by many scrimshanders. The ink, however, has the disadvantage that it dries out very rapidly on the surface of the material to be colored, so that it has to be removed by a damp cloth or tissue. A little saliva on a rag immediately dissolves the ink and works even better.

There are so many different coloring agents on the market, and they can vary so much from source to source in different countries, that it is impossible to list all the different possibilities here. I don't want to claim that any one is better than another, but I myself prefer oil or alkyd paints. Some scrimshanders also develop their own color mixtures, specially designed for their particular technique.

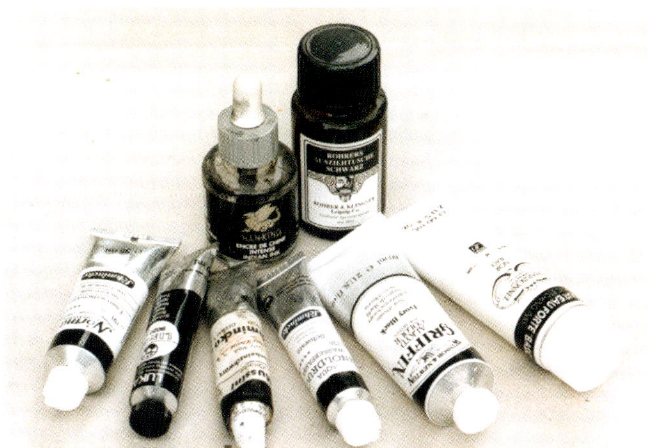
Photo by Halat

Various paint tubes and inks.

An important point when purchasing paints is the **pigmentation**. Paints are made with a binding agent and finely ground materials - the pigments - that can consist of earth, stone, various plant or animal substances, chemically-produced pigments, or even semi-precious minerals. Cheap paints do not have high pigment density and so do not cover a surface well. Moreover, the pigments are often too coarsely ground and so don't fit well into the grooves of very precise scrimshaw.

High-quality paints for artists are usually quite expensive, but the price scarcely matters when you consider how little you really need to color scrimshaw. The choice of black pigment is also important. There is ivory black, iron oxide black, and for example Mars black (the fantasy name of a black tone from Liquitex™). All of these black tones cover fairly well. Many are identified by proprietary names that vary from company to company, but ivory black is also still being made today from bone ash. Ivory black belongs to a class of blacking that is easily glazed. Mars black and iron oxide black are deep black and cover well.

In any case, pigments that cover well are essential for colored scrimshaw on black backgrounds. This property isn't always spelled out on the tube, but manufacturers have color cards that list the color fastness and covering ability of the individual paints. Except for white ink, India ink generally contains no pigment. It is a so-called tint. The color is dissolved from the source material. For that reason, India ink can penetrate the finest grooves. Filtered coffee is a good example of a tint.

I have thoroughly tested a few good coloring agents to see how quickly they dry and how well they will stand up to hard use. I simply used my finger to put a streak of paint on a piece of paper and then on a polished piece of mother-of-pearl, which doesn't hold paint as well as ivory or horn.

Although the name of the company and the color designations are different in different countries, the following list will give you some idea of the tremendous variety in the properties of coloring agents.

Waterproof black drawing ink initially adhered very poorly to mother-of-pearl and could be wiped off the next day with a finger. After about two weeks, a fingernail was needed to scratch it off. It is fairly waterproof and dries rapidly on paper. But on ivory it dries immediately and so firmly when coloring a piece, that, like oil paint, it can no longer be rubbed off. However, it comes off quite easily with a little saliva.

IlluColor™ **air brush paint** from Lukas™ is fluid ink. it comes in a variety of color tones, which can be mixed. It is absolutely waterproof, and its coloring behavior on ivory is comparable to that of India ink.

Basic etching ink supplied in tubes by Charbonnel™ dries slowly on paper. However, it is waterproof and dries faster than oil paint.

Water-based linoleum print paint ink dries quite hard, but it is always somewhat water soluble, so it is not really suitable for scrimshaw.

Griffin™ **alkyd paint** from Windsor and Newton™ is an oil paint that dries faster than normal oil paint because of the added alkyd resin. Initially, it dried slowly on mother-of-pearl, but after two weeks it could only be removed by scratching with a fingernail. It is absolutely waterproof and, for an oil paint, dries on paper with amazing rapidity. Any excess oil paint, regardless of type, can be wiped away with a dry cloth after coloring the surface.

Oil paints from Bloxx™, Norma™, and Schminke™ (unmixed with additives) dry poorly on mother-of-pearl, and like normal oil paint, were still somewhat softer than the alkyd paint even after drying for two weeks. They could also be scratched off, but they are entirely waterproof and harden quite nicely after a few weeks.

Of course, there are also other coloring agents, such as printer's ink, screen printing colors, and acrylics, which I haven't tested and which are sometimes used to color scrimshaw. The important criteria are basic pigment quality, color fastness, and often the ability to cover. In every case, it is especially important for scrimshaw coloring agents to be waterproof.

As a result of these tests, I learned an important lesson. You must let your colors dry thoroughly before delivering your work to a customer. This is absolutely essential if the scrimshaw is on an article to be used and not merely admired.

Technique

I distinguish between the production of "**utility scrimshaw**" done on objects intended for real use and "**display art**", scrimshaw created as pure art and not to decorate something used daily. Scrimshaw on the handles of collector knives is also a good example of display art. On objects that are intended for real use, I work more deeply into the material to ensure that the color will not wear off too rapidly. When you have to do detailed work for utility scrimshaw, the point of the needle should have a very narrow taper so that the point doesn't become too thick as you go deeper. This is perhaps comparable to photo-engraving scanning elements for printing; the finer the element, the finer the picture and color gradations.

If necessary, I will protect a completed scrimshaw work with a coat of quick-drying **lacquer**. This is especially necessary for pendants that will come into contact with skin. Ivory yellows very quickly if it is greasy, and sweat is extremely aggressive, so in time, the coloring agent might also dissolve out of the depressions.

In general, however, I do not think that it is a good thing to lacquer scrimshaw. First of all, the lacquer can change the appearance of fine scrimshaw. Moreover, lacquer can be misused to hide mistakes. For example, suppose that there is a spot on the material that doesn't have enough color, perhaps because it was overworked or perhaps because the points weren't placed close enough. This can be concealed by adding a little paint and, without wiping it off, fixing it with lacquer. However, scrimshaw is produced only by the color that remains in the scrimmed depressions themselves after it is rubbed in and the excess wiped off.

An example of "display art" on mammoth ivory by Viveca Sahlin.

Now on to the technique of scrimming. It is sometimes hard for a beginner to get exactly the right feel for working the materials, so right at the start, especially for neophytes in this field, I want to describe a few ways to scrim various subjects with different techniques and different tools.

It is important to hold the needle as close to the vertical as you can while still working in a relaxed manner. A line "scratched" at too much of an angle will only hold the paint on one side and you get a blurred effect. A point put in at an angle is no longer a round point, but an oval.

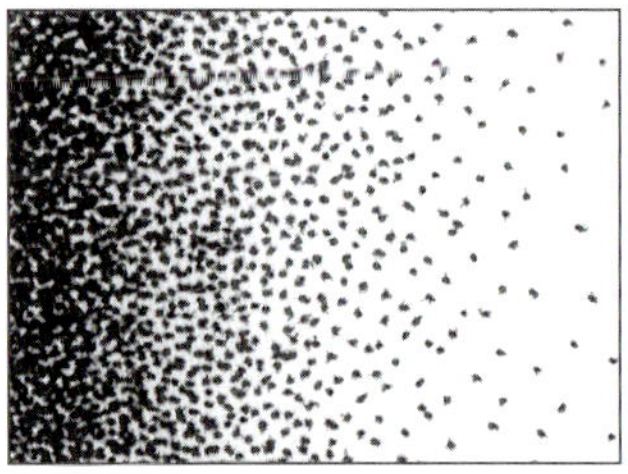

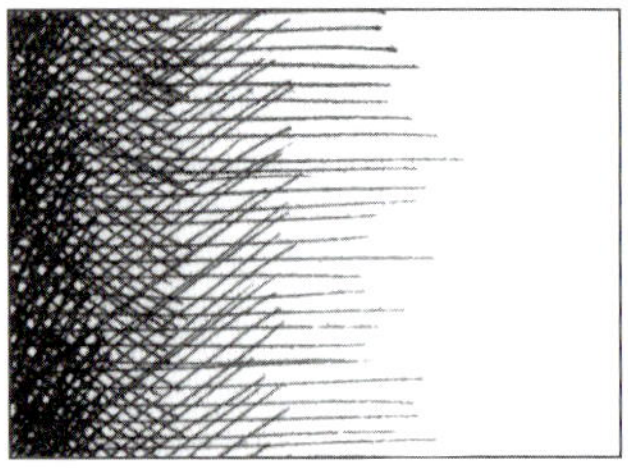

Gradation from dark to light using stippling method and line technique.

A good exercise to begin with is to take needle and scalpel and produce gradations from dark to light with both point and line techniques. The depressions for the dark spots need a little more pressure and have to be much closer together. But on the lighter surface, you use less pressure to make shallower depressions, and you decrease the density of the stippling.

It is also worthwhile to do a few **texture exercises** with different tools. It is best to practice on antler, bone, horn, or artificial materials, to save expensive ivory materials. You should keep the practice work to evaluate your progress by comparing it with your later work. I would always use stippling technique for human skin and all flat surfaces, for example flower petals, that don't have any texture of their own. Incidentally, it doesn't make any sense to try to give a fur pelt to a bear that will only be a few mm in size on the final piece. Although very fine stippling might seem suitable there, in reality the fur texture will also disappear a distance away.
Carefully examine the work of other good scrimshanders whenever you get the chance, especially in the original. Sometimes, if you ask permission beforehand, you may be given an opportunity to closely examine work at an exhibition. A hand lens is a useful tool for such examination, and they are available in various magnifications.

A needle may also be used to "scratch" lines to represent **fur texture**. Here it is important that the lines follow the natural direction of fur growth. They shouldn't go in just any direction. When you scrim subjects using line techniques, I suggest you follow the shape of the subject with the lines.
Fur or hair looks natural when the line becomes gradually thinner in its "swing" as you near its end. But even hair may be scrimmed using point techniques. It depends on the technique that you prefer.

To the degree the subject permits, I like to make **dark, bounded, unshadowed surfaces** with the pointed scalpel blade. For that purpose, you draw very clean parallel lines as close together as possible. Then you do the same thing again at an angle on top of the first set of lines.

Photo by Halat

ca. 1:1

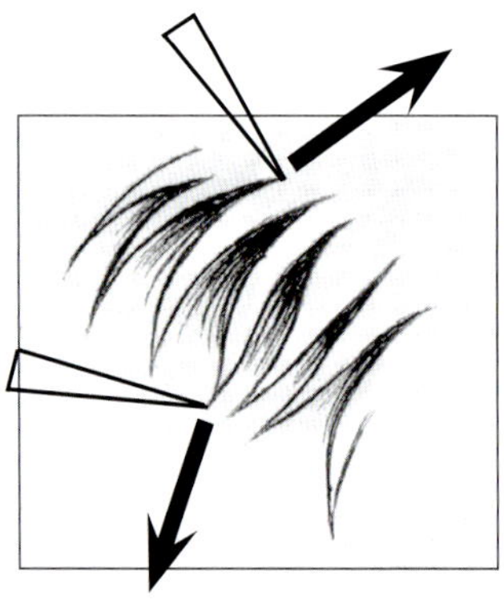

Hair portrayed using line technique must always first be scrimmed out toward the point. You have to work in the opposite direction where hairs come together and where there are shadows under the guard hair. The grooves there must also get gradually narrower. The bear's eyes, nose, and throat are done using stippling because of the relative lack of texture on those surfaces.

Generally, three or four overlaid sets of lines will suffice to give you a nice, black surface. But this technique only looks good where it is appropriate. You get an ugly effect when a surface with special texture, whether fur or feathers, is suddenly replaced by hatched lines in the darker places. Once you begin with a particular texture, you should keep on with it, in both light and dark. At the most, you may "mix" stippling with it. If an exact outline is to be filled with cross-hatching, for example in letters or working in line technique in general, the lines you cut have to begin exactly at the edge to get the necessary definition for a crisp and sharp edge.

Sketched example of cross-hatching for black surfaces.

It is sometimes necessary to scrim a perfectly straight line for an ornamental border, and you use a straightedge. You can pull the blade carefully along the straight edge several times to get a good, visible line. If you need a broader line, you make two parallel lines then fill the space between them with cross-hatching or with stippling. There are also templates for circles and other precise shapes. You can cut your own templates out of thick plastic packing material, for example, and fasten them to curved surfaces with masking tape. You draw curves with the needle. It slides around the curves better than a scalpel blade, whose flat, sharp edge tends to make it follow a straight line and cut into the template.

It can be a lot of fun to use the hooked blade to "stick" an evergreen forest in a distant background. For that purpose, I turn the subject upside down, "hook" into the material with the point of the blade and pull it up at a low angle. When looked at right side up, this produces a triangle in the shape of a tiny fir tree. When you do a number of such triangles together in slightly different sizes, the result is a beautiful, living, forested landscape.

The hooked blade can help when working on horn

This particular blade is also helpful when using the line technique for scrimshaw on horn. A needle is easily led in the direction of the fibers making up the horn, but if you cut the lines with the hooked blade as shown in the photo, it is not difficult to maintain the direction you want your line to take.

An important design element is the combination of black and white. Dark, high-contrast scrimshaw can be combined with lighter and finer scrimshaw, for example in themes with a landscape in the background. Light scrimshaw with little contrast is more representative of the background, like haze in the distance, when it

Photo by Halat

For this subject, the background is lighter and suggests great distance. The small firs along the ridge were produced with the hooked scalpel blade. Scrimshaw on mammoth ivory ca. 1:1.

is combined with darker subjects in the foreground. Again, examine the work of other good scrimshanders to realize how they use the contrast between black and white as a design element.

I tell every beginner that he has to practice and practice and refuse to give up even if his tenth piece of scrimshaw is still a disappointment. Scrimshaw is a traditional art that demands artistic skill, a lot of patience, and mastery of the craft. It doesn't fit today's pace and demand for instant results. Compare your work with that of other scrimmers and try different techniques. With time, your results will improve and, if you stick with it, you will eventually create a style of your own.

The water was scrimmed with lines; the bears still received some visible fur structure. This motif has a more sketched style than scrimshaw done purely in stippling. Scrimshaw by Eva Halat on elephant ivory, knife by Eberhard Kaljumae.

Surfaces

How do we prepare the surface of the material for scrimming? It is absolutely essential to have **smoothly polished surfaces** for scrimshaw. Sometimes you're lucky and get to scrimshaw knife handles. Knife grips almost always have a final polish, so you are spared the effort of preparatory grinding and polishing. Usually, however, the material requires a lot of preparation before you can start your "real" work.

When **sawing** ivory or horn, you have to be careful not to let the material get too hot. Band saws with narrow saw blades or good fret saws are better suited for our purpose than bandsaws with wide blades, which produce more frictional heat.

There are some merchants who sell ivory that has been specially cut by experts. If ivory is cut wrong, then cracks may rapidly appear at just the wrong places, or the material, especially large pieces (similar to wood), can be too strongly affected by changing temperature and humidity.

If you have more ivory than you really need at the time, you have to be careful that it does not dry out while in **storage**. A relative air humidity of 40 % is supposedly ideal.

Like wood, fresh material should be air dried before preparation. If the pieces are large, the cross-sectional surfaces should be sealed with wood glue. But even air-dried elephant ivory has a moisture content of about 15 % and for that reason will always "work" a little, depending on air temperature and humidity.

Depending on the state of the surface of the material, you begin with medium coarse and progress gradually to very fine **sandpaper**, sanding the surface so smooth that there are no abrasion marks visible to the naked eye.

The next step is to use a good, fine **steel wool**. There are several different grades of fineness, but they may vary in quality. Some 000 steel wool is so irregular and coarse that individual threads will put scratches in the surface. Instead of steel wool, you may also use one of the new Scotch-Brite™ artificial abrasive materials.

Finally, you use a **polishing agent** to give the surface a mirror-smooth finish. The fine polishing pastes sold commercially vary in quality. There is also a high-performance wax especially developed for ivory, which you can probably get only from companies that deal with ivory or from large abrasive manufacturers. The polishing paste is applied to a rag or to a machine with a polishing head, and then the surface is polished.

Polishing ivory with a polishing attachment on a drill press.

Naturally, machines, such as a belt sander or a drill press with a polishing attachment, will make this work much easier. There is a lot of friction because of the high speed involved, so if you work with machines, it is absolutely essential not to let the material get too hot. If frictional heat is allowed to dry out the material, it can crack, and the surface can become hard and brittle. You can avoid this if you don't use too much pressure while sanding, cool the material frequently, and work at low rpm.

It is harmful to inhale fine ivory or horn dust, and mother-of-pearl dust may even accumulate in the lungs. You must wear a **dust mask**. This is absolutely essential when you are working with these materials. The best dust masks are those that have filters that block harmful vapors as well as fine dust. A light mask with an intermediate layer of activated charcoal or a mask with interchangeable filters are both good. Masks with activated charcoal not only halt dust and vapor, but also keep out the bad smell that results from working ivory or horn.

Subject Selection

Let me say a few more words about the design of your scrimshaw. Even though the surface in front of you is now ready for scrimming, you still have to be patient before you can start. It's not a matter of just scrimming something on the material; you want to create a harmonious work of art.

The first thing that you have to consider is your choice of subject, and it must always fit the piece or object to be worked. A deer on a whole whale tooth is a matter of taste, but you will hardly ever place a lone standing marmot vertically across a horizontally-held knife handle. Rather, you will place it vertically on the handle when the knife is held vertically with the point down. If necessary, you can select a crouching animal as a model.

You are always creating a picture, even if only a very small one. You are not just sticking a subject in the middle of the surface. The entire surface is a part of the picture, including the background. Its shape has the same function as the canvas does for a painting.

Even empty spaces in a picture can be restful to the eye and yet provide interesting tension in the formation of the picture. A single subject can deliberately function as a vignette or be woven into the surface with a little help from landscape, grass, or ornamentation.

Remember, this is your work that will be judged. Let prospective clients know immediately if you think what they want won't turn out well. Propose an alternative to them. No one will remember later whose idea it was to do it that way.

I always find that cracks and streaks and veins of color in the material pose an interesting challenge. It is fun to fit these into the picture; sometimes they even suggest the subject. Long cracks can be made into effective trees, rivers, or parts of a landscape, such as horizon lines or ridges. Color streaks can also provide beautiful landscapes or natural borders for the subject.

There are some basic rules for **knife grips**, which determine the direction the subject is to face and the side on which the subject is to be displayed. You always

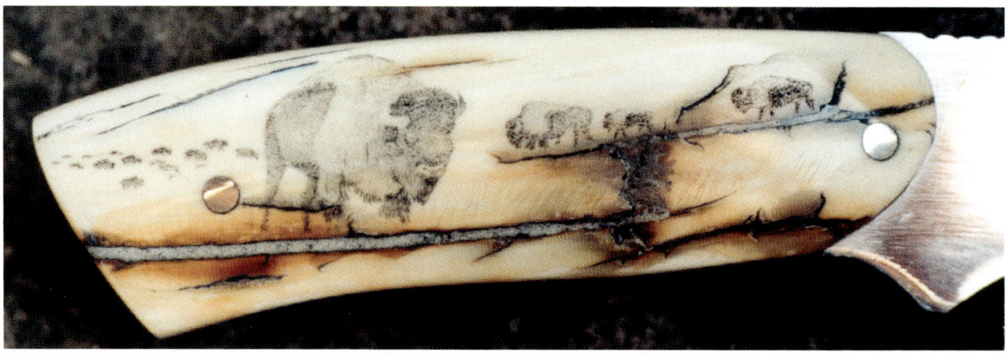

In the upper illustration, the numerous cracks in the mammoth ivory grip scale are still very visible. The beautiful coloring and the two large cracks provide the foreground for placing the buffalo. The fine cracks on the upper left become bluffs in the background. Scrimshaw: Eva Halat.

place it on the side where the knifemaker displays his logo. If you have a horizontal subject on just one side, the blade of the knife must point to the left with the edge down. For a subject that must be scrimmed in a vertical direction on a "standing" knife , the blade must point down and the edge is on the right side.

You must also protect yourself from the blade and protect the knife from damage. A piece of paper towel wrapped around the blade and held with tape keeps you from cutting yourself and from letting your mistakes - and there can be plenty of those - put scratches on the newly polished steel.

Of course you need **models** for your work. People always ask me if I work from a model. I can now trust myself to scrim a portrait of a wolf without a model, because I have painted and scrimmed so many, but a detailed "drawing" is always more natural and alive if you do it from a model. It's nice if you can use your own photos. Naturally this is a more individual approach. You can also find numerous subjects in books and on the Internet. You can add creativity to your work by placing your animal model in a different landscape or by grouping it with animals from other pictures so that you don't just make an exact copy of the original. A word of warning: Be sure that all the shadows of subjects in a picture are cast by light coming from the same direction.

When drawing an animal, you have to consider whether you want to show the whole animal or whether, because you're working on a very small surface, you would prefer to show only the face and make it a portrait.

An animal looks interesting and more alive when it reveals something by the way it holds its body or by its expression. For example, a cougar taking a comfortable nap on a cliff looks very different from the same animal stalking an unsuspecting prey.

The scale at which you have to work also plays a role in your selection of theme or subject. You will hardly try to show all of Noah's ark, including the crew, on a piece only two centimeters by two centimeters when you are working under double magnification. You will do much better with a single animal or an animal portrait.

If you are a beginner in art, the following possibilities might help you create good scrimshaw, because the transfer of subjects into scrimshaw technique is much easier for experienced artists than for the inexperienced. It is easiest if the picture or reference sketch that you use is black-and-white. Then you just have to "copy" the light and dark places. If you are still somewhat uncertain how to transfer a colored picture or a large subject, just transfer it into black-and-white in appropriate size using a copying machine or computer. It is helpful to make several detailed sketches before you begin scrimming, drawing the final size in pencil or in ink with a fine-point pen.

Workplace

Another thing that you shouldn't overlook is to be sure your workplace is comfortable. If you're sitting in an uncomfortable position, your hand, shoulder, and back will cramp and scrimming will become torture.

Your chair should be high enough so that your magnifier and working surface can be positioned so that you don't have to bend or stretch too much. If the piece you are going to work on is too small to be comfortably held in your hand, you can attach it to a larger piece with double-stick tape. Many scrimmers also use small bags full of cherry pits, rice, or the equivalent to easily hold and adjust the material in a comfortable position. This can be especially useful when working on three-dimensional objects such as powder horns or billiard balls.

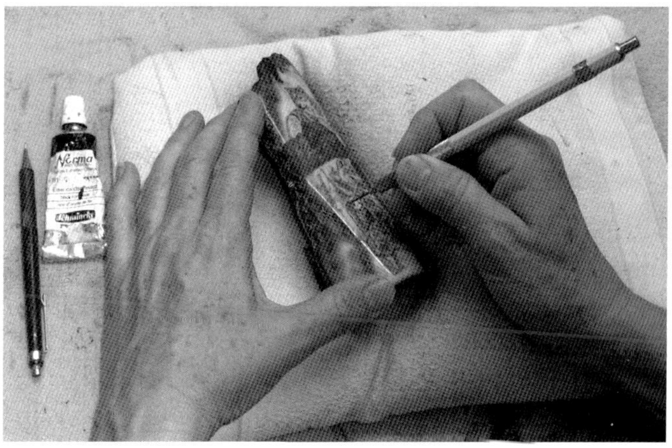

A "pillow" filled with grain is a comfortable rest for the scrimming hand and gives the object a safe and stable position.

When I have to work on a thick piece, I rest my hand on a book or small box to position it at the same height as the surface to be scrimmed. It is also helpful to place the material to be scrimmed on a piece of leather or some other soft surface.

Transferring the Subject

Soon you can start scrimming! But first the subject must somehow be transferred to the prepared surface or sketched on it. There are numerous ways to do this. Before transferring your subject to the working surface, it is advisable to first rub paint over the entire surface as a "surface test." If you can easily wipe the paint off the surface without leaving shadows or visible grinding marks, you can begin with the real work of scrimshaw. But if the surface retains even a trace of the paint, it must be prepared once again. Depending on how much paint is left, you may only have to polish the surface, but you may also have to reach for sandpaper once again.

Mostly, I sketch my subjects directly on the polished surface with a very soft (hardness 2B), fine-point pencil. You can only sketch the general outline, marking significant places for the proportions, because the pencil lines are thick and adhere poorly to the surface. There are also pencils for use on glass, which should work very well for preliminary sketches.

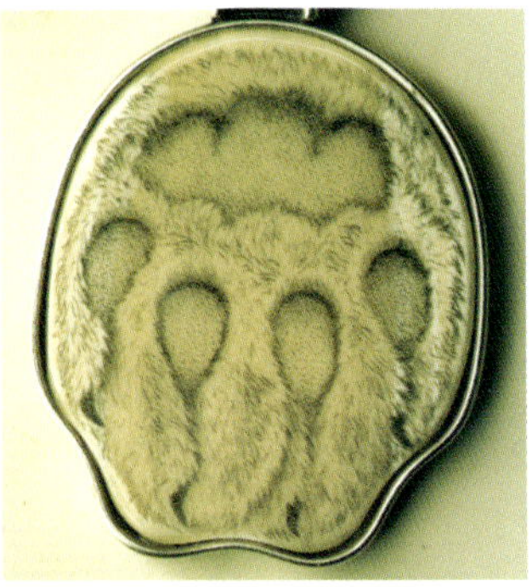

The pendant of mammoth tusk shown front and back at about the original size.

Preliminary sketch with pencil

The first lightly scrimmed outlines

After the first run

The completed subject

Photos P. 52: Halat

Another transferring method is tracing with carbon paper.

The transferred motif. The carbon paper's color adheres quite well to the polished surface.

Photos by Volker Alles

The first very fine lines are scrimmed and colored.

Then I put in the outlines by stippling with the needle or with very, very fine lines that can be easily worked over; then I ink it for the first time.

For animals with fur, you are on solid ground if you avoid sketching the first outlines with a single line, but use a number of small strokes. Fur really doesn't have a sharp boundary, and a visible outline remaining around the edge of the fur isn't very attractive.

After putting a sketch on a larger area, you can spray it lightly with a fixative for pastel chalk. This will keep your hand from wiping away the pencil lines while you're scrimming the initial outlines. Another possibility is to cover the surface with a thin coating of water soluble, white paint (for example, watercolor white), using only enough to give you a matte surface with the original surface showing through. When this paint is dry, you can draw fine, precise lines on it using little pressure or trace the subject on it, scrim the initial outlines, and then wash off the paint with a damp cloth.

You can easily make a sheet of transfer or carbon paper yourself. Take a soft pencil and cover a thin sheet of paper or the reverse side of the picture to be transferred with graphite, and then smooth this graphite surface with your finger to remove any extra graphite particles that would thicken the transferred lines. Now when you place the graphite covered side on the surface to be scrimmed, you can easily trace the outlines of your design with a hard pencil or ballpoint pen and scrim these transferred lines as your first fine outlines.

Another possibility for direct transfer of the subject is to reduce the subject to the desired size by hand, computer, or copying machine and to attach the paper to the working surface. Then, you pierce small holes through the paper along the outlines and at important reference points. This takes a little practice, because the paper will make it hard to judge the proper pressure to use with the needle and the stippling points that you get may be either too small or too large. After that, you fold the preliminary sketch to one side so that it can be flipped back to its original position if necessary, and then you color the scrimmed surface for the first time.

If there are a few places where the paper was not properly pierced and no points appear at those points after the first inking, then the sketch can be used to

Piercing the outlines

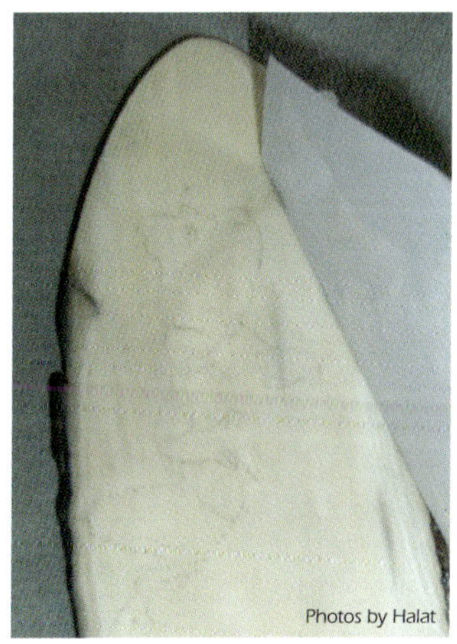

Photos by Halat

The barely visible points after piercing and inking.

"re-cover" the underlying surface, and the missing points are pierced once again. I generally use this method for transferring a subject when I am working with white scrimshaw on black buffalo horn.

I always keep the reference picture next to the work so that I can refer to it during the entire period that I am working on a particular subject.
Once the first outlines are visible, you can finally begin with "real" scrimshaw. If the picture is to have a dark background, you ought to begin with that. If you scrim the subject in the foreground first, you may make that surface too dark and later you will be unable to give it enough contrast against a dark background. A subject in front of a dark background must always appear light against it, because black-and-white scrimshaw lives from contrast.
However, you need not do the entire background all at once. It is enough to scrim a surface surrounding the foreground and later fill in the background, piece by piece.
In spite of your curiosity, you must take your time when coloring. If you rub the paint or ink onto a scrimmed surface too often, it can have the same effect as polishing the surface. The sharp edges of the fine grooves will be slightly rounded and will no longer hold the paint well. I usually do a "major run" working the entire subject, before I first apply the coloring agent. This makes it obvious where more work is required.

The first scrimshaw run before it is colored with oil paint.

Softly rubbing the color in.

Photos by Volker Alles

The finished scrimshaw.

After one or two more runs, the subject should be nearly finished. Then, all you have to do is work on those spots that have to be darker or more detailed. If a surface doesn't want to become really dark, you should examine it under greater magnification than the one you've been working at. It is amazing how much space you will find between the individual points for even more points to make the surface darker. Keep your needle very sharp. You can only get in between the dots already on the surface with a very sharp needle. Always resharpen it now and then during your scrimming process by turning it with light pressure at a flat angel on a sandpaper used for metal. A dull needle will slide back into the scrimmed depressions

White on Black

and more pressure is needed for stippling, which will give you cramps in your hand. So-called "negative" scrimshaw is not really a true negative. That would require the black-and-white picture to be entirely reversed from the original drawing. In scrimshaw, "negative" really refers more to the way we work.

Normally, we put dark surfaces on a light background. On a black background, you have to scrim the light surfaces and leave the quite dark areas undisturbed. On white surfaces, you have always scrimmed the dark parts, so when you begin to work on a dark surface, you will discover that your brain is set to interpret white as "empty" and dark as "something", so that dark is what you are used to doing. Now try to imagine that you are painting the highlights instead of the shadows as normally. That will help you to concentrate on the lighter areas.

Even here, one point is placed next to another.
Part of the horns and the background were done with line scrimshaw to incorporate fine cracks in the material into the design.
Overlay on a bow handle.
Scrimshaw: Eva Halat.
Size of the mountain sheep, about 6.5 cm.

Before you begin, it helps if you can sketch your subject on black drawing or sketching paper with a white drafting pencil. There's no problem if it's larger than the final size, the important thing is to find out where you have to leave the black. There is also a special cardboard in hobby shops or stationary stores that has a black surface. You can scratch lines in it, scraping off the thin black layer to get a white picture on a black background.

Negative scrimshaw is usually scrimmed on black buffalo horn. You can also do good "negative" scrimshaw on black paper Micarta™ and on pieces of the dark, outside bark of mammoth tusk. Oil paints and other pigmented paints are the best

On this black buffalo-horn knife handle the white transferring dots are quite visible.

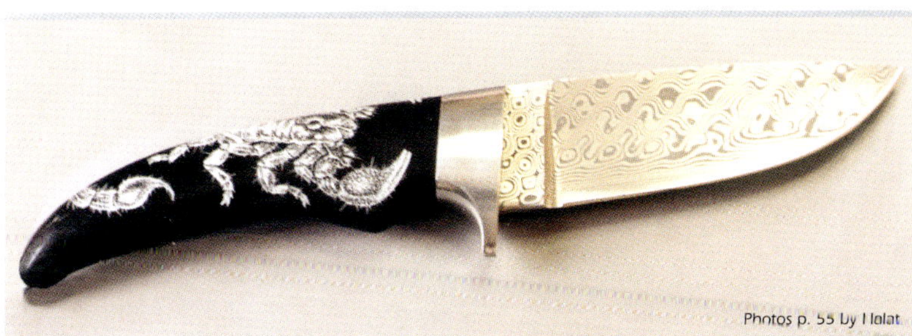

Photos p. 55 by Halat

The finished knife by Eberhard Kaljumae.

Tips for Corrections

for "negative" scrimshaw, because they cover the black background well.

But what happens when you make a mistake?
It doesn't happen that fast. You work so slowly when scrimming that you usually have enough time to think about what you're doing. But when a correction is necessary, it is usually for a place where you have done too much work, so the surface has to be cleaned off again. If it is a small mistake with deep "engravings", you have to enlarge the scraped area a bit to avoid the appearance of a pit, so that you get an undetectable shallow depression. After sanding or scraping the area with the rounded scalpel blade, you can try to polish it flat with steel wool. Then you have to go over it with a polishing paste until everything is as smooth as it was in the beginning.
You have to be careful not to overwork softer materials like horn. Too many uncontrolled lines or points on top of each other will make the surface so rough that it will hold the paint in "gobs", which show up unpleasantly as dark black places (or, with negative scrimshaw, shining white ones) without any detail.
Scrimshaw is normally never completely black. There is always a tiny narrow ridge of material left standing. You can try to shave off the color very carefully from such overworked places with a scalpel blade in the hope of freeing those tiny ridges. If that doesn't work, then you have to sand off the entire area where the mistake was made. Overworked very hard and brittle materials can be very obvious for the opposite reason. Working it too much breaks away the thin ridges, which should be left standing to hold the coloring agent in the grooves between them, and an "open" surface can appear that can barely hold the agent. The only thing that you can do here is to grind it off, polish it, and redo it.

Working in Color

Traditional whaler's scrimshaw was mostly colored in black and sometimes in shades of brown. You very seldom see any antique scrimshaw in color. However, since Bellingham, colored scrimshaw is no longer an exception and has become a special challenge for many scrimshanders.

As always, there are still artists who work in black-and-white in the traditional whaler's style, scrimshanders who have raised their black-and-white technique to the pinnacle of perfection and who do nothing else. In contrast, other scrimmers work almost entirely in color. I have my own, more or less tested technique that I use to make colored scrimshaw, but I would hesitate to claim that it is the only correct one.
Because each artist develops his own individual style and technique, it's not really possible to describe it more precisely. As with many other arts, the secret of success and the creation of a personal style and technique are based on years of experience. Every artist depends on his own experiments, especially for such an unusual art as scrimshaw. If, in the course of time, someone discovers a special procedure,

I can well understand that he would be unwilling to casually give away his hard-earned knowledge to somebody else.
The following introduction only describes the principles and demonstrates a few of the technical possibilities. There are many techniques that I haven't tested myself, but I want to encourage every beginner to experiment. When you get down it, there are probably as many different ways of going about it as there are scrimshanders.

The art of scrimming is the same for colored scrimshaw as for black-and-white scrimshaw. You can use stippling, combinations of stippling and lines, or scrim other textures. As always, it depends on the intent and style of the artist.
However, for the same degree of detail, colored scrimshaw is more time-consuming than black-and-white. In black-and-white work, you can leave light surfaces only slightly worked or quite free of scrimming to get good contrast, but in colored scrimshaw the entire area of the picture may be completely full of different colors. The contrast you get in black-and-white scrimshaw by "scrimmed" versus "empty" surfaces is obtained for two adjoining areas in colored scrimshaw by contrasting colors. That means that both surfaces must be completely worked.

Colored scrimshaw looks most attractive if the paints are neither too gaudy nor too bright, unless expressly required by the subject. Especially primary colors that are too bright often lack the necessary flair and, even with scrimshaw, have a cheap effect. So it is always better not to use too many primary colors in a single picture. A color mix with few primary colors gives the entire theme a unity of color and holds the picture together optically.
A good exercise to give you a feeling for color is to take a few primary colors and mix the entire remaining color palette that you need from them. A bright, clear yellow, a middle blue (sky blue), a shining ultramarine blue, and a magenta red are a good basis. Mixing sky blue or ultramarine blue with a bright yellow gives you two completely different shades of green; and yellow, red, and blue, mixed in the proper proportions, will give you brown.
It can really be a lot of fun to experiment and mix them any way you want. It is a little adventure to discover how many different colors you can get from the different mixes of primary colors. Naturally, you must also use primary colors where they are required. Flowers or bright feathers look great in shining colors.

There are good books for beginners on the use of color in painting. As we pointed out at the beginning, a knowledge of drawing, and for colors, painting is a considerable help in getting good results relatively quickly in your scrimshaw.
Now for the technique: You can do colored scrimshaw in many different ways. However, the basic principle is always to scrim the area for each new color, put in the paint, and only then start to work on the next color. There are scrimshanders who claim that it is better to begin with the lighter areas of the subject and do them before the darker ones. Others prefer to begin at the darker places. I work with

both approaches. (The step-by-step illustrations on page 67 are good examples). After the transfer or preliminary sketch of the subject, I color the initial reference stippling with the appropriate pale colors. If these first outlines are too dark, they will show up in the lighter areas of the finished piece.
If the subject has a few dark areas in just the same color, I will usually begin with that one and scrim it completely. Often I prefer to begin with the background, even when it is lighter than the rest of my subject. If the background frames the entire subject, I can color it without worrying about anything else because there are still no other worked surfaces. For scrimmed surfaces with shadows in the same color, I begin with light paint and only put in the dark shadows as a second coat in the passages that have to be darker.
If the subject requires very dark places, another possibility is to first scrim the darker parts and shadows and begin to color them with either black or with some dark color that suits the subject, such as a dark brown or a gray-blue. It won't matter if they initially get into the lighter areas, because you will always be blending those colors, and bit by bit you let it get increasingly lighter. You can get a nice gradation from dark to light in this way.

You need greater magnification to work on colored scrimshaw, especially for small detailed work, than you do for black-and-white scrimshaw. The different colors must be clear and separate from each other with clean edges, otherwise the entire picture will look blurred and more like a watercolor than crisp scrimshaw. While working on a scrimshaw miniature, you need very strong magnification to get the precise clean lines it requires. For that reason, I work with four- to eight-power magnification right from the start.
Each area, scrimmed in sequence, must be very carefully colored with a fine brush right after the scrimming and before the next area is prepared for the next color. You paint under the same magnification as you scrim.
Sometimes while painting, small air bubbles, visible only under a microscope, can appear; these keep the paint from getting into the grooves. You then have to help the paint soak in with a brush (size 01 or even 00), which must, without exception, have a really fine point. Good brushes are not cheap, but a poor quality brush looks like a shaving brush under the microscope, and it is impossible to paint the surfaces properly with a broad brush.

Oil paints are really the classical medium for scrimshaw work in color. They can be thinned a little with additives, and you can use other additives to make them dry faster. Personally, I would rather avoid the use of inks in colored scrimshaw. Because of their low viscosity, there is always a danger that capillary action will draw them from the areas you are coloring into adjoining, already colored areas. But many scrimshanders do excellent work with colored inks.

Once you have carefully put paint on the area to be colored, you must remove the excess paint just as carefully. In every case, just as in black-and-white scrimshaw, you must avoid wiping it straight off. For larger areas I use very light and careful circular movements at exactly the same spot with a cloth or hand tissue stretched over a fingertip. You can "wipe up" small surfaces with Q-Tips™ or with tissue wrapped around a brush end. You can even use a toothpick to pick up excess paint or to carefully wipe it off. You should never leave any paint in the spaces between the points or lines. After all, we're making scrimshaw, not ivory paintings.

Now it will become evident that it is often safer to begin with dark colors. When paint happens to get into adjacent areas, it is not so bad if it is a lighter color over a darker one. However, a brush with black touching a yellow surface can be a real problem. We have to be very careful that the grooves are filled completely with paint and that there is no room for other paints. But this doesn't mean that you can wipe paint over other colored areas. If you do, you may get ugly changes in an area, especially a light-colored area that has already been colored, because a thin film of the new paint will stick to the first.

Perhaps it would be as well to allow each color to dry completely before continuing your work. However, oil paints need a couple of days to thoroughly dry, and that would really try the patience of any scrimshander. The attempt might be worth it, but I have never had enough patience to try. Maybe printer's ink or other fast drying paint works better.

Some artists give themselves additional protection while painting by spraying an already colored surface with a fixative spray before scrimming the next surface to be colored. This is an attempt to make it easier to remove any paint that accidentally gets onto already-colored surfaces. I haven't tried this yet, and I am not really sure that it wouldn't harm the overall appearance of the work. This would certainly put a great number of coats of the fixative spray on the places you colored first. If you think that this technique might work for you, you should simply try it out. Maybe it works when there are only a few colors involved, but it shouldn't be necessary to fix the colors already in place if you go about your painting carefully enough.

Although ivory carving and painting really have nothing to do with scrimshaw, I would still like to mention them just for the sake of completeness and show some examples without going into detail. These are classic techniques, like scrimshaw, and sometimes there are scrimshanders or carvers who combine scrimshaw and carving.

A quite unusual ulu, the Eskimo skinning knife. The polar bear is an Asiatic carving, the blade by Michael Staubach.

Photos by Halat

Ivory and bone have been used for **carving** far back into the dim mists of antiquity. Many antique carvings have been found around the world, in China and East Asia and throughout India, Syria, Egypt, and Africa. Walrus and mammoth tusks and bones have also been used for carving in Russia and among the Eskimos. Ivory carving existed in northern Europe over 1500 years ago, again mostly on walrus tusks.

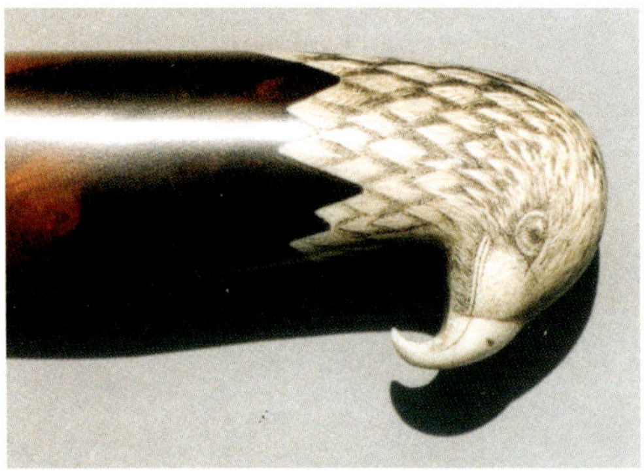

Shaped ivory combined with scrimshaw on a knife by Eberhard Kaljumae.

There were elephants in China until about 1000 years ago, and the Chinese have a very long tradition of ivory carving. On the other hand, ivory carving didn't begin in Japan until around 1600. Today Asia is the greatest producer of ivory carvings and one of the principal importers of ivory, including elephant ivory, mammoth ivory, and walrus tusks.

The world-famous portrait of the Empress Sisi, here immortalized on ivory. The original miniature is about 10 cm high and colored.

Ivory was very popular in the 18th and 19th centuries for miniature **paintings**. In Paris, you could get a specialized education as an ivory painter. Ivory painters mainly painted portraits, using watercolors or gouache in such thin coats that the background surface showed through, giving a certain softness to the delicate paintings.

The colors were not waterproof, so these small pictures were always framed under glass. Their owners also have to protect these valuable ivory paintings from bright sunlight, as there is a danger that the colors will fade.

Today, there are very few ivory painters.

Petra Bergoint

Petra Bergoint was born in 1962 in Aschaffenburg, Germany. From 1979 to 1982, she trained in the rare craft of ivory carving at the Vocational School for Wood and Ivory and took her master's examination in that field in 1991.
She has her own studio and is a participant in the exhibition and restoration workshop at the Deutschen Elfenbeinmuseum (German Ivory Museum). Her work has been shown in numerous exhibitions.
Mainly, she carves mammoth ivory, and she deliberately allows the veins and colors of the fossilized material to appear in places, integrating them in the designs she creates. Black figures carved out of horn, for example nocks for bows, can also be found in her studio. She carves her own designs but is happy to carve ideas suggested by her customers. She also specializes in the restoration of old ivory figures.

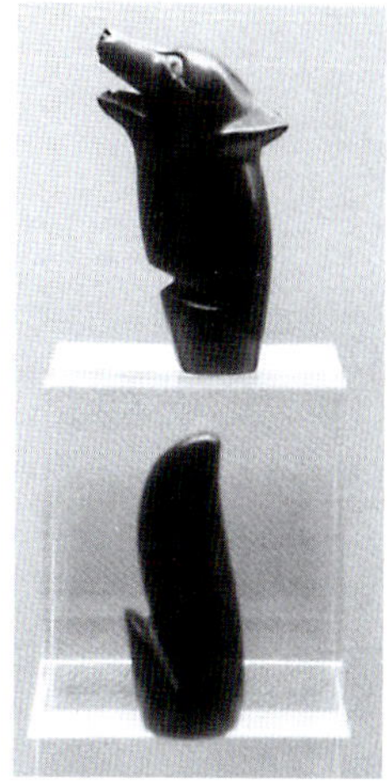

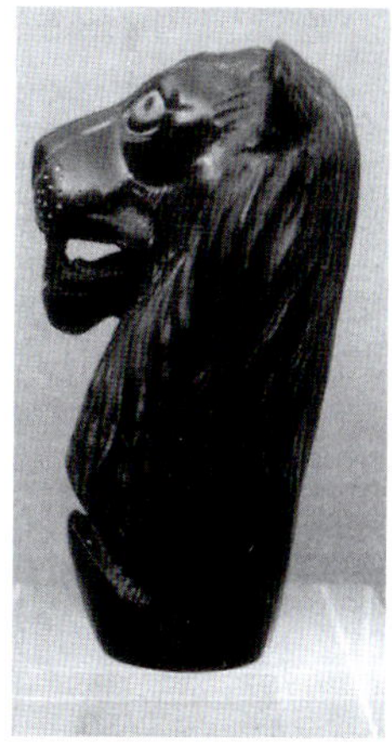

Bow nocks of Nigerian horn. The wolf is 6 cm high, the lion 7 cm.

Interesting ivory knife grips, carved by Petra Bergoint. The blade of the buffalo knife is by Hassel. The blade of the dagger is from Damascus steel by Manfred Sachse. Both pieces assembled by Michael Staubach.

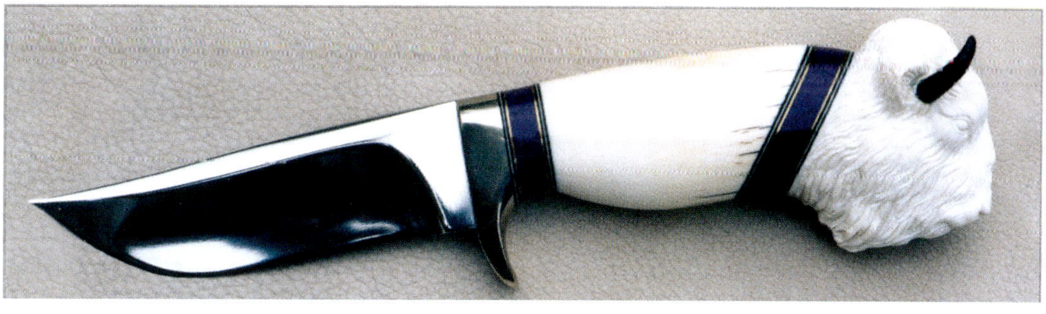

Eduard Stamm

Eduard Stamm was born in 1943 in the Erz Mountains in Germany. He developed a love of nature and forest animals at an early age, wandering through the forests near his home. Paired with his artistic gifts, this experience made it possible for him to develop his talent in sculpture by himself.

Eduard Stamm is fascinated by every natural subject, whether animal, plant, landscape, or human portrait. He creates sculptures and scenes at exact scale in very tiny spaces. He works mostly with horn, but he also uses wood, stone, ivory, and plaster of Paris. In 1993, he won the "Golden Basket" for miniature sculpture at the Westminster Gallery in London, and other prizes followed in 1994, 1995, and 1998.

This tiny tobacco or powder container was carved out of an old billiard ball and is decorated all around with hunting scene microcarvings. 8 x 4.5 cm

A Hunting Bear. Carved out of a moose antler rosette.

Mammoth ivory transformed into a beautiful cameo brooch. Size: 9 cm.

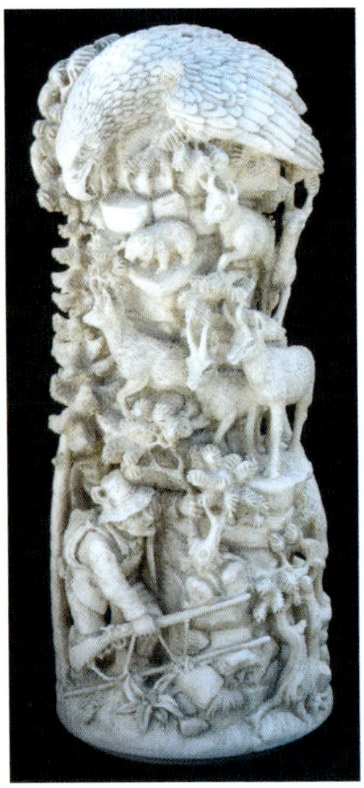

This unbelievably detailed sculpture serves as a salt and pepper shaker. Size: 15 cm.

The container with lid in an alpine motif is also carved out of mammoth tusk. Size: 16 cm.

David Warther

David Warther is an active fifth-generation carver. His ancestors came from Switzerland, and his great-great-grandfather was a wood carver and cabinetmaker. His grandfather carved historical steam engines out of ivory and wood. David began to carve at the age of six and, even as a teenager, produced display works for the Mystic Seaport Maritime Gallery.

David specializes in extremely detailed ship miniatures, true to the originals. Even the rigging is of ivory and sometimes measures only one ten-thousandth of an inch (0.0025 mm) in diameter.

His research covers all of the precise details of ships from different regions and periods of history. Famous historical ships can be found among his many different models, such as the Mayflower; Columbus' flagship, the Santa Maria; cogs from medieval Europe; and the elegant ships of ancient Egypt. David uses scrimshaw technique for the individual details of many surface features.

David's works are exhibited in the land of the Amish People in Dutch Valley, near Sugar Creek in Ohio, and he works on his ships every day in public there. He refuses to sell his work. He wants visitors to the exhibits to enjoy them and further generations to learn from his models.

Sunbeam Whale Ship U.S. Lagoda

18th Dynasty Ship, Egypt Star of Memphis.

All of David's work is intricately scrimshawed.

Left: Detail of the medieval Baltic ship, the Danzig, 1400 AD

Right: Detail of Roman grain ship Neptunus of Ostia, 200 AD

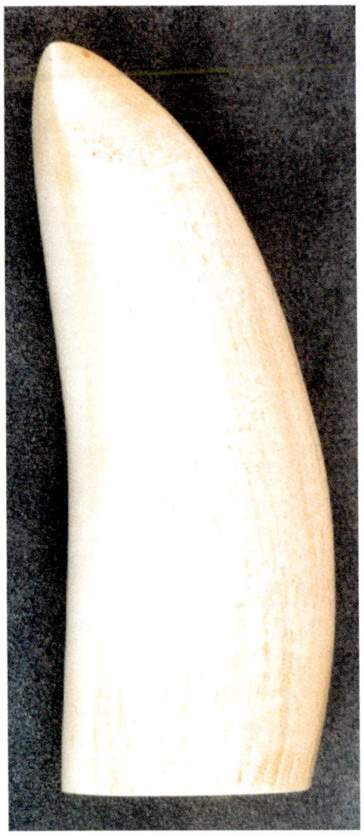

An "Artek" tooth made of polymer. Below in the hole at the end you can read "Artek Blank". It would be nice if all replicas were labeled like this.

Although this book deals with contemporary scrimshaw, there are many scrimshaw collectors and others interested in the art who would be delighted to acquire genuine old scrimshaw from the whaling period. Very high sums are paid for rare old pieces of original scrimshaw with documented provenance. For example, an antique whale tooth scrimmed in color by the famous scrimshander, Edward Burdett, fetched 60,000 dollars at auction, and another tooth by Frederick Meyrick was sold for 40,000 dollars.

It isn't just antique scrimshaw that fetches such high prices. A lot of work by living scrimshanders is already a very good investment. Works by living artists are normally always signed and it is easier to test their authenticity. Either the artist's style is well known, or you can ask him yourself if the item is being sold by someone other than the artist or a reputable gallery. This is the only way to be certain when large sums are involved.

Even when dealing with smaller pieces of antique scrimshaw, you still want to be sure that they are genuine before buying. You will be somewhat disappointed if you hope to make an unexpected profit by finding old works of scrimshaw in flea markets, attics, or even on the Internet (where they are very rarely offered, and then they are not cheap and there is a lot of fake among them). The sums mentioned above are exceptional, and of course they made headlines in the press. Almost all scrimshaw was done by unknown seamen and as a rule will fetch prices that won't make anyone really rich.

Old scrimshaw was seldom signed or provided with a date. It is rare that a technique can be attributed to a specific artist and relatively easily identified, and it is especially difficult to detect that a new "antique" work is new, when it has been done on antique ivory in an old style. Moreover, there are methods for rapidly aging new ivory or to make it appear old artificially.

There is also "old" scrimshaw on artificial materials. Replicas of genuine old scrimshaw on artificial materials are often sold in museum shops, but they are generally marked as replicas. The Artek™ company, which produces such replicas for museums, marks the pieces with their company name. These teeth also have a short cylindrical hollow in square-cut bases.

Photos Page 64,65: Halat

Other companies also make official replicas that are not marked as such and that can be resold as genuine by unscrupulous dealers. One buyer even purchased an "Artek" tooth under the impression that Artek was the artist's name!

There are a number of methods you can use to detect artificial materials or antique style scrimshaw on new teeth and determine whether an object is genuine or false. I present them here in the order of their practicality.

Antique-style scrimshaw was done on this artificial tooth. In places it is unclear and looks as if it were worn with time. Unfortunately, there is no marking in the hollow below to indicate that you are dealing with a replica.

Careful exterior examination: In antique scrimshaw, you are generally dealing with the whole tooth, so the easiest way is to pick up the tooth and, if possible, compare its weight with that of a known artificial tooth of similar size. Ivory is a little heavier than the artificial materials and does not conduct heat as well, so it feels a little cooler. Anyone with experience handling real whale teeth will never be fooled by an artificial imitation.

The exterior hard layer of enamel has been worn away at the tip of most teeth, which reveals a wave-like band of ivory layers around the upper part of the tooth. A real tooth also has a certain number of fine, lengthwise cracks, depending on its age and how carefully it has been stored and cared for.

Electrostatic charge: Artificial materials take a static charge faster and hold it longer than real ivory. This is an especially good test in dry air. You rub the tooth carefully with a silk or soft wool cloth, and if it attracts dust, ash, or small pieces of paper, you can suspect that it is artificial. If artificial materials have been treated with antistatic solutions, this test will not work.

Heat: Heat a sewing needle red-hot (holding it in pliers) and push the point against the material at a suitable spot. If it is genuine ivory, the most that will happen is that

Transferred into black and white, the wavelike layers of tooth enamel are quite visible on this antique sperm whale tooth.

the hot needle will make a tiny black spot on the surface. The artificial material will melt and you can push the needle in. If you have the chance to shave a small piece of material from a hidden place, you may be able to smell the characteristic odor possessed by many, but not all, artificial materials. This works even better if you heat the shavings. Anyone can distinguish the characteristic odor of burning ivory from that of artificial materials.

Magnification: Under very strong magnification, artificial materials sometimes display tiny bubbles that occur during production. Artificial materials really have no internal structure, because they are a homogenous mass, but "concretions" are visible in real ivory.

If you examine an old tooth under a microscope, you will be able to see whether the scrimmed lines cut cross the fine cracks in the material or whether those lines are broken by the natural cracks that occur as the material ages. If the lines of the subject cut through the natural cracks, then the lines were scrimmed after the cracks formed, and this is most likely new work on an old tooth.

UV light: When you compare artificial material with ivory under longwave ultraviolet, real ivory will shine more brightly.

X-rays: You can even x-ray the tooth, and if it's a real tooth, the root canal will be visible for almost its entire length.

These are a few of the possible tests you might use, especially on entire teeth, but they are not one hundred percent certain. If you still have any question about the authenticity of a particular piece, a mariner's museum will usually be able to tell you where you can get old scrimshaw tested for authenticity. They might even be able to give you an expert opinion on the piece.

This is a small sperm whale tooth with scrimshaw by Dorinel Stoica. These teeth can vary a lot in size and shape, as one can see from the scrimmed ones in the gallery section; but the different layers of dental material are usually visible, especially on their top end.

There are also artificial products, mostly grip scales for knives or belt buckles, that have a scrimshaw subject either printed on them or put on by some other kind of technical process. These reproductions are then offered for sale under a misleading term such as "scrimshaw-style designs". Generally, the price will tell you immediately that these objects can't be genuine, original scrimshaw.

The subject looks like this after the first application of color. The water and sand were done with stippling and colored one after the other.

Here I worked over the sand a little more and made the color darker. The sea grass was the next step.

The first color application for the sea horse.

The completed work. The shadows on the sea horse were done with stippling and colored, and additional stippling was used to make the background darker and give it more depth.

A pair of elephant tusks. Usually the color is lighter than that of these tusks, which have a beautiful brownish stain.
The tips are often striped with fine longitudinal cracks; similar "veins" can be found on walrus teeth.
The ends of such teeth are hollow and taper until the material is quite massive.

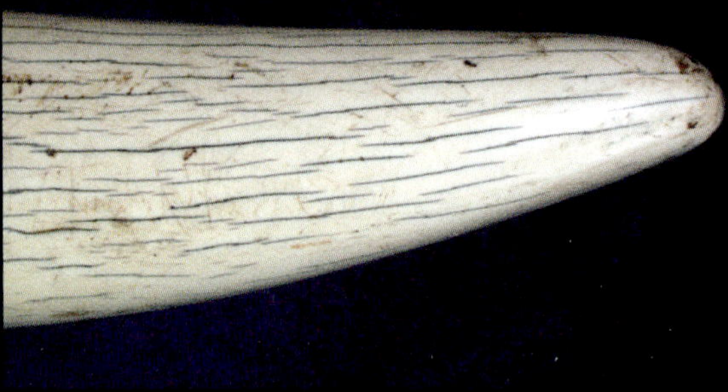

On these old ivory billiard balls, the Schreger lines are clearly visible, identifying them as real ivory.
Right: Mammoth ivory bark pieces.

Warthog tusks in different shapes and sizes.

Hippopotamus upper jaw tusks are usually curved like this tooth. The surface has many fine lengthwise grooves.

Walrus tusks can vary greatly in length and thickness. In these tusks, it is also clearly visible where they were inserted into the jaw and which part was outside. At the end they are hollow, but with a shorter taper than elephant tusks.

A finely detailed scrimshaw by Attila Harmat on a tagua nut.

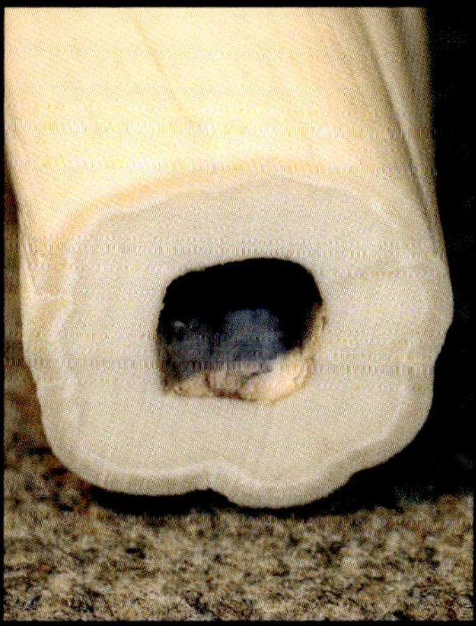

Cross-section of a narwhale tusk. The outer layer is cementum; the inner material is dentine. Between them is the thin "transition ring".

Some whole narwhale tusks.

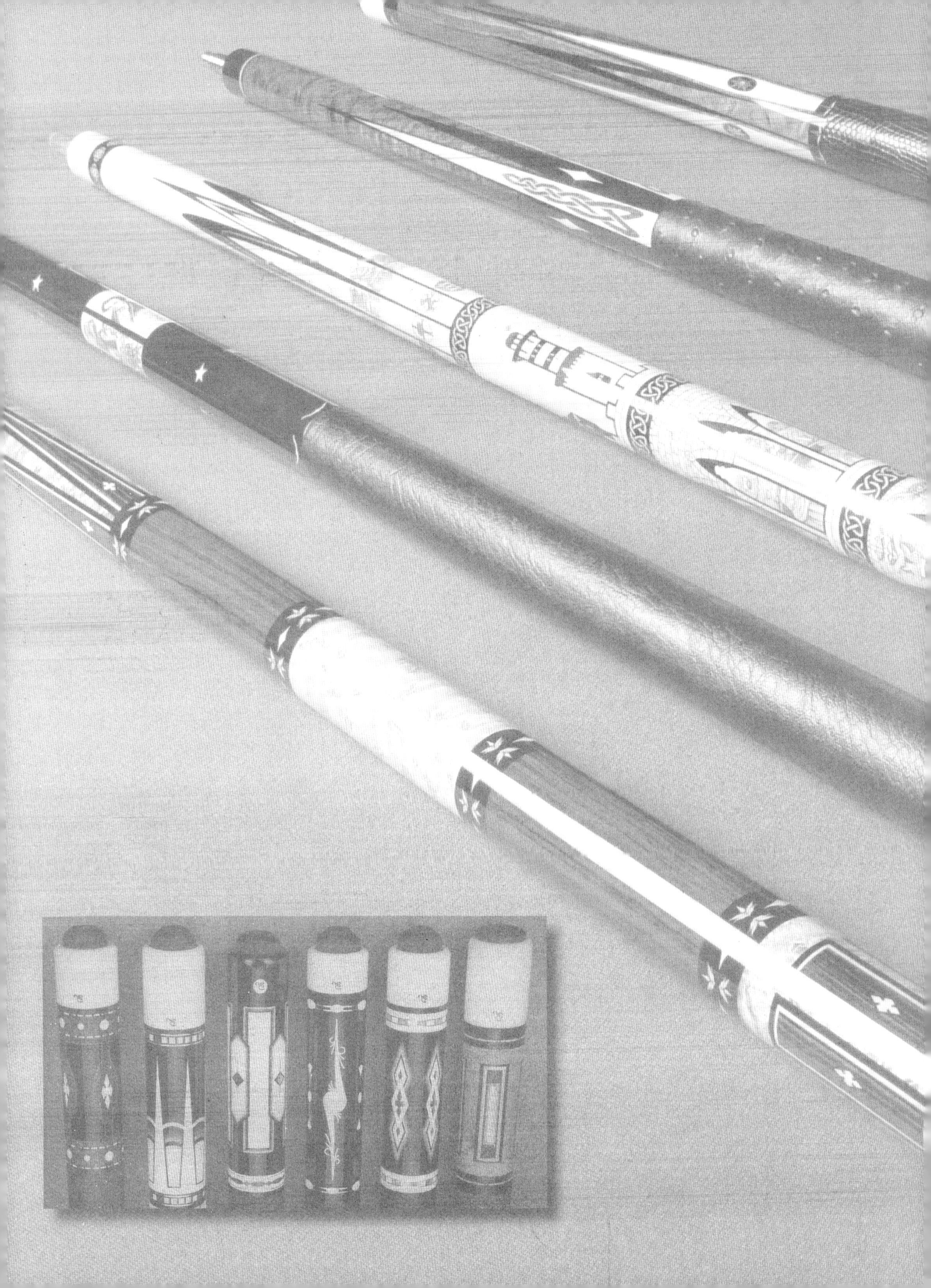

Billiard Cues

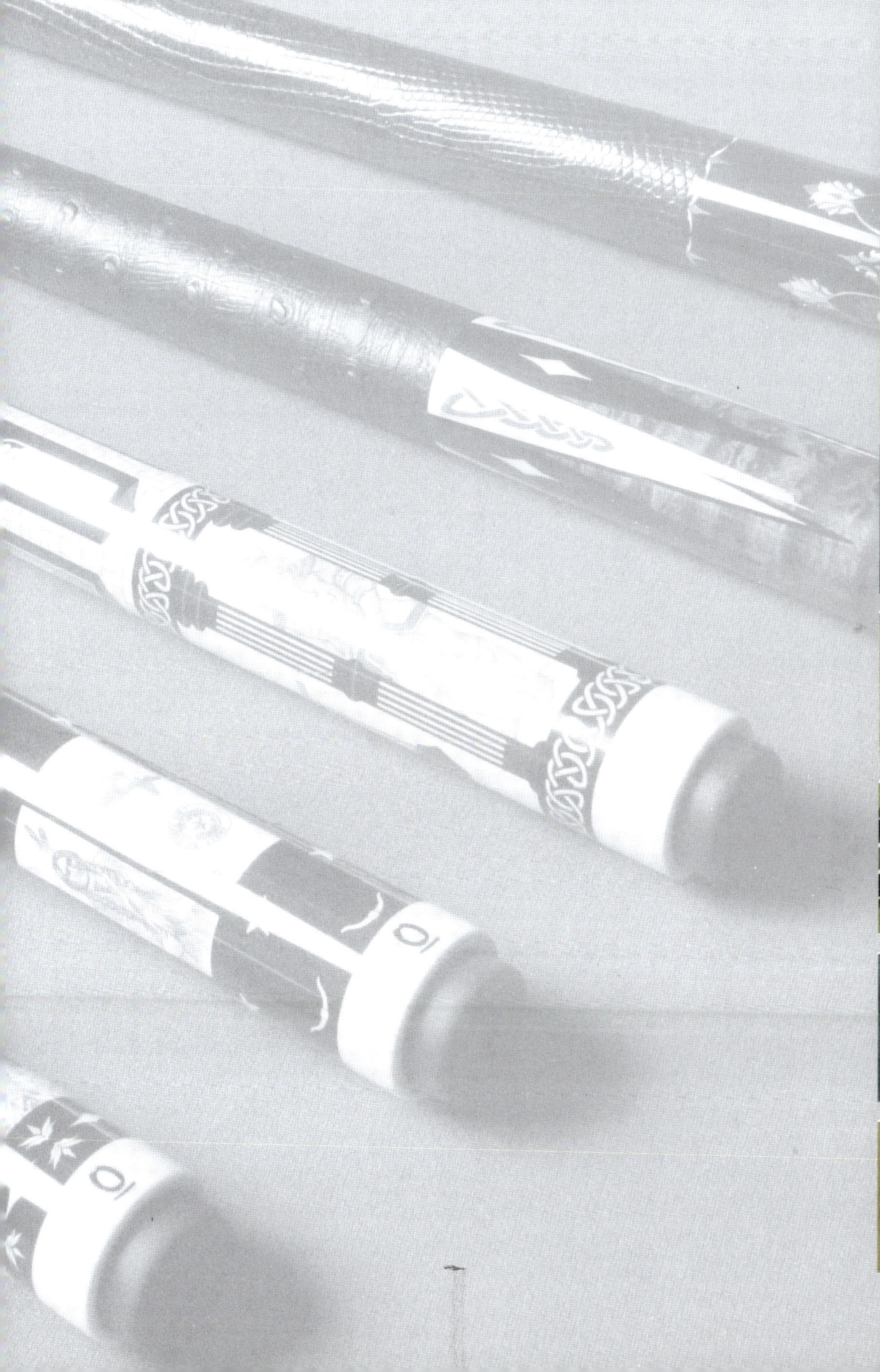

Billiard Cues

Besides artworks from the maritime world, knives are probably the best-known objects connected with scrimshaw. A further, perhaps less well known, realm where scrimshaw is used, as a decorative element, is that of billiard cues. There are cues that are decorated with small individual motifs, and others with elaborately made colorful scrimshaw, with a motif winding around the entire lower end of the cue.

For simpler transport, a billiard cue is made of two parts, the lower part (butt piece) and the upper part (shaft). The threading with which the two parts are screwed together must be made very precisely, since the entire cue must exactly form a straight line.

The cue as a whole is slightly conical, and the ball is pushed with the end of the thinner upper part. This shaft is usually made of high-quality hard rock maple. In general, long pieces of seasoned wood are used to make cues, and a cue must never warp, for it would then be absolutely worthless and unusable.

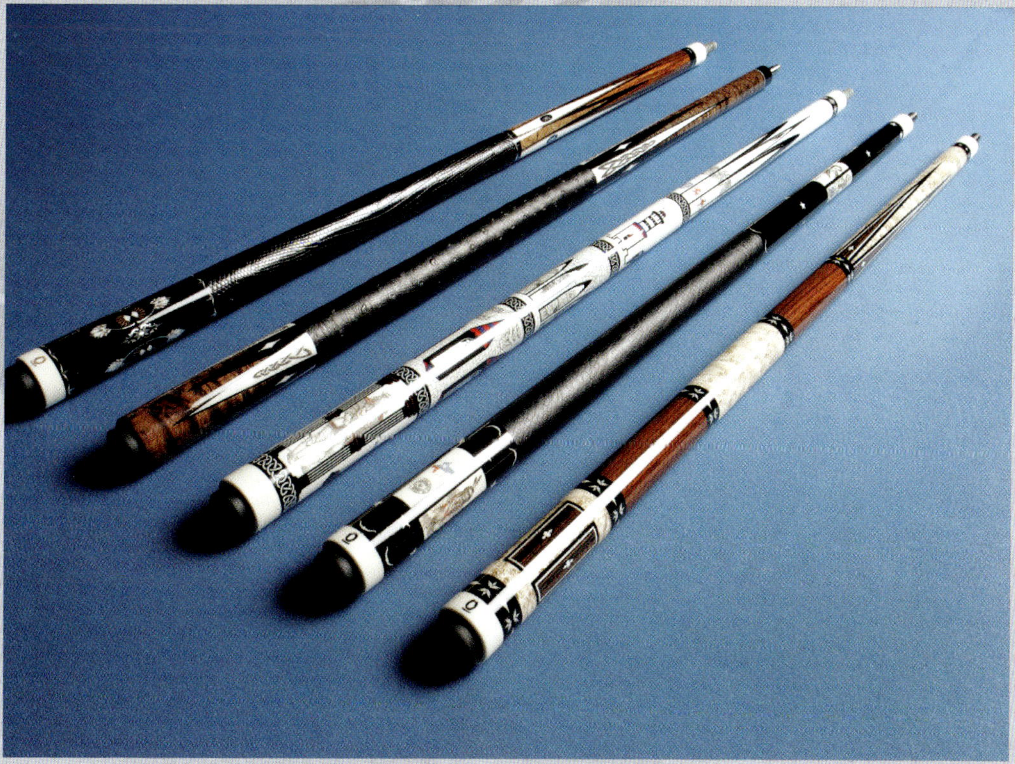

Various elaborately made cues made by the German cue maker Marcus Dienst of Arthur Queue, sometimes with wrapped handles or handles decorated with inlays and scrimshaw work.

An important criterion for a good cue is its play behavior. The total weight and the shifting of the weight must agree, and when orders are filled, the diameter preferred by the client is considered.

The lower part of a cue is the part that can be adorned with all sorts of decorations. The butt of an expensive cue is made or rare hardwood. The butt is usually made of three pieces: the forearm, from which the screw projects; the handle, which on simple cues usually has a wrapping that can be replaced when it gets worn, and the butt sleeve, the end piece of the cue. Most of the decorations, such as inlays of rare wood, semiprecious stones, sterling silver, ivory, scrimshaw, and even gold or small diamonds, are usually found on the butt sleeve, the thickest part. But the handle and the forearm of expensive cues are also specially designed. Over the years, every cue builder develops his own personal tastes as to the use of inlaying materials, and every good cue builder, like an artist, also develops his own unmistakable design style.

There are classic forms of inlays, such as points, long forms that run to apexes, where the challenge is to make the point as fine and thin as possible. Rectangular inlays of ivory are, like miniature canvases, predestined to give the cue a personal note of the owner via scrimshaw. There are no limits for the cue builder in designing inlays. The intricacy of the inlay and the amount of filigree depend upon an artist ability. The parts must fit together to the hundredth of a millimeter. The number of inlays plays a major role in setting the price of a cue. There are fairly exact principles as to how much a cue may cost with how many inlays. The making of a particular cue, what with the necessary seasoning times between the individual work processes, takes from 9 to 12 months.

Various beautiful inlay work on butt sleeves. These cues were made by Ernie Gutierrez of Ginacue, USA. Ernie Gutierrez' cues are desired all over the world, and he was the first cue maker who was honored by inclusion in the "Cuemaker Hall of Fame" during his life.

The parts that are scrimmed are made of legal ivory from old supplies. For making billiard cues, Elfordyn is also being used. It has the same coloring as ivory and can also be used for scrimshaw, but for high-quality scrimshaw work, equally high-quality ivory material is still being used here.

Mammoth ivory can also be used for inlaying work, but it is scarcely usable for large sections of cue material, since large, crack-free pieces are needed to "turn" round material for cues, pieces which are as good as impossible to obtain from mammoth ivory.

The most laboriously worked collectors' items clearly rank among the highest-quality billiard cues. These cues are made primarily as works of art, and are almost never used in play. Such collectors' items are always unique works. Collectors contract some of them, with the buyer more or less providing the pattern; others arise only from the ideas of a cue maker, or are made with special subjects as theme cues for shows or other events.

Such a "custom cue" can cost a lot of money. Cues from the thirties to fifties, which cost $30 to $50 US at the time, are sold today for as much as $8000. Newer cues with striking designs, made by well-known makers such as Bill Schick, Ernie Gutierrez, Tod Kohara, Richard Black or Bill Stroud, to name only a few, can increase considerably in value in just a few years. The "Celtic Prince" cue made by Thomas Wayne brought an unbelievably high price at an auction. This cue has 1500 individual inlays of ivory and ebony, forming a pattern of Celtic knots around the lower part. The bidders bid each other up to the price of $103,000 US.

Cues with scrimshaw are usually theme cues that present a definite subject in their overall formation. For example, Paul Drexler's famous "Hustler Cue," which was auctioned off at a benefit event for $30,000, is a good example. Its subject is that of the film ***The Hustler***. As an inlay, a roll of film wraps around the lower part of the cue, and the actors in the film (including Paul Newman) are scrimmed into film clips as individual pictures from their film roles by Sandra Brady. Another theme, which was provided for the exhibitors at the Cue Collector Show, was a cue in a Greco Roman design. How the theme is developed is left to the creativity of the individual cue builder. For some years this Cue Collector Show has been held annually in various areas of the USA. Twelve cue builders of the world's elite are invited and bring along their high-end cues. Cue collectors also display parts of their collections there. Cues with the most elaborate inlays and scrimshaw work, with values from $3000 to $50,000, can be admired there. To date this event has been only for invited guests, but in 2008 it is to be open to the public for the first time.

For some twenty years there has even been a billiard-cue museum in the USA.

Ten Roman emperors were immortalized in scrimshaw for this Greco-Roman theme cue. The butt sleeve shows portraits of Zeus, Neptune, Diana, Apollo, and Ares from the realm of the Greek gods. Marcus Dienst, of Arthur Queue, made this cue of ebony and ivory for the 7th Cue Collector Show. The scrimshaw work was done by Eva Halat.

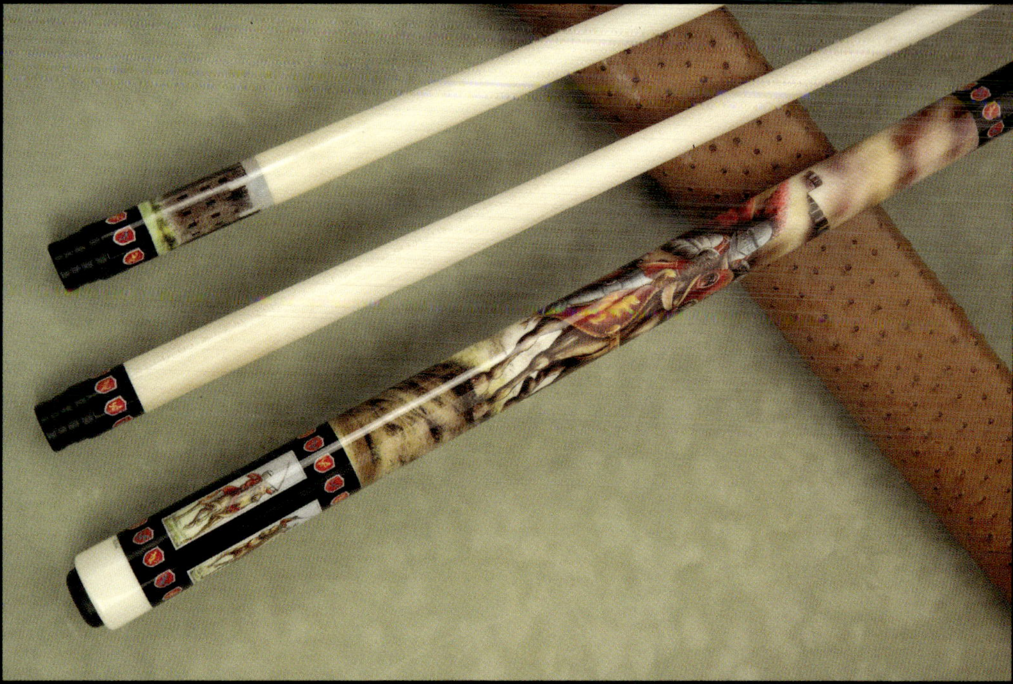

This cue was made by builder Paul Mottey in 2007. The client and owner of the cue, Will Prout, provided the theme for the cue and chose the wood for it. He also provided the patterns for the scrimshaw work, from cigarette boxes of 1909 with pictures of medieval knights. The well-known scrimshaw artist Salman Rashidi used them to create this superbly colored scrimshaw work. (Photos: Paul Goodwin)

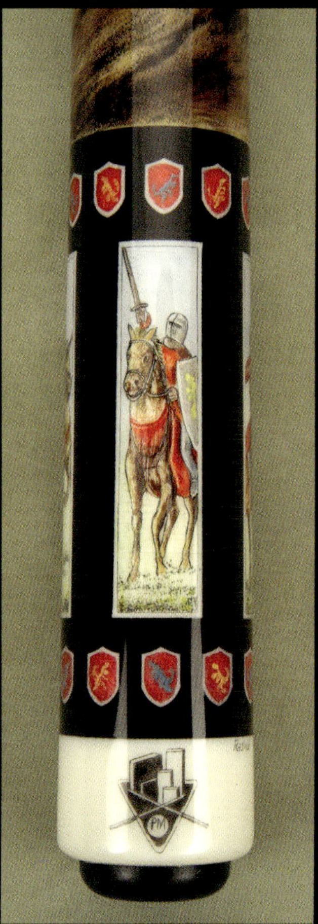

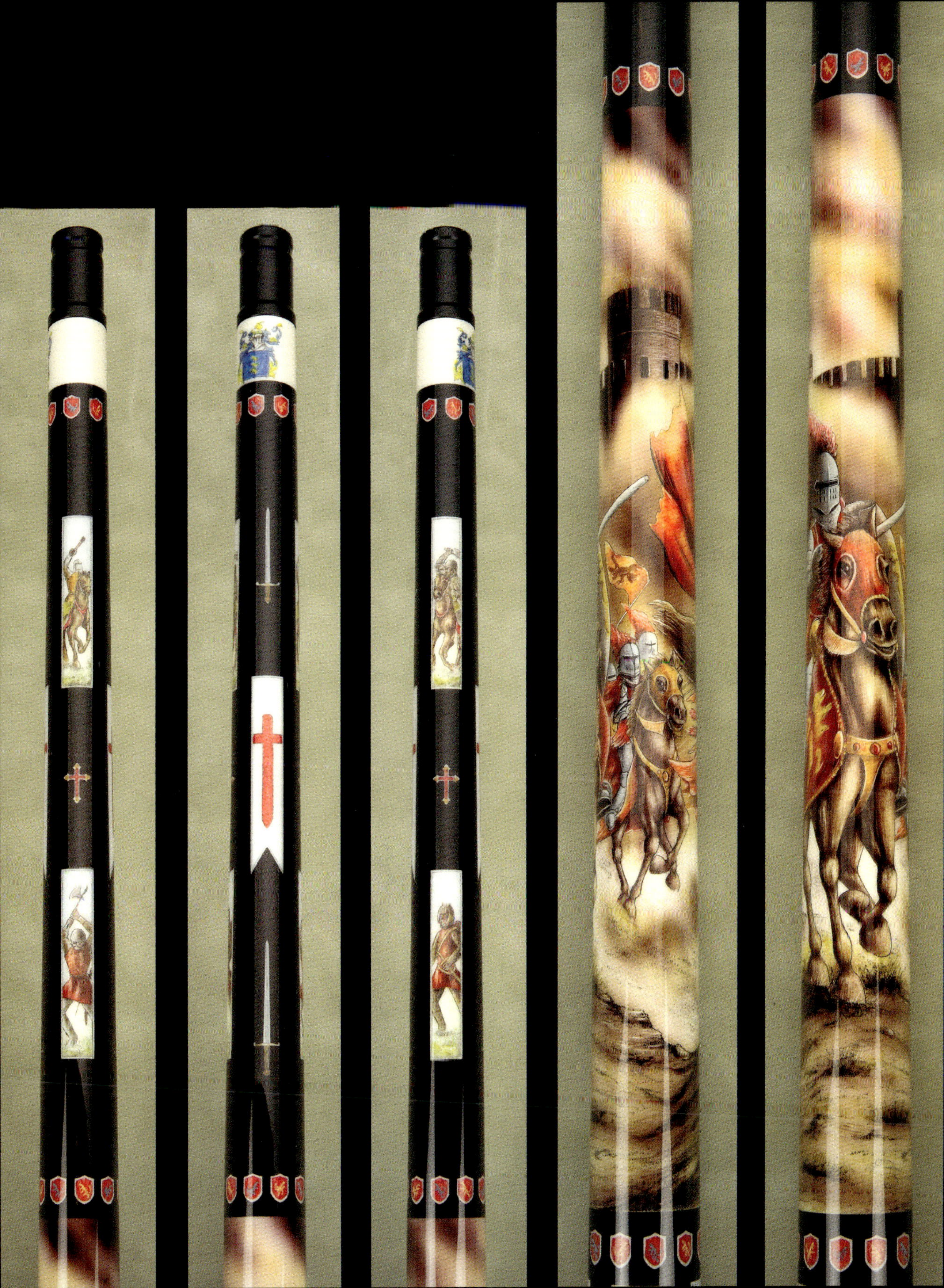

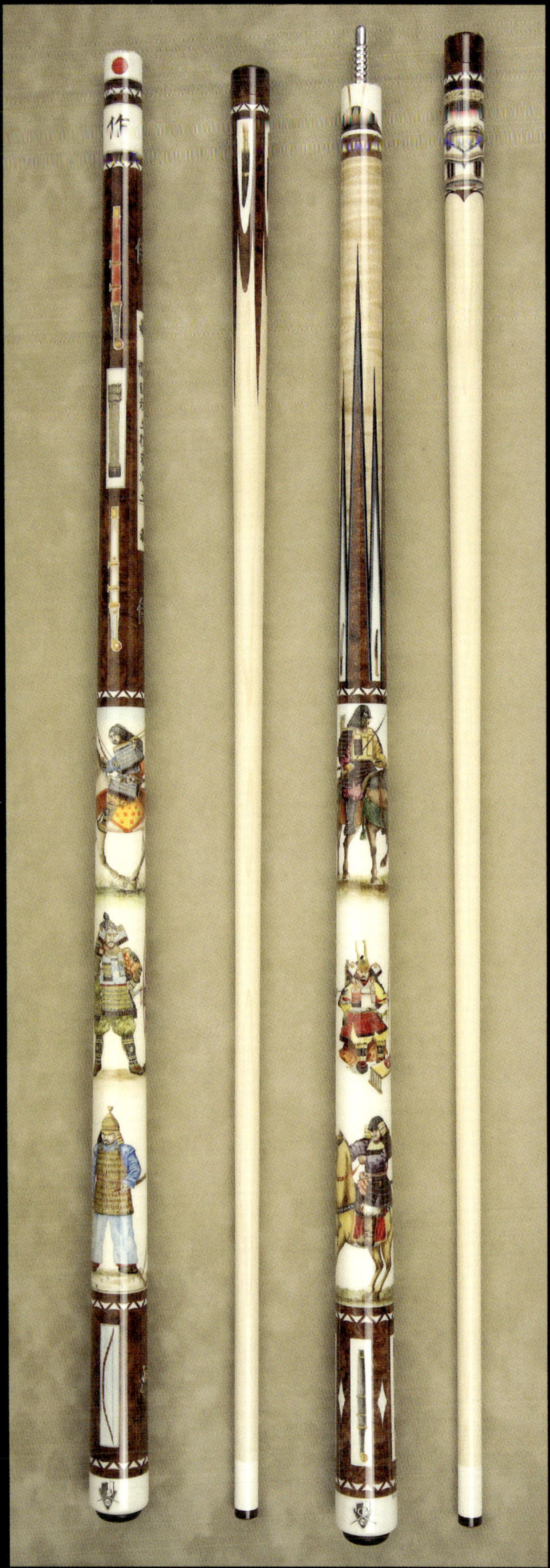

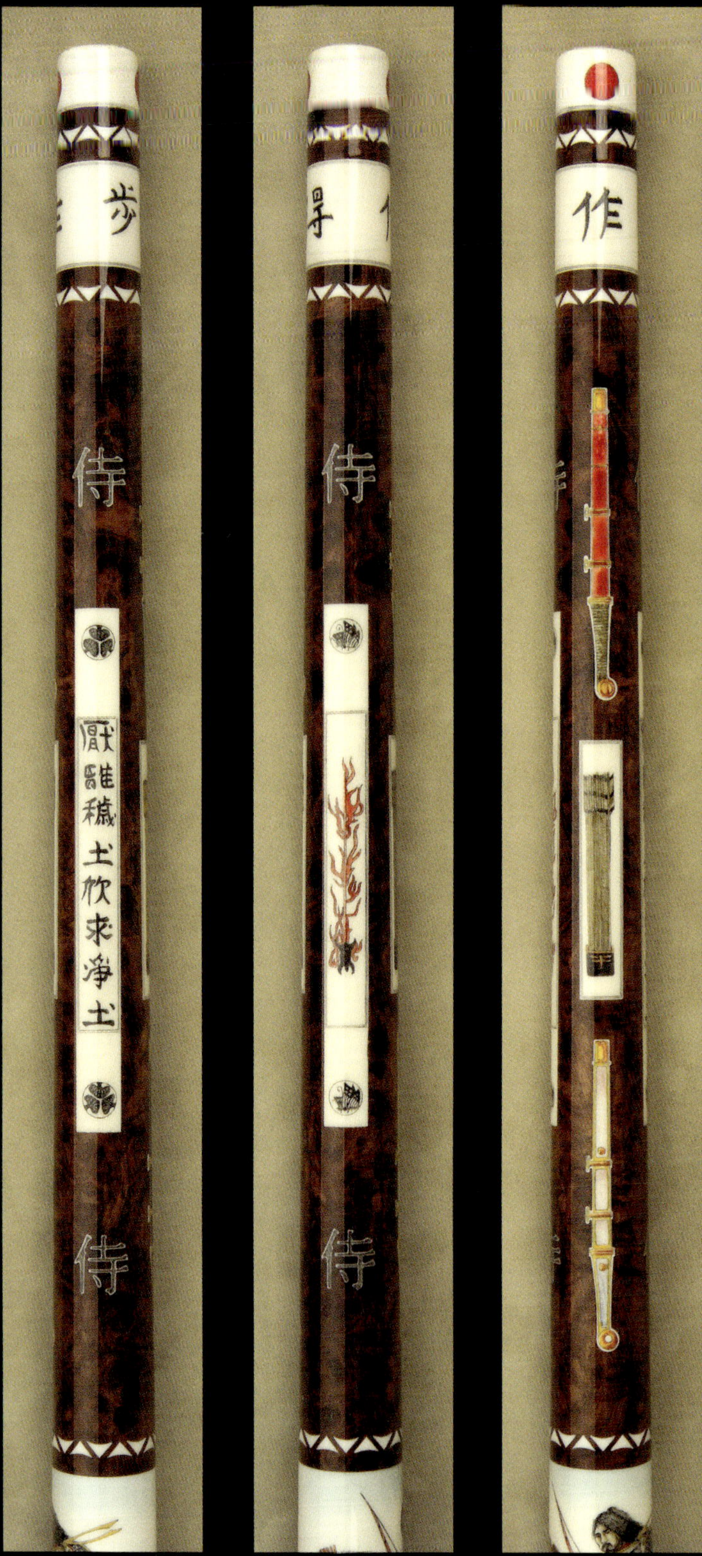

A matched pair of beautiful cues, with samurai warriors forming their theme.
These two cues were also made by Paul Mottey, a renowned cue builder from the USA, in 2000-2002. Salman Rashidi was also chosen to do the scrimshaw work. The two cues are in the collection of Will Prout. (Photos: Paul Goodwin)

The
Four
Horsemen
of the
Apocalypse

"The Four Apocalyptic Riders"—Paul Drexler, who also ranks among the greatest cue builders of the USA, has developed this theme. The owner, Will Prout, commissioned this cue in 2006. At his wish, Paul Drexler modified the inlay work with silver inlays and, after a discussion with the owner, the scrimshaw work was made by artist Sandra Brady. (Photos: Paul Goodwin, kindly made available by Will Prout)

The notes on the inlay are a great idea. This "music cue" showing a piano player is also half of a pair of cues. The owner, Will Prout, bought the first cue, without ivory in the handle, from builder Paul Mottey in 2000, and six years later he had this second one made to complete the pair. The scrimshaw work was made by Salman Rashidi. The case was made by Whitten Custom Cases. (Photos: Paul Goodwin)

This stylish cue from the firm of South West Cues was made in 2006. The Ferrari shown on it, scrimmed by Salman Rashidi, is, like the cue itself, owned by Will Prout. The case is also by Whitten Custom Cases.

A child's cue with cobras and lizards, which a father had made for his son. The reptiles were scrimmed by Eva Halat.

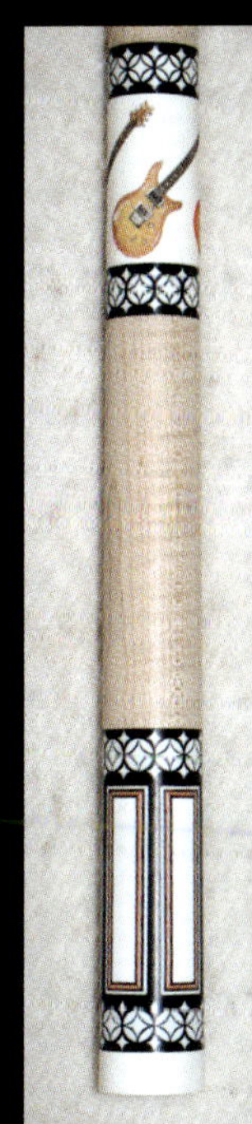

The second hobby of a billiard player: three Paul Reed Smith guitars that belong to the owner of this cue were scrimmed on the cue from Arthur Queue by Eva Halat.

The "Pharaoh Cue" was also made by Marcus Dienst of Arthur Queue for the 2006 Cue Collector Show in Las Vegas. Using illustrations from ancient Egyptian temple columns, Eva Halat created the scrimshaw work after consulting with Marcus Dienst. The straight zigzag line pattern on the curved upper section was a particular challenge.

All the symbols, pharaohs, and gods depicted, like the scarab, the Sphinx, the sun god Ra or Tutankhamun are intended to bless the player with good energy, health, sovereignty, and clear sight. For example, Horus and Seth, who fought with the pharaoh, who tried to preserve balance for dominance in the world, symbolize the player's inner harmony when playing, or the starry sky, symbolically portrayed with blue rings, is meant to give the player guidance in unclear moments.

More than 600 inlays of lapis lazuli, coral, and 14-karat gold were set into this cue.

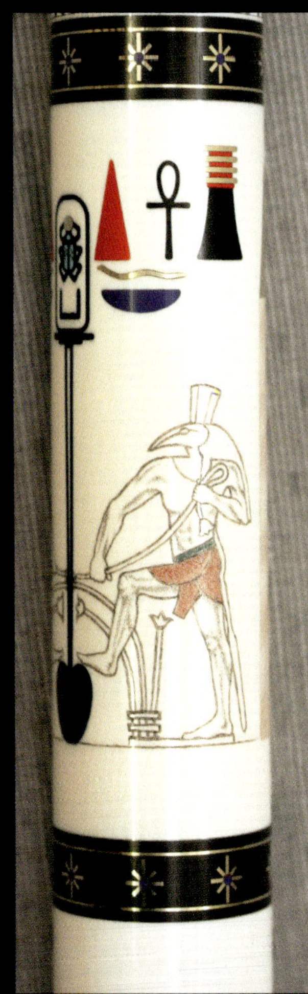

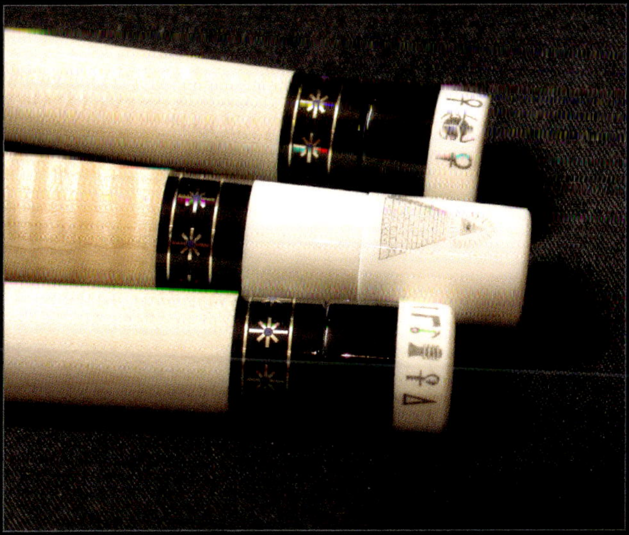

Here too, Egyptian symbols are used. On the screw protector is the well-known pyramid with the eye, based on the design on the dollar bill.

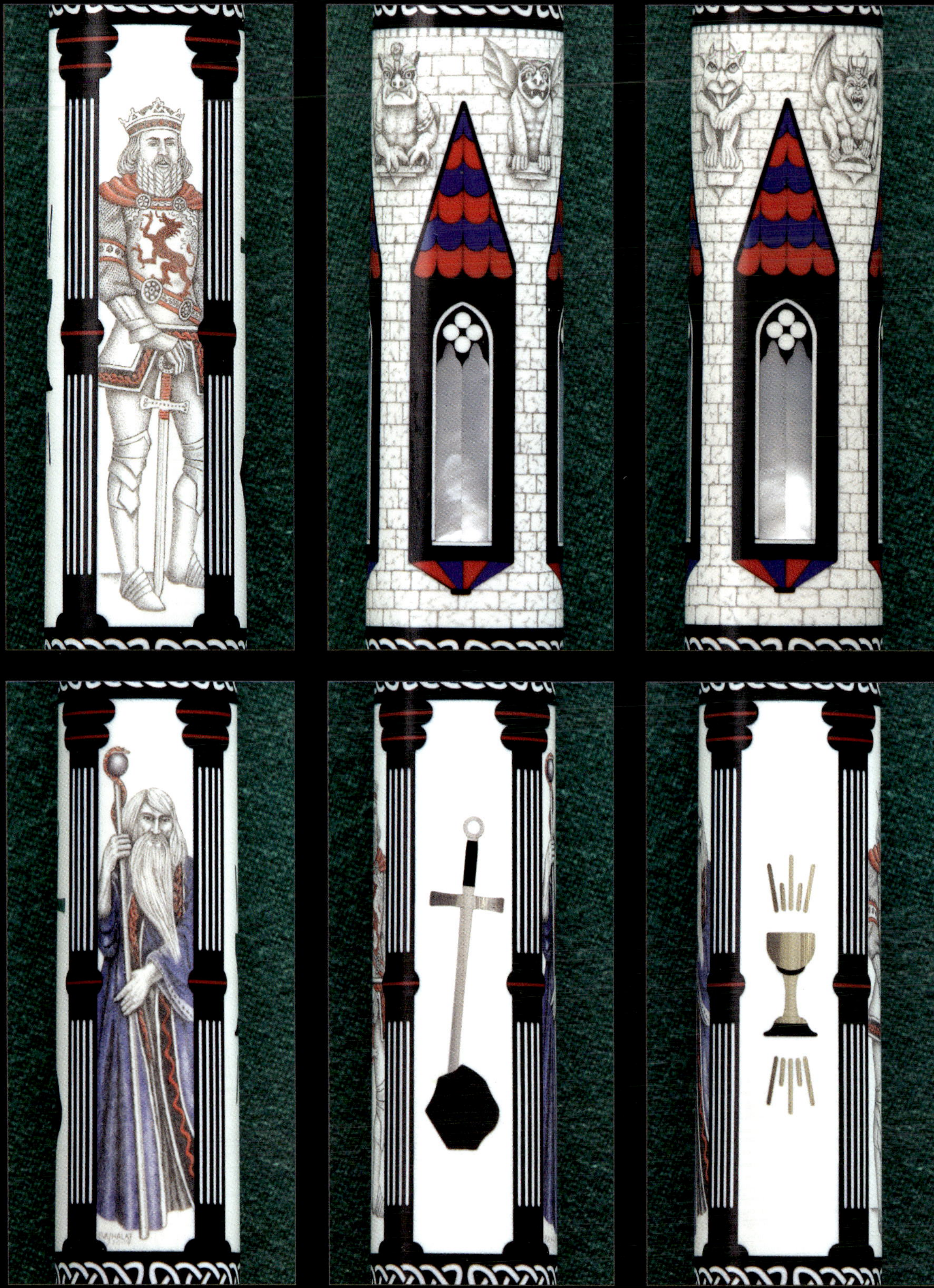

The "King Arthur Cue," a collector and theme cue, was made by Arthur Queue. Exactly 898 inlays were used. "King Arthur" was first displayed at the 2007 Cue Collector Show in Houston, Texas.

The individual panels are separated by ebony rings decorated with intricate Celtic knots made of inlaid ivory. Between the inlay columns on the butt sleeve are King Arthur and Merlin, with Arthur's sword Excalibur and the Holy Grail inlaid in silver between them. Above them are windows of mother-of-pearl with brickwork and gargoyles in scrimshaw technique.

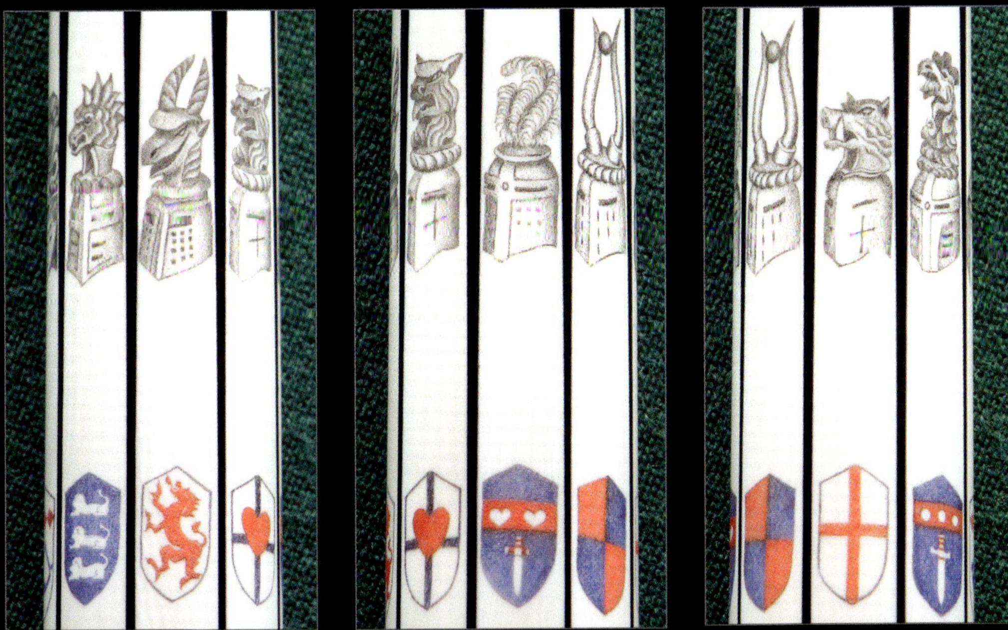

In the third section, fifteen knights of the Round Table (seven seen from the front and eight with their backs to the viewer) and King Arthur himself are seen through the windows. Above is a section showing the uppermost part of the castle, with towers and battlements. Finally, the coats of arms and helmets of the knights are scrimmed. King Arthur can be recognized by the crown and the dragon on the armor, flag, and coat of arms.

The scrimshaw work on the design of this cue made of ebony, ivory, and silver was done by Sandra Brady; it was built by Dan Dishaw, and is a theme cue in ancient Greco-Roman style. Four athletes, winners of the first Olympic Games, stand atop the columns: a javelin thrower, a charioteer, a sprinter, and a discus thrower. On the butt sleeve, the Olympic flame is shown under the archway of the Coliseum.

Decorative traditional ornamentation is also put to use in cue formation, as here with scrimshaw oak leaves done by Eva Halat on a cue from Arthur.

An Indian cobra in four different views, scrimmed by Sandra Brady on this cue by Ar... Cantando. The wood of the butt sleeve is snakewood, combined with ivory.

ROGERS

Gallery

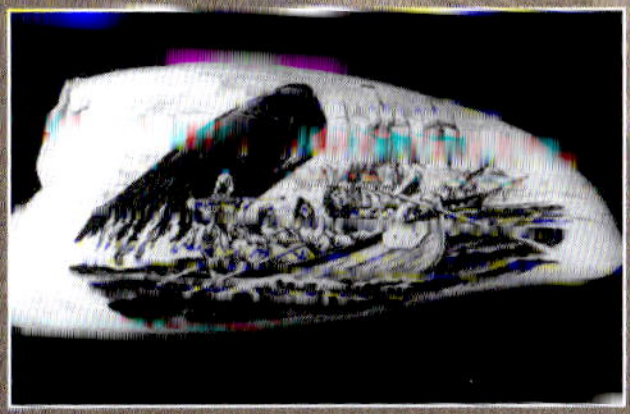

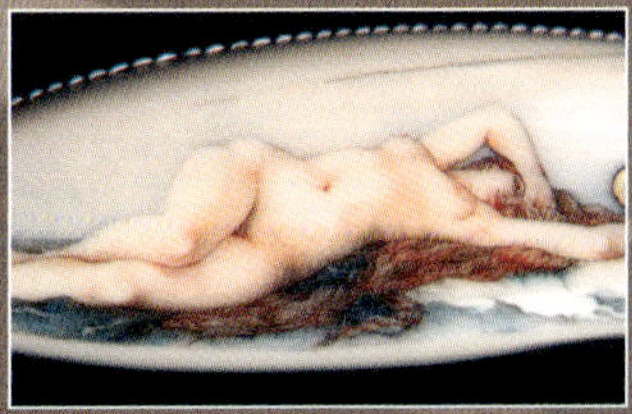

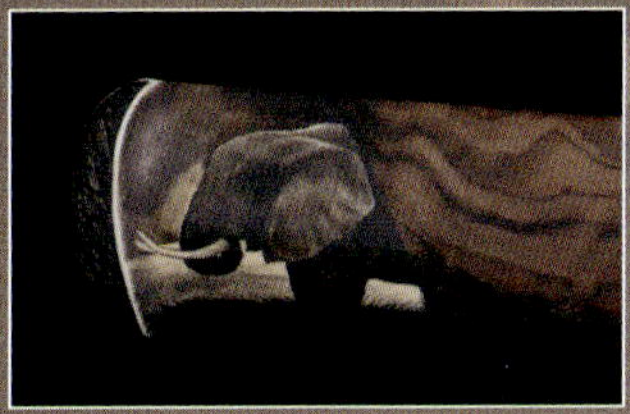

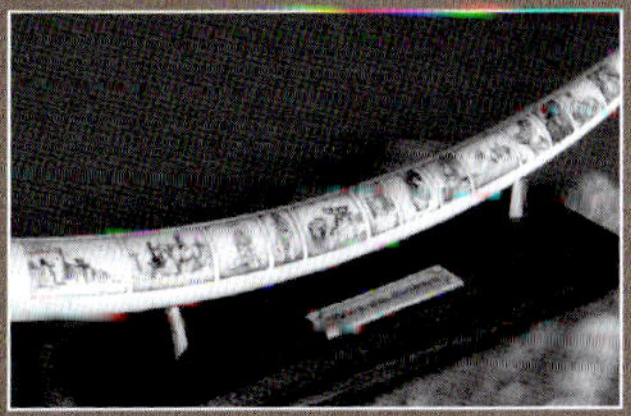

Gaétan Beauchamp

Gaétan Beauchamp grew up with seven brothers and sisters in l'Abiti, a wild region of Quebec. In his youth he spent much of his time in the wilds, where he ran a trap line, usually traveling by canoe. He loves to do creative work with his hands. Earlier, this artist had already tried his hand at pottery, painting, and canoe building, and he is an enthusiastic archer. Gaétan married early and had to earn a living for his family, but didn't have much luck at a variety of jobs. The unfortunate part was that he had to move frequently with his wife and family whenever he changed jobs.

All that changed when he began to make knives and to scrim. Scrimshaw interested him as much as all the other creative things he had done earlier. A friend, skilled in this art, showed him the first steps. Gaétan was delighted and wanted to continue with it. He began with mammoth ivory and Micarta™, but now what fascinates him most is to work on a dark background like buffalo horn. This "negative" technique was seldom seen at the time, but he specialized in it, working in white and color on a black surface, while continuing to do scrimshaw on light materials. For scrimming, he uses diamond needles in a variety of sizes.

As more and more people became interested in his art, Gaétan decided to make a living with scrimshaw. At that time, he was still unknown as a knifemaker and getting too few orders for his knives, so he decided to combine the two activities. With increasing success, he became swamped with work, and his wife, Denise, finally quit her job to help her husband make knives. Now Gaétan Beauchamp is a well-known knifemaker and scrimshander and a frequent participant at knife shows in the United States and Europe.

Steak knives with a series of Indian chiefs scrimmed in white color on water buffalo horn.

Chief Joseph
on a knife by Gaétan.
Grip: water buffalo horn
Total length: 20 cm.

Left: A twin pair
of knives by Gaétan
with the portrait of a wolf.
The grips are of water buffalo horn
and mammoth ivory,
the blades of Damascus steel.
Total length: 18 cm.

Below: Chief Quannah Parker
as white scrimshaw on a piece
of water buffalo horn.
Dimensions: 20 x 13 cm.

Gaétan Beauchamp

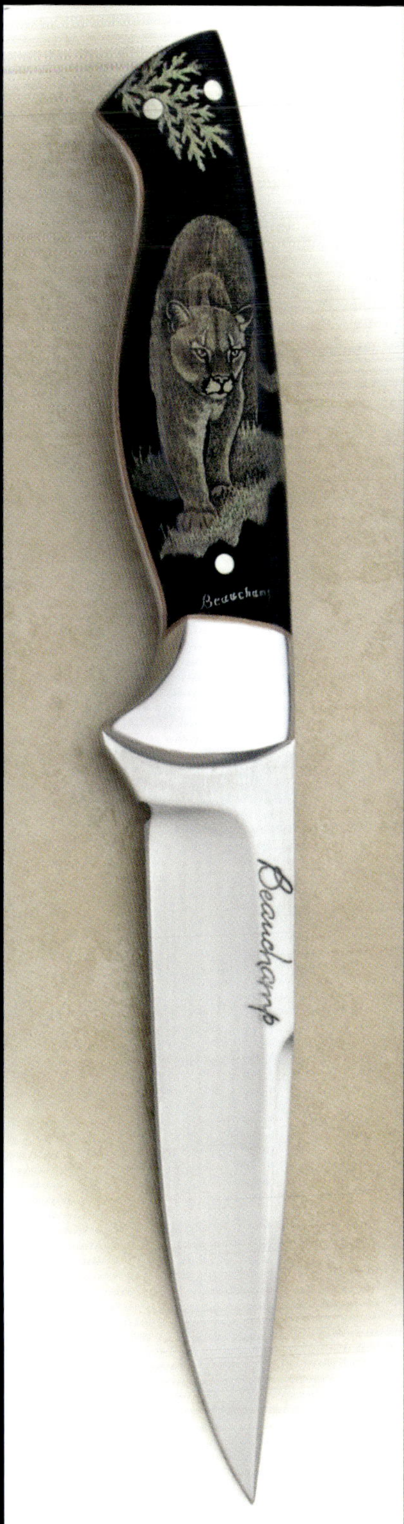

Gaétan has experience with color scrimshaw on black water buffalo horn. This knife also has a grip of this material and is 23 cm long.

Above: Two bolo ties made of mammoth ivory.

Large colored work on a piece of water buffalo horn. Dimensions of original: 20 x 12 cm.

Gaétan Beauchamp

A second set of twin knives, here with a leopard head. Grips: Mammoth ivory and water buffalo horn. Blades: Damascus steel. Lengths: 23 cm. Miniature knives: 4.5 cm.

Top: These orcas are scrimmed on mammoth ivory, as is the Eskimo on the sheath. The knife is 24 cm long.

Below: A masterpiece on a water buffalo horn section. Dimensions: 20 x 13 cm.

Margaret Blake

Margaret Blake was, to be sure, born in Utah, USA, but also regards Colorado as her home. She left Brigham Young University with a BS and MS in the field of physics and art. Margaret has spent most of her life as a teacher, set designer, and artist, while also raising eight children.

Margaret, and her husband Karl, moved from Colorado to Park City, Utah, eleven years ago. She loves to play tennis, go hiking and canoeing, play music, and take good care of her family and friends. Along with all her activities, she sometimes also finds time to be an artist, specializing in scrimshaw, watercolor, and oil painting.

Scrimshaw fascinates Margaret because the materials are so unique. She loves old ivory and works mainly with mammoth ivory or fossil walrus tusks. Every piece of ivory seems to have its own unique spirit, which she respects and keeps in mind when she works on it. She has been a scrimshaw artist for twenty years, and in that time she has produced over 200 large and small works of art.

Here again, the motif suits the walrus tusk, with scenes of the Inuit world, which is also the realm of the walrus.

Human portraits are favorites of Margaret Blake. She scrims very sensitive works in a very personal style on mammoth ivory.
(All photos: www.HawkinsonPhotography.com)

Margaret Blake

The American aborigines are an ever-popular motif. The picture of the trapper comes from the same era. Both works are scrimmed on mammoth ivory.

This work is a combination that one very rarely gets to see: Scrimshaw combined with relief carving in ethnic style. This gives the portrait a beautiful and interesting frame, and the contrast between the two styles is charming and effective. (All photos: www.HawkinsonPhotography.com)

Sandra Brady

Sandra Brady majored in art at the University of Toledo, concentrating on anatomy and the human form. This artistic training enabled her to create and define a style uniquely hers, one that sets her apart from her contemporaries in the field of scrimshaw. She is well versed in a number of artistic techniques, for example, drawing, hand printing, oil painting, and pastels, but her true artistic passion will always be scrimshaw.

"My special strength is wildlife scenes," she states candidly, "although recently I have also received commissions for many pieces depicting Greek and medieval mythology. I enjoy working with the human figure. It can be a little more challenging, and for that reason it can also be more fulfilling." She gladly accepts commissions, whether for a piece of old elephant ivory jewelry, for a rare piece of thousand-year-old walrus ivory, or for a handmade collector's knife, and a customer can also purchase a "stock item" directly from her.

Sandra Brady now lives and works in Toledo, Ohio, with her husband Jim Fray and their children Nick and Emily.

Left: The two nudes on this pair of knives by Tommy Lee are on antique elephant ivory. (Photo: Weyer of Toledo, Ohio, USA)

Below: "Einstein", scrimshaw on antique elephant ivory. The interesting folding knife with the Damascus blade is by Hugh Bartrug.

The grip of the "Cosmic Centum" knife by Don Lozier shown above is of mammoth ivory. (Photo Weyer of Toledo)

Below: These three knives by George Herron are part of the millennium series, which consists of 20 knives. Sandra Brady has scrimmed a number of composite scenes of the events that changed the world during the last 100 years.

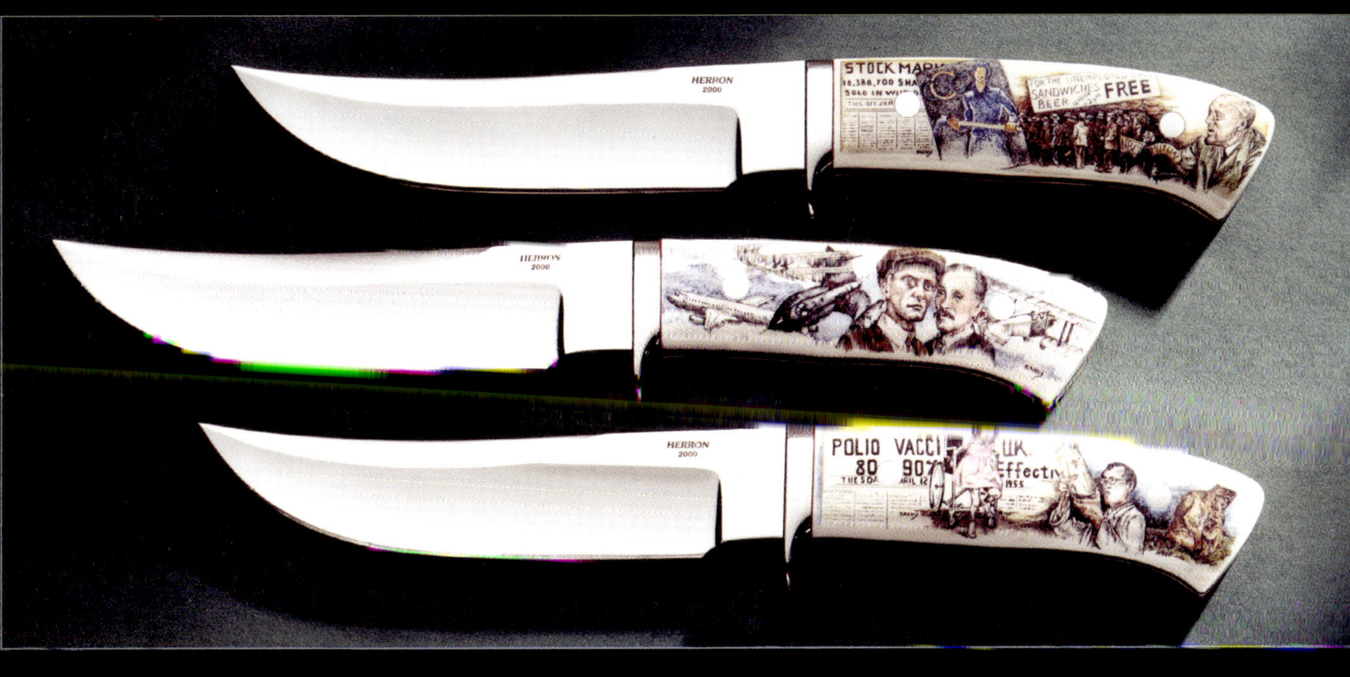

"Company for Dinner", a big, wonderfully decorated arching hippo tusk.

Right: A gun too precious to use with a knight on horseback scrimmed on the grips and gun engraving by Michael Dubber.

Sandra Brady

Special billiard cues are sometimes decorated with scrimshaw, like this beautiful "Hustler Cue", with scrimmed pictures and portraits on an inlayed "film roll".

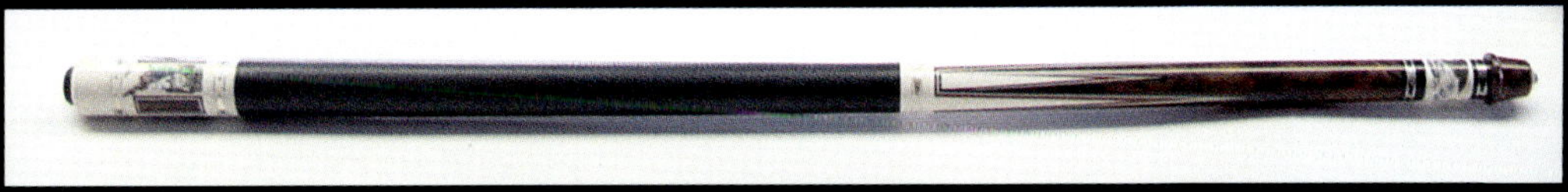

"The Freedom Cue", also a finely decorated cue. Scrimmed with different freedom symbols of the United States. Cue made by Richard Black (Blackcues)

Thoughts on archaic scrimshaw.

From time immemorial, man has needed to express himself and to communicate, not just with his own kind, but with all of creation. Most shamans maintained this connection between their tribes and the world they lived in. Survival would scarcely have been possible without it.
The development of self-awareness brought a desire to show individuality, to decorate yourself in order to separate yourself from others.
We can divide old bone engravings (scratchings) into two groups:
1) Ornamentation, consisting mostly of simple geometric figures
2) Shamanistic signs and pictures, which were used for a special reason known only to their possessor, but usually for awakening or maintaining certain characteristics or abilities.
These archaic ways of expressing the human spirit have exerted a hold on Phillip Branschi since he first encountered them. Unusual for the Swiss, because of their devotion to precision, he delights in using the simplest tools, without measurements or sketches, to reestablish a little of our original connection with the rest of creation.

Philipp Branschi decorates the grips of his knives in an independent and archaic way. He likes to use antler and bone as the material for his grips.

Roberto Bruci

Roberto Bruci lives and works in Cecina on the Tyrrhenian Sea in Tuscany, Italy. After a number of jobs, he spent several years painting, giving free rein to his love of the sea and sailing. He also restored some old sailing boats, which gave him an opportunity to see old carvings and engravings done by seamen on materials such as whale teeth and walrus tusks.

He became fascinated with this art and his enthusiasm for it flared up a few years later. Inspired by American, Italian, and German scrimshaw on valuable knives, he found the necessary patience and dedication to develop outstanding skill in this art. He does detailed, precise, delicate work, mostly of nature and hunting scenes on knife grips of horn and ivory. He uses tools he makes himself, acrylic and oil paints, and a magnifying lens.

Today Roberto Bruci is a recognized and highly regarded artist in Rome, Parma, Romana di Lombardia, and Lugano. His scrimshaw has also received a great deal of recognition in various publications dealing with the art.

Incredibly fine "dots" were necessary to create such a delicate tiny portrait.

Two similar scenes on staghorn. The different appearance is attributable in part to the different black-and-white treatments given the sailing ships and their backgrounds.

An extravagant scrimshaw on ivory after a hunting scene by Paul Rubens. Roberto Bruci first slightly altered the format of the scene in a sketch to fit the knife grip. The precision and detail in the work can easily be seen in the enlargement. The knife by D. Barban is made of stainless and Damascus steels.

A swimming tiger on mammoth ivory. Knife by Max. Damascus steel.

Ships in Genoa Harbor, immortalized in ivory on a knife by L. Gigante. The blade is made of ATS 34 steel.

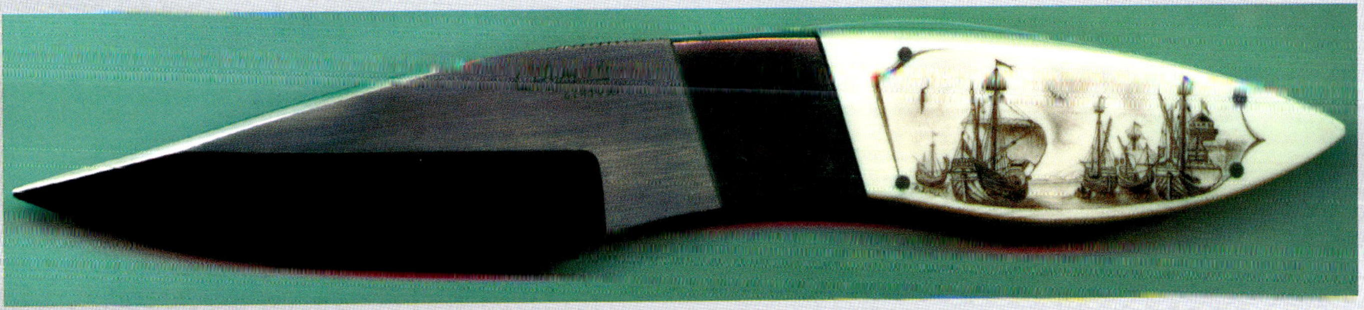

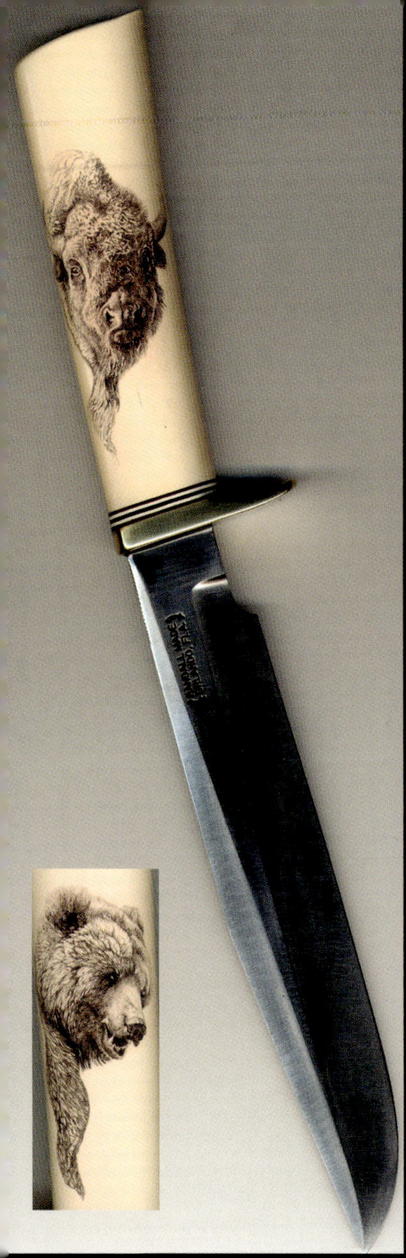

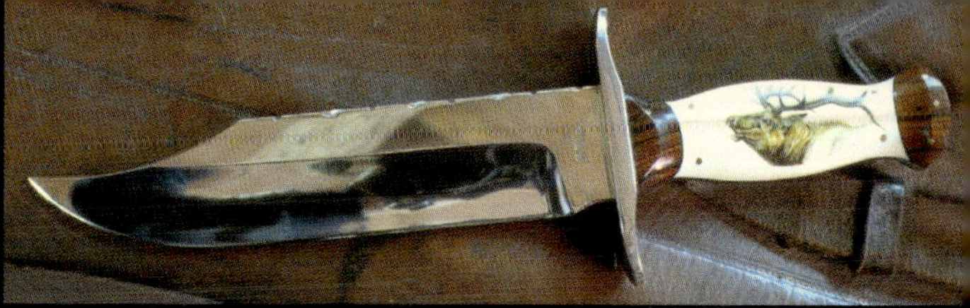

Scrimshaw on the mammoth ivory grip of a knife by L. Fin.

Top: It's interesting how Roberto "wraps" the dragon around the grip of the knife.

Left: A "Randal" knife decorated with bear and bison in brownish color.

Roberto Bruci

A simple scene, but the sensitive treatment of the color and shadowing in the material gives it a beautiful feeling of early morning autumn mist.
The knife is by I. Corsi.
The grip is made of staghorn.

He also scrims Indians on pendants and bolo ties

Another of his Native American portraits, of which Robert Bruci is a master, on the grip of a knife by L. Fih.

Enlarged scrimshaw of an Indian woman on a knife grip.

Sharon Burger

Sharon Burger qualified as a fine artist, specializing in sculpture, and received her National Higher Diploma in Fine Art in 1992 at the Technikon, Natal in South Africa. As a student, she had numerous exhibitions of her work, but over the next several years after qualifying, in order to make a living, she had to take a variety of jobs involving wrought iron furniture, gates, balustrades, and business signs. Finally she found her niche in scrimshaw, the exact opposite of the massive objects that she worked on earlier.

While attending a knife show in Durban in 1995 with her father, a knife maker, she was introduced to the scrimshander Toi Skellern. Sharon had always resisted her father's urging to make scrimshaw, because she thought that scrimshaw had nothing to do with "proper" art and was really more of a "craft". Her introduction to Toi and real scrimshaw changed Sharon's opinion. She had to admit that scrimshaw was not a merely a "craft" but a legitimate art form requiring a great deal of study, practice, talent, dedication, and above all, patience. Toi's work, her enthusiasm, and her willingness to share her knowledge persuaded Sharon to try it at least once.

After Sharon had done a few practice pieces on ivory, she visited Toi and examined her work under Toi's microscope. She was devastated when she saw her "exercises" under magnification. She says that her stipples looked like craters. She hadn't realized that you weren't supposed to use that much pressure when stippling. Sharon had a talent for scrimshaw and the fault was easy to correct, but although Toi encouraged her to continue, she was so depressed that she vowed never to try scrimming again. For two months she didn't pick up a needle, but her father wouldn't let her give up. He gave her a knife to scrim for him. Thinking, "Why not? It's now or never!", and without practicing first, she went straight to work on it. Her father was pleased with the result. Sharon knew very well that she had a long way to go, but at that point she was ready to practice and learn.

Handles of a carving set featuring young women on wart hog tusk. The dimensions of the subject are ca. 7.5 x 2.5 cm.

Sharon did more work for her father and other knife makers. In 1997, she was inducted into the Knife Makers Guild of South Africa, and today she is a full-time scrimshander.

Sharon works with two different techniques: stipplings and "cutting" (line scrimshaw), but she prefers stippling, because this technique is more precise and permits greater tonal range than line techniques. Her favorite subjects are portraits and figure studies, including animal portraits in close-up. She says that she is obsessed with fine detail, especially when she scrims eyes.

Sharon does black and colored scrimshaw on materials that include ivory and whale teeth (both only for domestic sale and use), wart hog tusks, hippopotamus teeth, buffalo horn (reverse scrimshaw), and fossil ivory. She doesn't limit herself to any particular subject, and it makes no difference whether she works from a client's photograph or finds the appropriate photos herself. Most of her work is done on commission for knife makers and collectors. However, she also does display-art pieces, framed works, pendants, earrings, brooches, and bolo tie pieces.

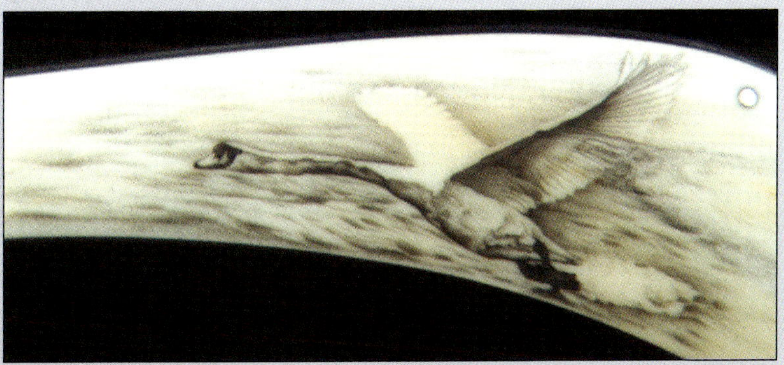

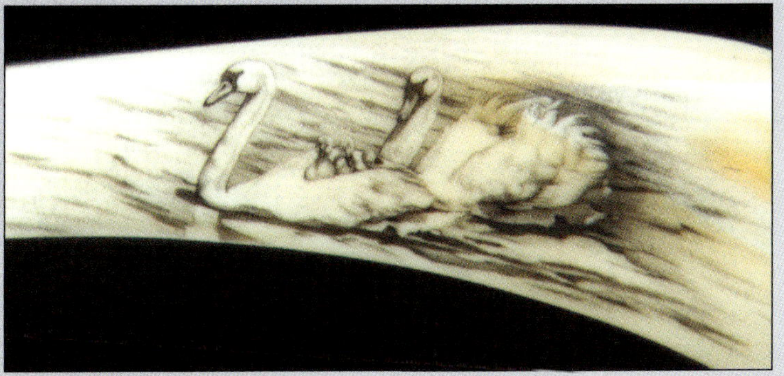

Two swan themes scrimmed in fine stippling technique on a carving set. The grip scales are of wart hog teeth. Dimensions of the subject: ca. 7.5 x 2.5 cm.

The dimensions of the original elephant scene are 6 x 3.7 cm. It is scrimmed in stippling technique on elephant ivory.

Sharon Burger

"Big Five", a favorite African theme, scrimmed here in stippling technique on elephant ivory. The dimensions of the subjects run between 3.5 x 2 cm and 4 x 2.5 cm.

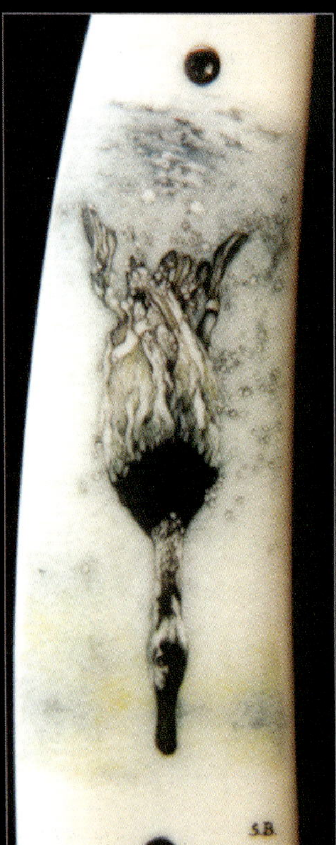

A diving canvasback duck in delicate color shadowing on a folding knife. Elephant ivory. Subject dimensions: ca 5.5 x 2 cm.

The leopard is scrimmed on elephant ivory and is ca. 6 x 2 cm in size. The difficult fantasy scene with the gnomes is on a knife handle of hard hippopotamus tooth. The dimensions are about 7 x 2.5 cm.

Sharon Burger

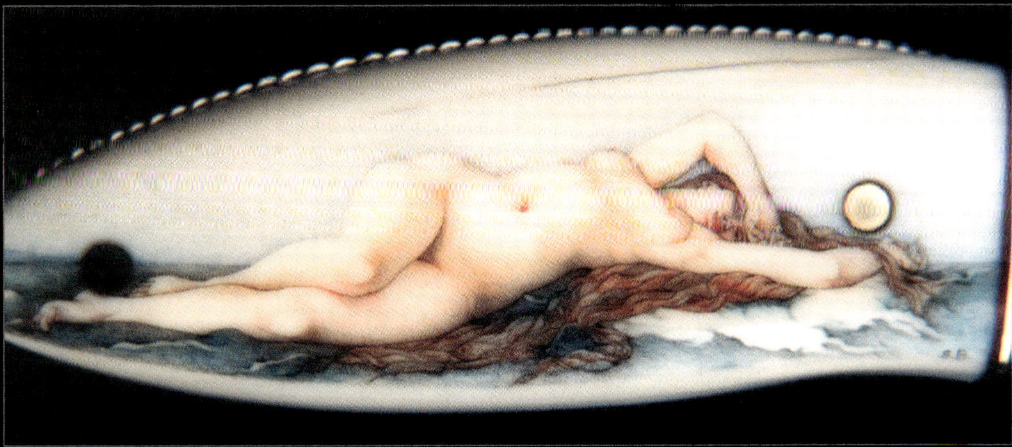

Cabanel's Venus on a knife handle of hippopotamus tooth.

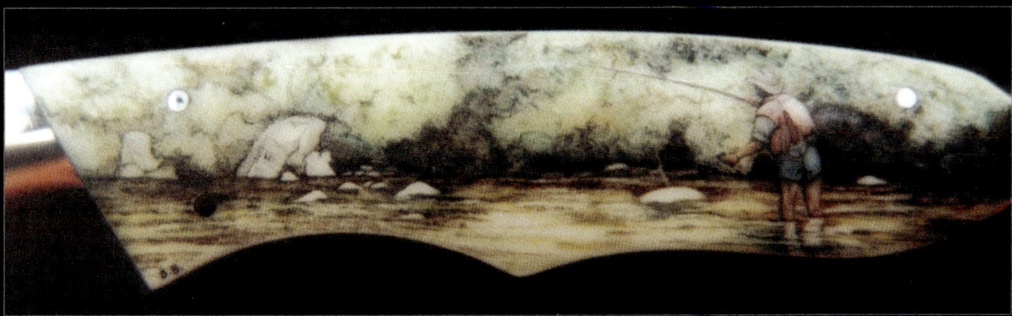

A fishing scene on a knife handle of elephant ivory.

A Staffordshire terrier on elephant ivory. Dimensions: ca. 3.5 x 2 cm.

This couple is scrimmed on both sides of an elephant ivory knife handle. Dimensions: ca. 3 x 2 cm.

Jean Pierre Coudert

Jean Pierre Coudert is a teacher by profession. In his spare time, he makes artistically handmade knives and does scrimshaw. He is an enthusiastic archer, and he was the European Champion in Traditional Archery at the European Master's Tournament in Portugal in 2002.

The logo on his knife blades displays a target and arrow with Coudert's name. He doesn't call himself an artist, although he is proud of his ability to produce realistic, true-to-life animals and nature scenes. He began scrimming portraits successfully a short time ago.

Jean Pierre Coudert uses only stippling technique for his scrimshaw work. He believes that this is more durable than lines on a knife handle, where the scrimshaw can lose its color over the years from wear and the friction of handling. Mainly, he uses ink for colored scrimshaw, but for buffalo horn he uses oil paints. He begins by putting in the outlines with stippling under 4-power magnification. After he has colored the outlines and added more stippling, he does the detail work under a stereo microscope.

Two detailed pictures of Jean Pierre Coudert's knives with his own scrimshaw work. The original diameter of the inlay with the owl is 1.5 cm.

Necessity is the mother of invention. Cracks appeared in the material when Jean Pierre began to work on one of the bolo ties above, so the originally planned roebuck became this doe. Jean Pierre inlaid a decorative disk of turquoise at the location of the defect.

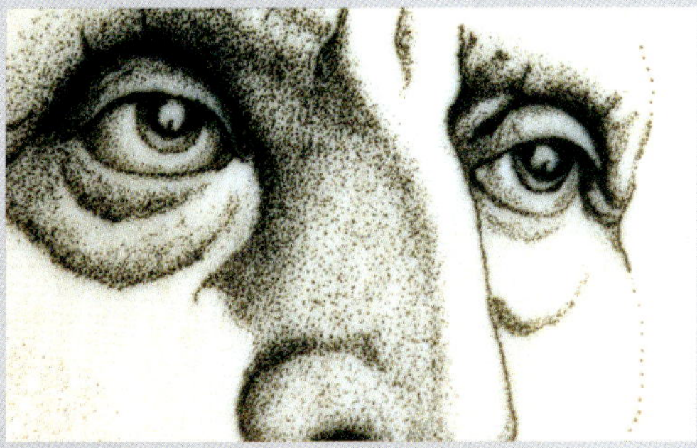

Left: An extremely detailed piece, just this part alone of the Indian portrait required seven hours. It is shown at about the original size next to the completed work, which took another 45 hours.
Below: A bighorn sheep on the grip of a folding knife. The picture is shown enlarged.

Jean Pierre Coudert

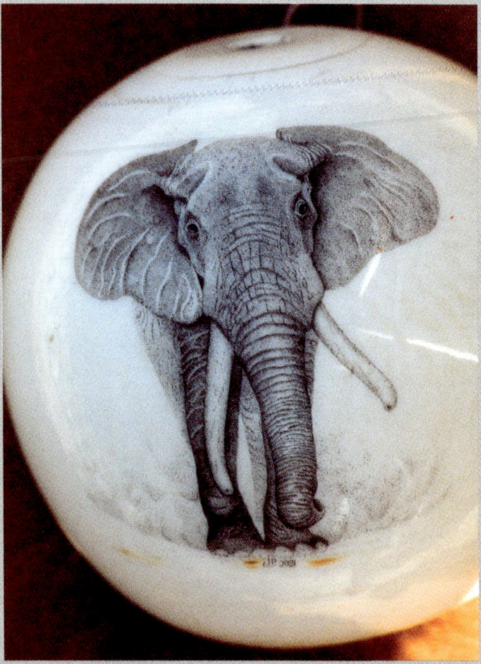

Jean Pierre says that this elephant on an ivory billiard ball was one of the trickiest pieces he has ever done. The picture changes according to the perspective from which it is viewed, so he had to alter the proportions to compensate for this effect.

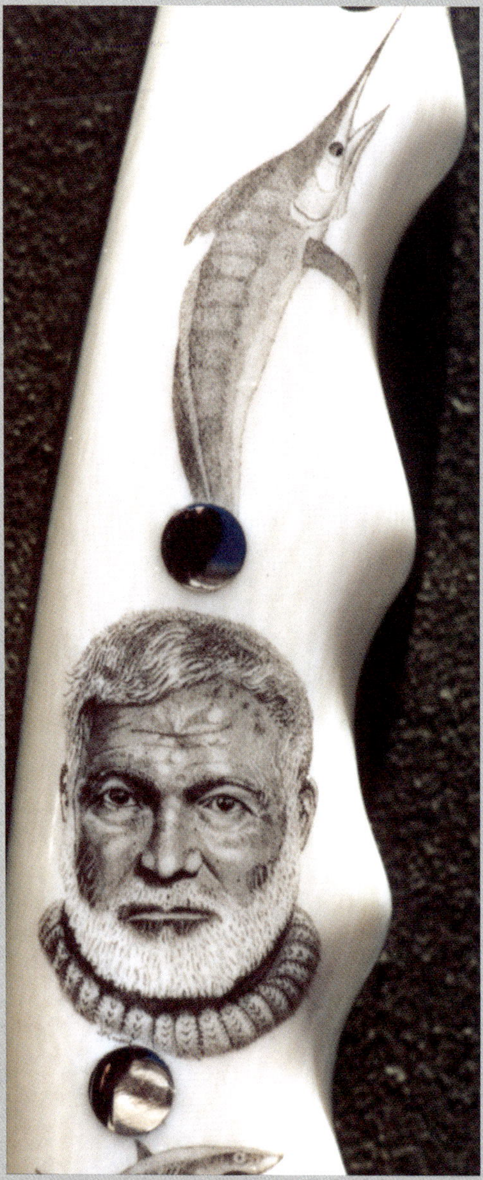

Top: Hemingway step-by-step. The picture with both eyes done already makes it easy to imagine who it will be at the end.

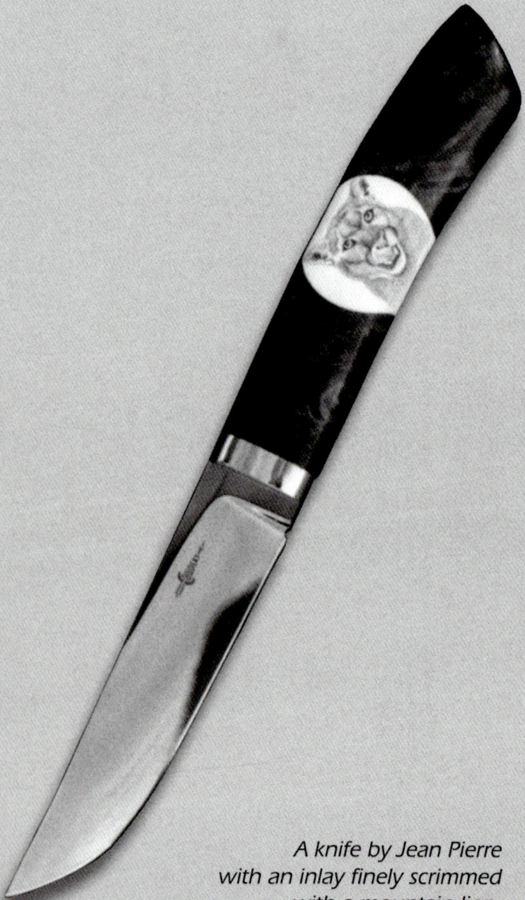

A knife by Jean Pierre with an inlay finely scrimmed with a mountain lion.

A portrait of a cat, scrimmed on buffalo horn and colored with oil paint. When he wants to reduce drying time, Jean Pierre sometimes uses acrylic paints on a black surface.

This capercaille on ivory is colored with ink. The picture is greatly magnified.

It is also possible to include the natural structure and color of mammoth ivory in the subject.

Stefan Dohnke

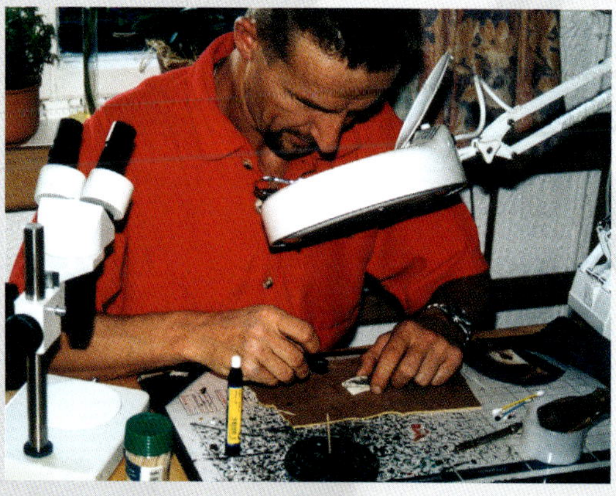

Stefan Dohnke was born in 1962 in Sonthofen in Germany. His attention was first drawn to scrimshaw toward the end of the '80s, and he tried this new activity for himself, spurred on by a friend who made valuable Damascus knifes.

He read a great deal about scrimshaw (mainly books from America). Talking to artists at various knife shows was a discouraging experience for him. In fact, Stefan says that they gave him the impression that the skills were family secrets. So in order to learn how to do it, he had to experiment with it on his own. At the beginning, he limited himself to simple subjects and worked mainly during the morning hours to get the quiet he needed to work undisturbed.

The surfaces on which he scrims have increased in variety with time, but he works only on natural materials. As models, he uses subjects from hunting magazines and books, and he is allowed to do studies in a taxidermy studio. For his scrimming, he uses a tool he made himself out of a specially ground diamond needle from an old record player.

Most of his scrimshaw is produced under 3.5-power magnification, and he uses a binocular microscope at 6- to 8-power magnification only for the final inspection. Objects that will have to stand up to daily use, such as pendants, lighters, and belt buckles are protected against wear with a coat of clear acrylic lacquer.

His clients are mainly hunters and traditional archers. Stefan will scrim any subject they want.

Two scrimshaws on red deer rosettes. The portrait of a Native American is used as the clasp for a bow cover, and the fox is on a belt buckle.
In the middle, a lynx head on a knife guard.

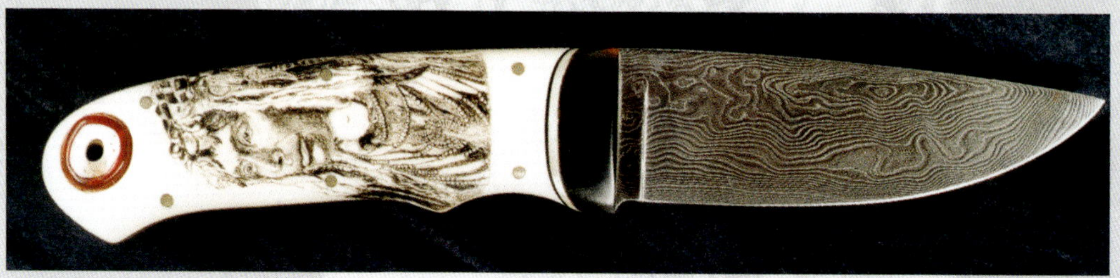

An ivory brooch with a lynx head, next to a cigarette lighter (1:1) with a bone appliqué on which Stefan Dohnke scrimmed a wolf.

An original display for the fish on camel bone. The slice of agate resembles a small lake in both color and shape.

Enlargement of a subject on an Indian knife. The knife is made out of 448-layer Damascus, the grip is buffalo horn, silver, and ivory. An old pearl is the bushing for the lanyard hole. The height of the original is 5.5 cm.

An elephant with young worked on ivory. The puma on the knife handle to the right is 3.5 x 1.9 cm.

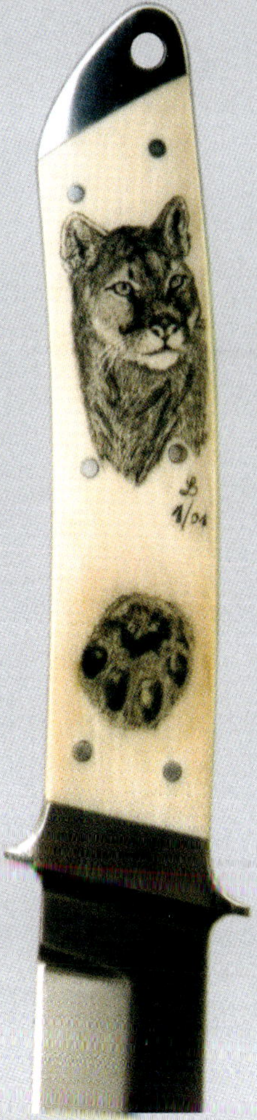

Andrey Dolenko

Andrey Dolenko was born in 1951 in Sevastopol on the Crimean Peninsula on the Black Sea. In 1959, he moved to Vladivostok, where he later entered the Russian Merchant Marine Academy. He received his degree there in the industrial management of fishing fleets.

Andrey and his family have spent much of their lives at sea on whaling vessels; his grandfather as a harpooner, his father as an engineer, and his mother as a ship's dentist. In the Antarctic, Andrey sailed on the same whaling ship as his mother.

He was first exposed to scrimshaw in 1985, when his ship was in port in Singapore for repairs. He was so excited by this art form that, from then on, he wanted to do nothing but make scrimshaw.

It was hard for him to learn the technique, because scrimshaw is not very well known in Russia and there were very few books available on the subject. Andrey had done etching and engraving earlier for minting bronze and silver coins, and he quickly discovered that both techniques had one thing in common: There is no room for error in either!

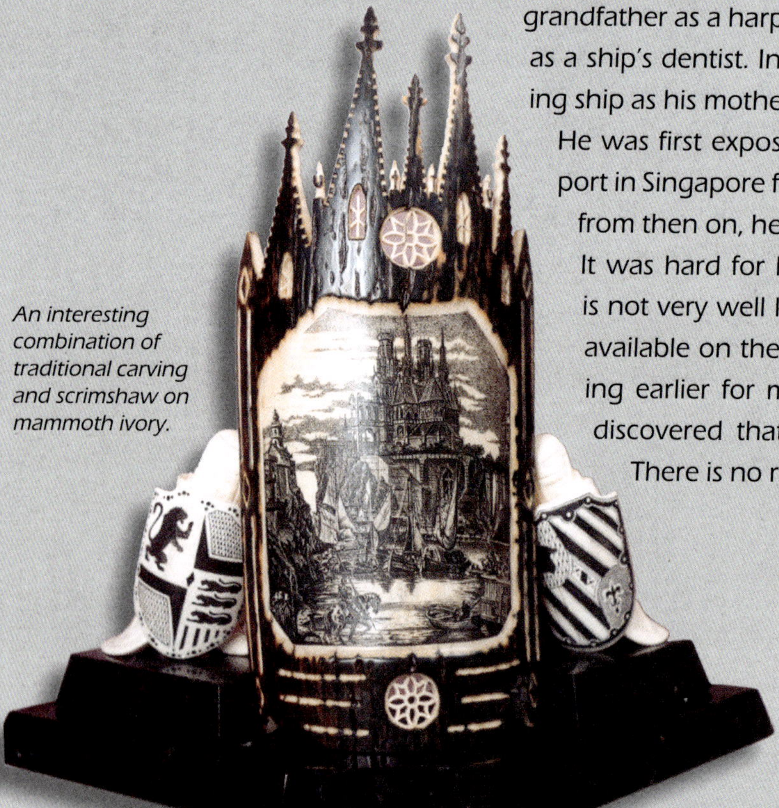

An interesting combination of traditional carving and scrimshaw on mammoth ivory.

"Portsmouth Harbor" on mammoth ivory measures 15 x 10 cm.

This piece is 35 x 12 cm in size. The lighter gives a feel for the original size.

Andrey Dolenko won first prize with this work at the International Scrimshaw Competition in Hawaii. Dimensions: 35 x 15 cm.

Tiger family. 15 x 10 cm. Both tiger themes are scrimmed on mammoth ivory.

There are 100 animals scrimmed on this noble piece. Andrey won second place in the 2001 International Competition in Hawaii with it. The dimensions are 34 x 16 cm.

Sprinting tigers. 20 x 8 cm.

For "Warriors Way" on mammoth ivory, Andrey won first place in the 2000 International Scrimshaw Competition in Hawaii and received the "Niihau Award".

Maihkel Eklund

Maihkel Eklund lives in Sweden and earns his living from his work as a nature painter, knife maker, engraver, and scrimshander. The idea of doing scrimshaw came to Maihkel while he was studying art and working with graphic technique. He thought that he could make good use of those skills for his knives. Only later did he discover that the technique already existed.

Maihkel says, "The technique that I use is very simple. I build a picture out of small points, a bit similar to making tattoos. The only difficulty is placing the points in their proper places!"

He colors his works step by step in order to watch his subject develop. Normally he uses black or brown oil paints, but he may also use a variety of colors in one subject.

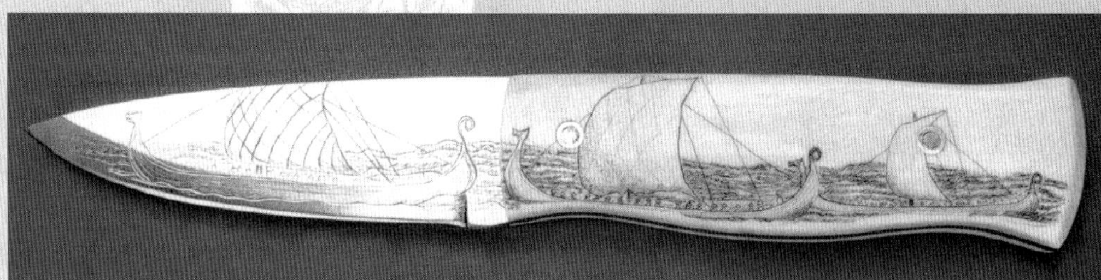

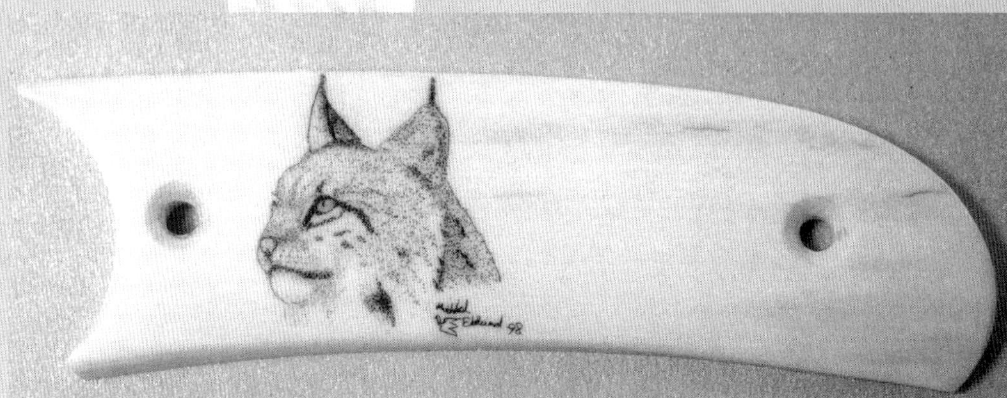

On his knives, Maihkel likes to carry the theme of the engraving on the blade over onto the grip as scrimshaw. The knife grip is of whale tooth. The lynx head is on a grip of mammoth ivory

Maihkel Eklund

One of Maikhel's knives with a Native American portrait on mammoth ivory.

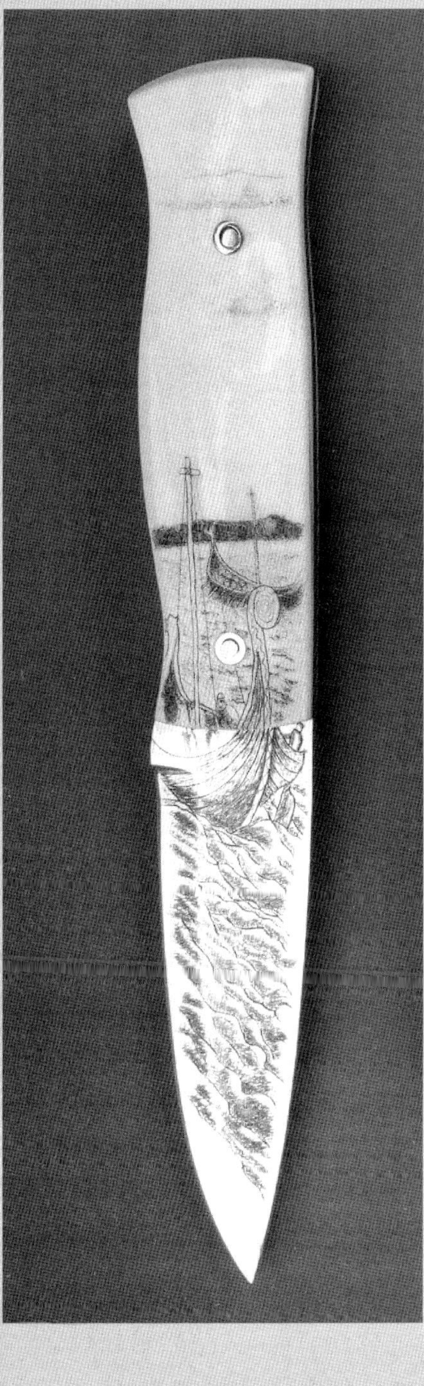

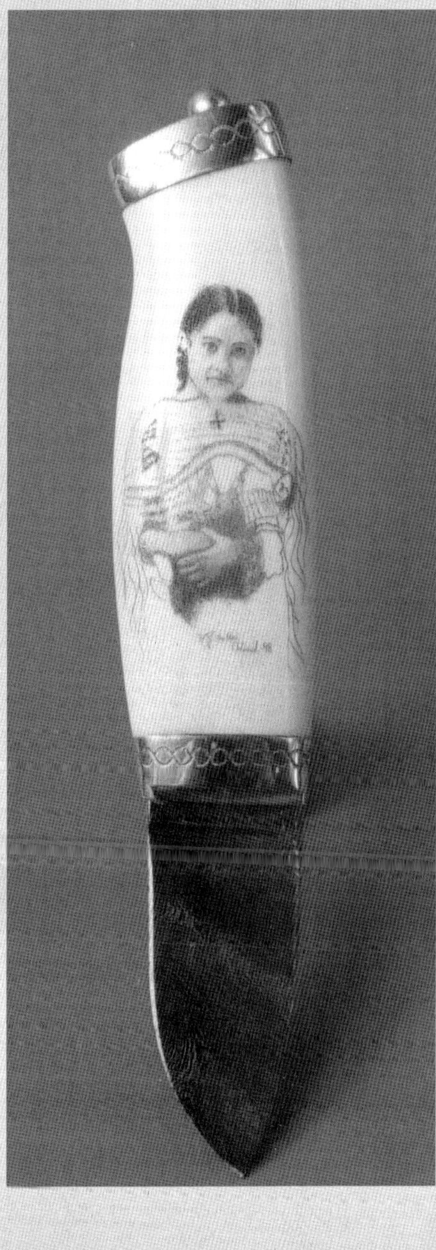

The knife grips are made of sperm whale tooth, narwhal tooth, and mammoth ivory.

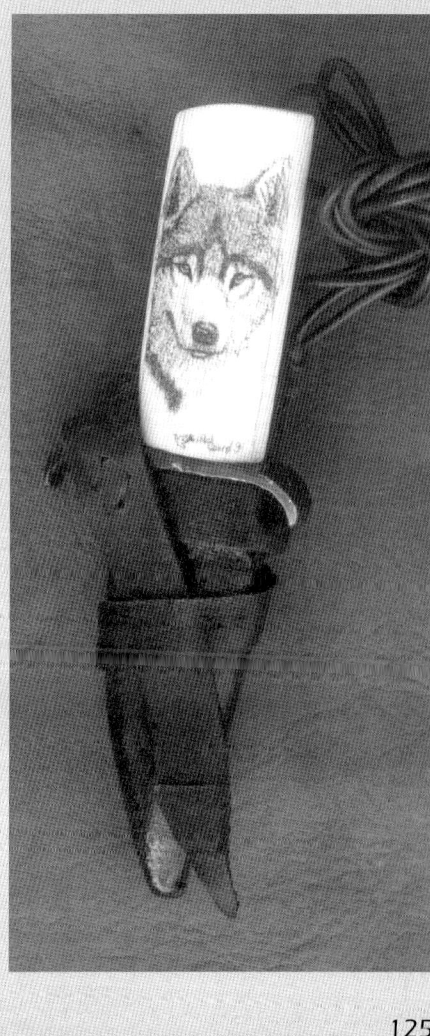

Gary Fiedler

Every artist can remember the moment when he decided which art form was the one for him. Gary's moment was that day more than 25 years ago when he saw his first engraved powder horn at a muzzle-loading rendezvous. He knew then that he had to learn how to do it. He had a background in art and had planned to become an illustrator, but somehow he had become a policeman instead! He had always enjoyed working with pen and ink, but he knew scrimshaw would be a real challenge. There was no one in his area who could show him the finer points of engraving, so it has been a self-taught, trial-and-error process to get to where he is today.

Gary has worked with several kinds of materials over the years, including fossil ivory and antler, but his work with powder horns seems to be what keeps him the busiest. His engraving fits very well into his hobby of Revolutionary War reenactment, where men would rarely be caught without their powder horns and rifles. Almost always, the horns are engraved with battle campaigns, maps of their homelands, or the owner's name.

Gary enjoys creating that special horn, one that will be passed down for generations to come, just as they were hundreds of years ago. As the saying goes, "It's all in the details", and that is very important with this kind of work. He takes great pride in getting even the smallest detail just right. Whether it's a mast and rigging on a ship or feathers on a bird, he doesn't consider it done until it's as perfect as he can make it.

Gary works with a homemade scribing tool and a standard lighted magnifier, and he uses only black ink. Although the colors being used today are stunning, he prefers the more traditional look and simplicity of black on white.

Gary enjoys every aspect of engraving, but he is happiest while working with animals. Getting that special look to the fur and a sparkle in the eyes is not as easy as you might think, and when he is told, "it looks so real!" it makes all those hours that were put into the piece time well spent.

Gary's work was mentioned in a nice article on powder horns and engraving published by *Muzzle Blasts* magazine in December 2002. He is also honored to have some of his illustrations hanging in the museum at Fort de Chartres, Prairie Du Rocher, Illinois.

The art of scrimshaw has been around for hundreds of years. Gary is proud to be a part of keeping this beautiful artwork alive.

This piece is one of the very first items that Gary scrimmed. He says that when he compares it with the work he does now, he can see his improvement over the years.

Top: Three pieces with animals. Gary and his wife are nature lovers; the playful and curious otters are some of their favorites and were done especially for Gary's wife. Otters: 13 x 8 cm, baby cougar and coyote: 7.5 x 5 cm.

Horner James Adams made this map horn. The engraving was done by Gary as a privately commissioned order. It has a Lewis and Clark theme on it with a map of their journey from St. Louis to the Mandan village. The name of its owner, Hollis Ross, is engraved on it.

Right: The whale's tooth is a privately commissioned piece. Its length is 16 cm.

"Fox Family", also a commissioned horn with ornaments and nice carvings.

Far left. Gary did this cougar for his wife. They both love cats and they live together with three of them.

Left: This portrait of Buffalo Bill Cody was done on ivory micarta many years ago. The yellowing is due to the age of the micarta, but gives the piece an interesting look.

Below: This priming horn was made by horner Mark Toigo. Gary has engraved it with the H.M.S. Victory, Lord Nelson's flagship. Nelson's portrait is on the reverse side. Gary has kept this piece as his own private horn.

At the end of the '70s, Wolfgang Fubel began exploring the fur trade era in North America as a hobby. He made his first moccasins and buckskins himself, started doing bead-and-quill work, and read numerous books on the trappers and voyageurs. He devoted himself to the colonial era in American history and is very careful about authenticity.

When Wolfgang began to produce map horns, he found it essential to use only the best and most authentic material. When you sort through a hundred horns only to find that just five of the pieces are suitable for making map horns, you very quickly realize the importance of finding the right source of supply, which isn't easy.

The literature dealing with powder horns is skimpy, as many scrimshanders have found, but Wolfgang was forced to rely on it for his research. He knew no one else who was producing these expensive horns.

Wolfgang is now motivated to make these horns by the requests he receives. There are now enthusiasts and collectors in both Europe and the United States waiting for him to produce more horns.

An English map horn. The heart is a silver inlay. It was a frequently used symbol on hunting bags, clothing, jewelry, and many other items. Size: 28 cm.

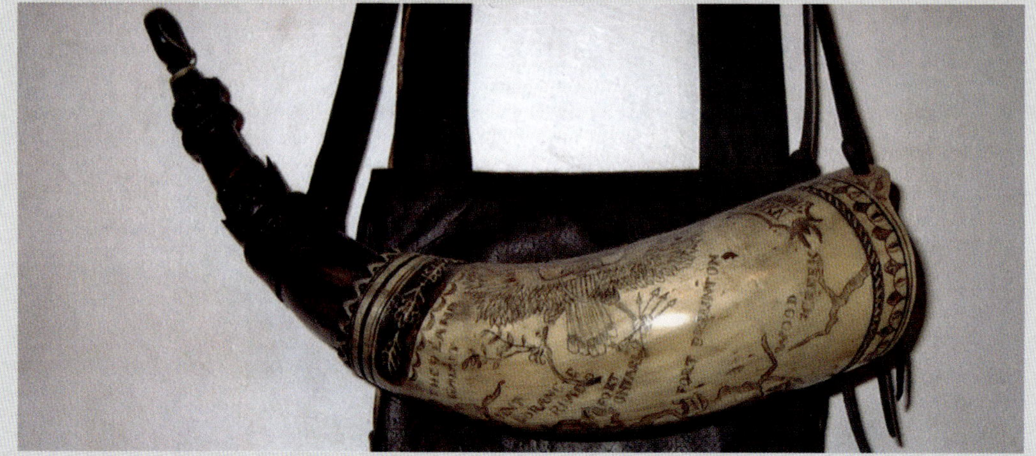

The style of this powder horn is from about 1755. The eagle isn't a fitting motif, but it was the customer's wish. Length: 32 cm

Wolfgang Fubel

This is a replica of a powder horn from the period of the English-French colonial war in Canada about 1755-1770. It was made after detail sketches from a flat projection. Very few horns possess the necessary attributes to produce such a powder horn. The dark end isn't attached or stained, it is the dark layer that sometimes appears when the light yellowish surface is worked down. Only the eye of an experienced horner can select such horns before they are worked. The windrose is a silver inlay. Size of the horn: 32cm.

Paul Gonzalez

For forty years Paul Gonzalez has lived in Aix-en-Provence, the hometown of the renowned painter Paul Cezanne and the author Emile Zola. Twenty years ago Paul began to get interested in knives, with his main interest in the art of scrimshaw. He was soon ready to produce some work.

Later he decided to produce his own knives, so he could present his scrimshaw work better. To do this, he studied smithing with Dominique Bargiel, a French expert in Japanese smithing work.

Paul's first scrimshaw work appeared in 1990. It was a drawing of a mammoth on a piece of jawbone. He kept it as a souvenir. After this first attempt, Paul taught himself practically everything about scrimshaw work by collecting information, materials, and equipment everywhere.

He began then to work with a headband loupe, but has also used a microscope with fivefold magnification since then.

As time passed, Paul Gonzalez developed a style that he himself says is more portraiture than anything else. He is interested in history, especially the history of the Native Americans.

His favorite materials are mammoth ivory and buffalo horn. At the beginning of his career, he signed his works with a Japanese ideogram. Several years ago he changed to "Paul G."

Paul can earn only half his living with knives and scrimshaw; also both are really a passion with him. He produces only five or six knife units per year, but one must not forget that he makes the entire set by hand: knife, sheath, and scrimshaw.

One of Paul's latest works, the portrait of a small child.

Right: A trapper scrimmed into black buffalo horn.
(Photos: Frédéric Combe)

This big Bowie knife has a partly hardened Damascus blade and a handle of walrus ivory. Two Indian medicine men and a warrior are scrimmed on them by Paul Gonzanez.

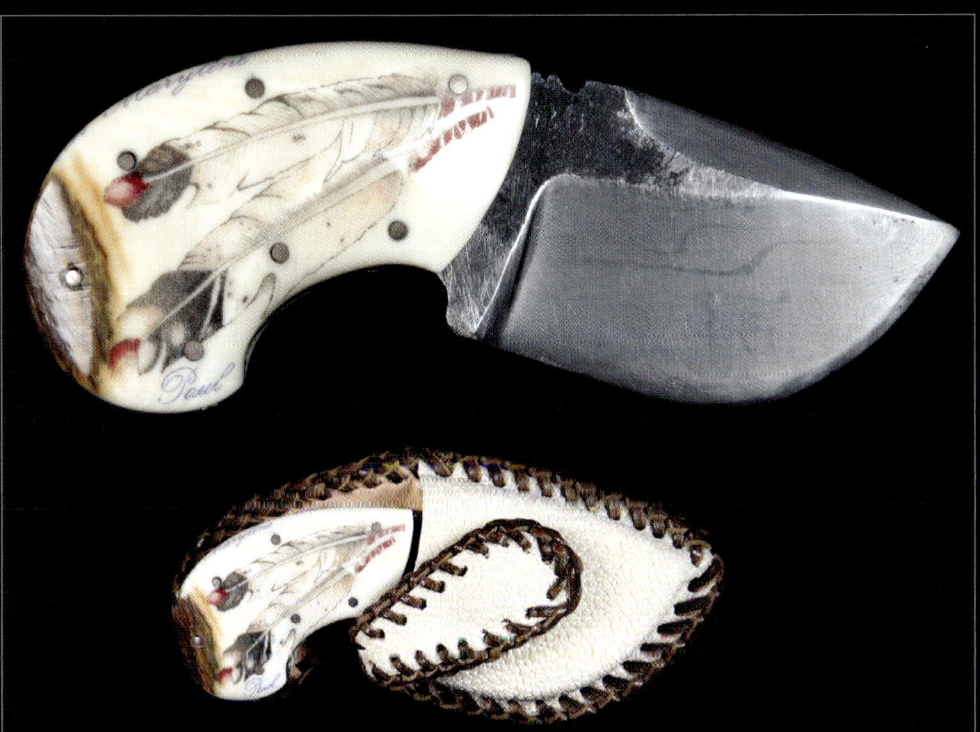

This knife handle is also made of walrus ivory and colorfully, suitably decorated with scrimshaw Indian eagle feathers. (All photos: Frédéric Combe)

Eva Halat

Eva Halat began to paint before she could really walk or talk, and she swiped colored pencils from her older sister's school bag. She comes from a family of artists, and fortunately her parents encouraged her obvious talent. She was trained as an illustrator and graphic artist from 1970 – 73 at the Johannes Gutenberg School in Stuttgart and in 1978 had the first exhibition of her paintings.

After that, Eva worked as a freelance illustrator for advertising agents. She drew with pencil, pen and ink, and chalk, painted with oils and acrylics, and did a lot with airbrush on paper and vehicles. In 1984, she received first prize for vehicle airbrush design at the "Erster Autosalon Stuttgart" (First Stuttgart Automobile Salon).

Whenever she had any time left over from work, household chores, and raising her two sons, she painted and displayed her work at exhibitions. In 1988, Eva took up traditional archery, and she discovered scrimshaw when she met knife enthusiasts and knife maker Eberhard Kaljumae among the archers. Then around 1992, she was asked for the first time whether she could do scrimshaw on an inlay for a knife handle or a bow.

After some initial trials on pieces of polymer in a scrimshaw kit from the United States, she scrimmed her first knife. The knife belonged to a friend, who at the time didn't know what "real" scrimshaw was supposed to look like. When Eva looks at the photograph of that job today, she can only advise the beginner never to give up, but to keep practicing and studying the work of other scrimshanders.

Since then, Eva has done a great deal of scrimshaw. She works by hand, mainly using stippling technique, but she also scrims in fine lines when required by the surface of the subject. She prefers oil paints, both for black-and-white and for color. She does most of her work on commission, but from time to time creates scrimshaw from her own designs.

The pendant is decorated on both sides with Stone Age people.

Trout swim on this fish knife made by Daniel Vally.

The inlays on one side of the extension are decorated with a badger watching a snake, eye-to-eye with a ground squirrel. The motif of two sleeping lynx on the customer's knife (see below) is repeated on the extension's rear side at his request. The knife was made by Eva's husband Eddy.

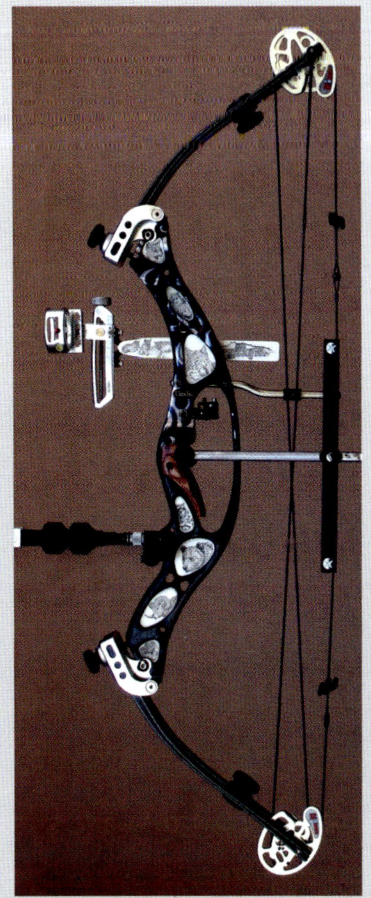

Wildlife of the Rocky Mountains on an unusual object for scrimshaw. This Hoyt UltraTec compound bow came as consignment work and it was a joy to create.
12 thin inlays of antique elephant ivory with 19 animal portraits are fixed in the holes of the bow handle with silicon putty. They give the bow only 80 grams more weight. This bow is surely one of a kind.

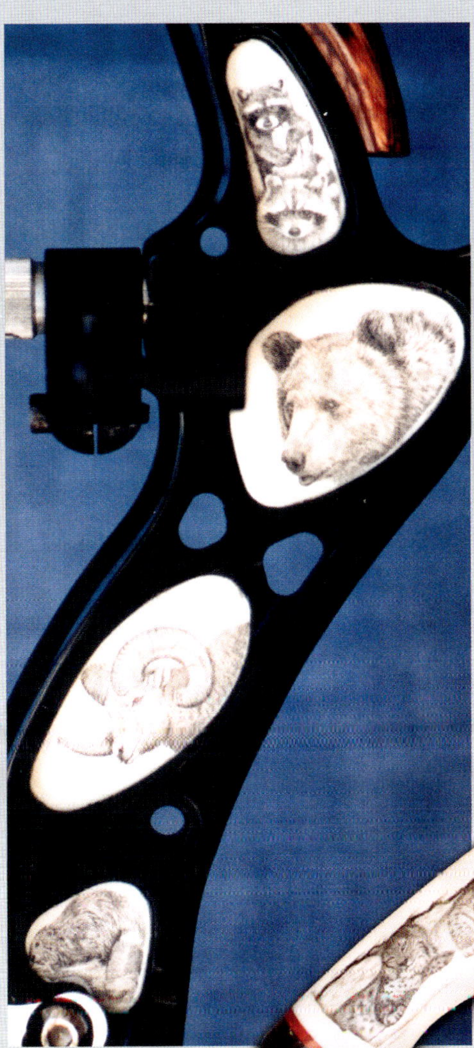

Eva Halat

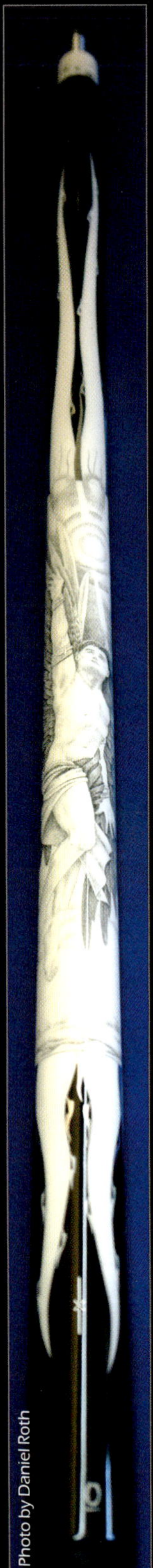

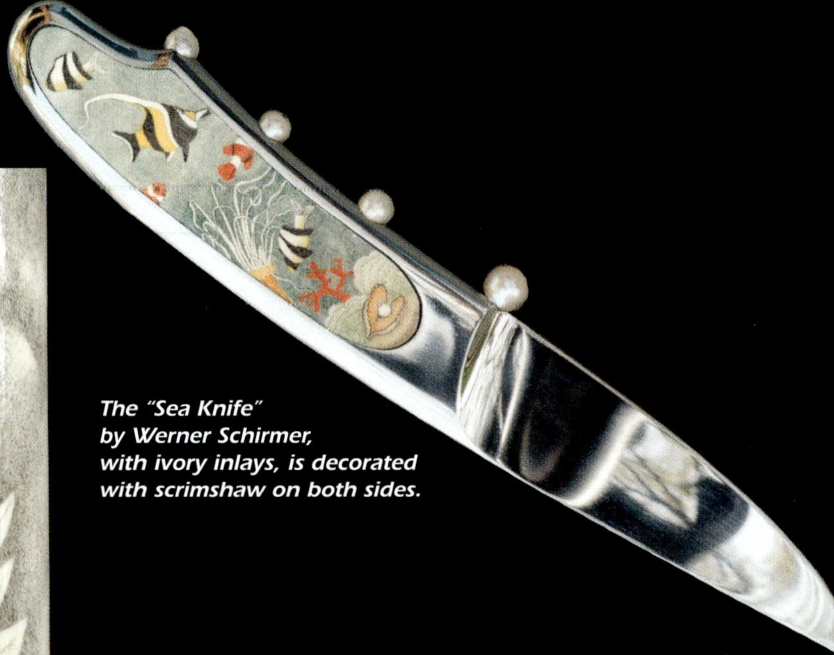

The "Sea Knife" by Werner Schirmer, with ivory inlays, is decorated with scrimshaw on both sides.

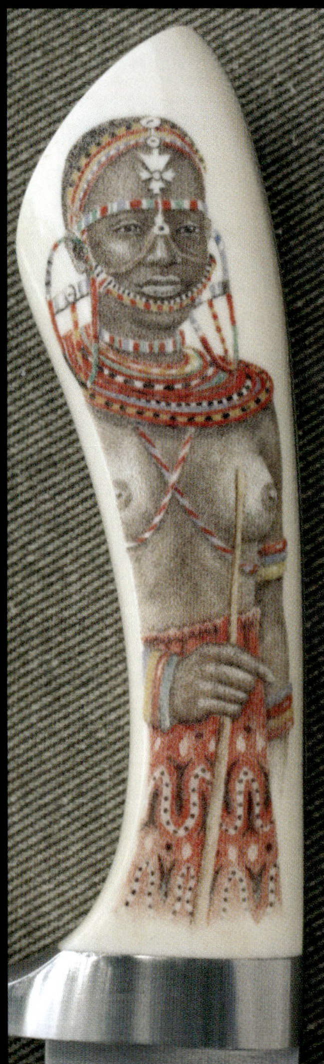

Above: Both sides of the grip of the "Massai" knife by Eberhard Kaljumae from the book's front page.

Left: Detail views of a custom billiard cue by Arthur Queue company, Germany. The Ikarus is scrimmed on elephant ivory. The cue is made of ebony and ivory with sterling silver inlays.

Left: This display piece was done on consignment as a gift donated by the hunter to the dog's owner for tracking the deer.

A knife by Werner Schmer with nudes after Bruno Bruni scrimmed on both sides of the elephant ivory grip scales.

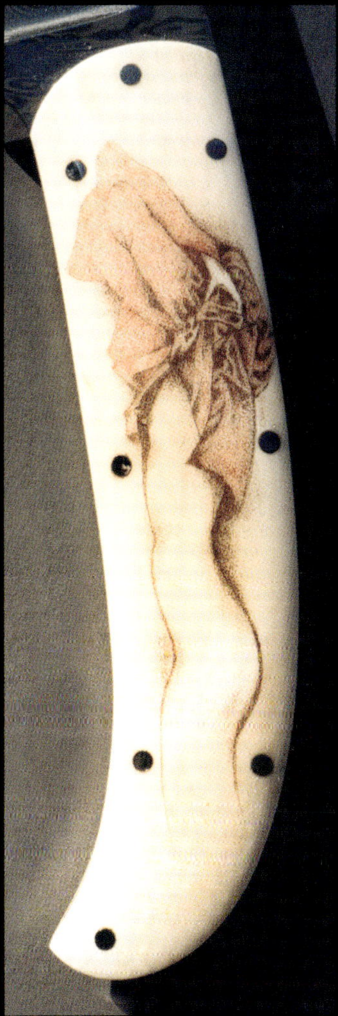

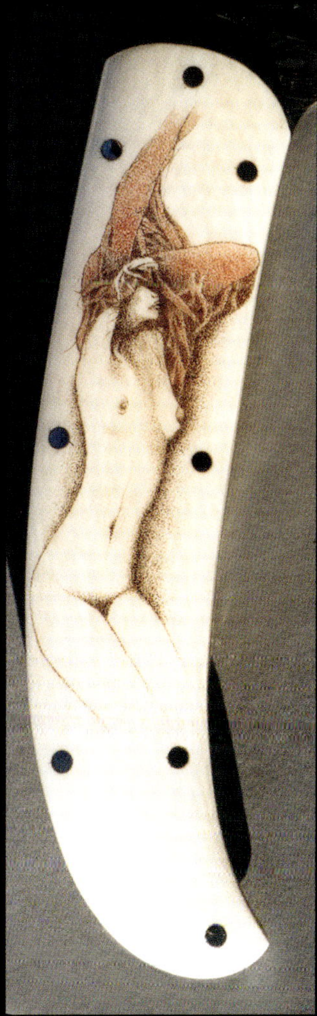

Tiger on mammoth ivory. Size: ca. 1:1.

Attila Harmat

Attila Harmat, born in 1968, lives in Kisdobsza, a small city in Hungary. By training, he is an art teacher, but at the moment he is not working in that profession. Instead, he illustrates books and does metal engraving and scrimshaw. He prefers to work in black-and-white on a variety of materials, including mammoth, mastodon, and elephant ivory, walrus, whale, or hippopotamus teeth, and buffalo horn.

He has no preferred subject matter. Usually he draws or engraves wild animals, fish, horses, or birds, but he also likes to work with human anatomy and often scrims scenes from ancient mythology and, of course, beautiful girls.

Two big cats on mammoth ivory. Size: 15 X 9 cm.

"Satyr with Nymph", a scene from Greek mythology (original dimensions: 14 x 7.5 cm) repeated on a knife with gold inlays by Ferenc Tumpek.

Attila Harmat

Above: Knife with elephants from the "Big Five" series by Ferenc Tumpek. Size: 23 cm, mammoth ivory and stainless Damascus steel.

A tiger stares out of the grip on a knife, also made by Ferenc Tumpek.

Right: A very finely scrimmed woman on mammoth ivory. Size: 11 x 15 cm.

A salamander on mammoth ivory, size: 14 cm.

A beautiful knife by Tumpec Ferenc with African scenes, lions and cape buffaloes. Size: 23 cm, materials: mammoth ivory, RWL-34, blue carbon steel insets with gold inlays. The gold inlay and metal engravings are also Attila's work.

Bob Hergert

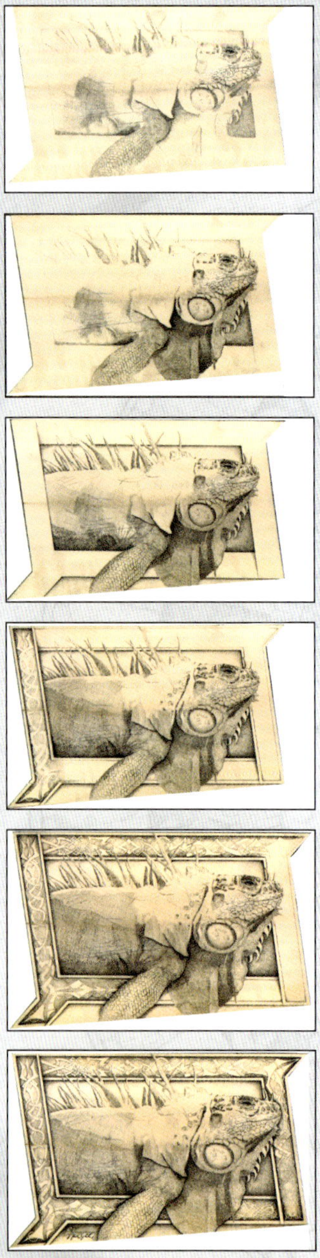

Bob Hergert was born on September 22, 1952, in the United States in Portland, Oregon. Soon after, the family moved from the city to the small town of Beaverton. In 1958, there were still beavers in the creeks around the town. Much of his childhood was spent in the orchards and forests during the warm summers, and reading and drawing during the long months of rain and cold. When he reached his 19th year, he got wanderlust and left for Mexico. A couple of years later, he took a nine-month trip through Central and South America.

Some say artists are born with their talent. This may be true, for by the age of 9 or 10, Bob was drawing in pen and ink - portraits, cars, monsters. With no formal art training, he was learning the basics of perspective and shadows. He took his first art class late in high school, and he took a few classes in painting, drawing, and printmaking during the short time he was in college.

When his portfolio permitted him to land a job in an advertising agency, he left school for the working world and took jobs as a technical illustrator, mural painter, and school bus driver when unable to support himself as a freelance artist.

His strength in art was his ability to draw, though he was competent in painting and airbrush. The difficulty at that time was finding a niche for pen-and-ink art. He reprinted his drawings and sold the prints in galleries and shops, but only in a desultory way. In spite of the lean times, he felt that art was the inevitable path he had to follow. It was at this time (1978) that a jeweler who owned and sold some of his prints suggested he try scrimshaw. The jeweler provided ivory cabochons for him to "scratch", then the pieces were set into bracelets and pendants. Soon he introduced Bob to his ivory dealer, who gave him a broader view of the scrimshaw world. He was able to see the work of the best scrimshanders around.

Bob was then introduced to Gary Kelley, who wrote for *Blade Magazine* and who was a co-founder of the Miniature Knifemakers Society. Gary took an interest in Bob's career and helped him in countless ways. Before long, Bob's work was featured in many knife publications. It wasn't until Bob had been doing scrimshaw for almost 15 years that he finally became a full-time scrimshander. Most of what he does is commissioned by art and scrimshaw collectors. Occasionally, he sends work to galleries.

Bob's technique is generally stippling, that is tiny points or dots incised into the surface of the ivory. His carbide tool is so fine it can cut a point as small as a dust particle. He works on fossil ivory, as well as on some of the imitation ivories. He fills his incisions with oil paint, mostly black, in the traditional method of the early scrimshanders. He specializes in portraits and figures, but he doesn't limit his subject matter and has done cars, motorcycles, buildings, wildlife, etc. Recently he began working with a couple of custom guitar

"Iguana". The step-by-step production of a fascinating work.

makers. One of their guitars was made for Warren Haynes of the Allman Brothers Band, and recently he did work on a guitar for The Beach Boys.

Bob attends a number of the West Coast knife shows and gives demonstrations each year at the Oregon Knife Show. He is always happy to share tips with other scrimshanders or to talk with anyone interested in this amazing art form. He is an avid promoter of scrimshaw and works to educate the general public about the timeless quality of the art. He welcomes comments and correspondence.

He now lives with his two dogs on the southern Oregon coast in a town of only 1000 people with few distractions - other than its natural beauty. He drives the community ambulance, and his other interests include playing guitar, camping, canoeing, photography, traveling, and, as he himself says, "watching the stars and acting the fool".

Scrimshaw work on the buttons of a custom guitar. The material is mammoth ivory.

"Aztec Calendar", a box made of elephant ivory with an extremely finely worked motif from the Aztec culture, with an enlarged view at the left. The oval dimensions are 8 x 10 cm.

Bob Hergert

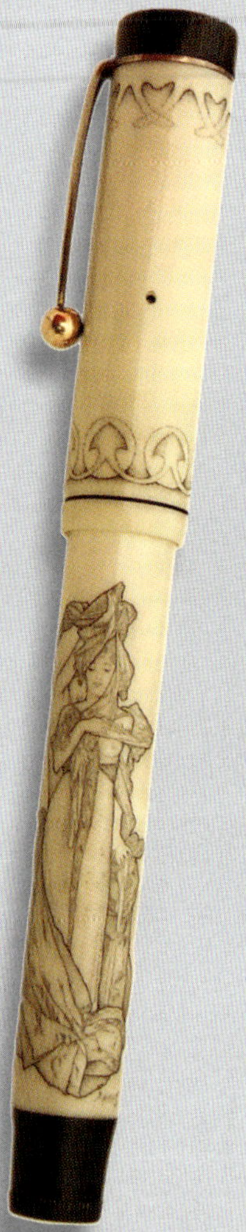

Young maiden on an elephant ivory pen.

Above: Two folding knives by David Boye.
Below: Angels and devils, A clever and intricate piece of scrimshaw on an old billiard ball.

Bob plays the guitar, and this is evident in his choice of subjects. Above, the guitarist and singer Neil Young on a folding knife with mammoth ivory, on the right Elvis Presley on a Zippo lighter with a mastodon ivory overlay.

Bob Hergert

Turkey and duck scrimmed on black Micarta™.
Below: "Cave of the Storm Nymphs", mammoth ivory, ca. 7.5 x 12.5 cm. Bob has hidden a small book in the picture with the title "Micro-Scrimshaw" (Bob's informal name for his company).

The ivory piece is ca. 12 cm in size.

"Boyd's Forest Dragon" on mammoth ivory, ca. 7.5 x 12 cm.

Bob has scrimmed a scene with coastal Indians from the American Northwest on an artifact, a piece of fossilized walrus ivory.

Hans Peter Jensen

All of the extraordinarily detailed and artistically perfect works by Hans Peter Jensen are originally in color, including this blonde on an ivory inlay on a knife by Wolfgang Dell.

Hans Peter Jensen did his first scrimshaw in December 1998. He still remembers it well: "At the time I was visiting my brother-in-law and he proudly showed me his newest acquisition, a beautiful knife by a well-known German knifemaker, decorated with a wolf's head scrimshaw. Jokingly, I told him that only the body and legs were missing, and I offered to supply the missing bits. I can still clearly remember his horrified expression."

So Hans spent some time with scrimshaw literature. He found Bob Engnath's books *Scrimshaw Connection I and II* especially useful. His first scrimshaw in line technique was in black-and-white, but immediately after that he began to work in color. Today his style is a combination of stipple technique and engraving. He says that he prefers this because the color contrasts that this style allows are the only way he can get the three-dimensional effect and the extremely fine detail he wants.

He uses a stereo microscope with 10- to 20-power magnification. A quality, colored scrimshaw requires four to five times as much working time as one done in black-and-white. Depending on the difficulty of the subject, that can mean 150 to 800 hours of highly concentrated work under the microscope for Hans.

A chain pendant in the style of a bolo tie on a piece of mammoth ivory bark.
Left: Shown in approximately original size, with an enlarged section next to it.
The puma and the Indian are both scrimmed on knife grips on mammoth ivory. The dark blue-green material is the exterior layer of a tooth.

A woman in leather on a mammoth ivory grip. Knife by Jockl Greis.

Hans Peter Jensen

A folding knife by Andre Thorburn. The grip scales are blue mammoth ivory bark pieces.

The colors of this scrimshaw match the knife by Jockl Greis perfectly. Scrimmed on mammoth ivory.

"Little Big Horn", a dagger with scrimshaw on the grip and sheath, shown at a somewhat reduced scale.
Below: An enlarged section of the piece. The material is elephant ivory.

Top: Two nudes. Hans Peter Jensen has perfectly mastered this subject. The bather to the left is done on mammoth ivory. The nude on the right is done on elephant ivory, and was a very time-consuming job, taking more than 800 hours of work.

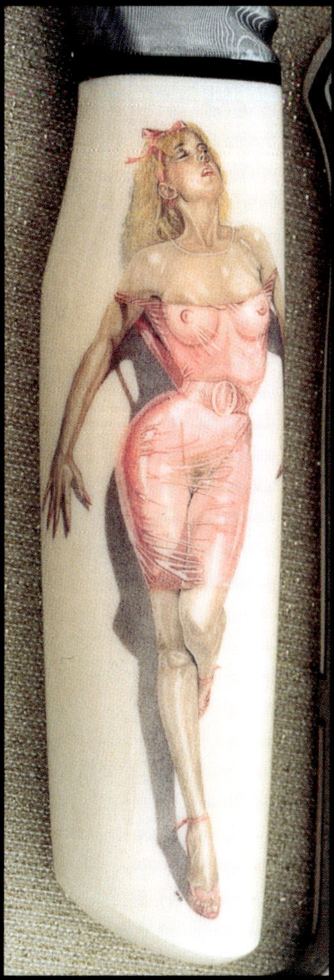

"Lady in Pink" on mammoth ivory

Top: The tiger's fur melts interestingly into the Damascus steel's pattern. A fantastically designed knife by Johannes Ebner with a black buffalo horn grip.

Left: The jaguar is worked on a knife grip of hard hippopotamus tooth. The elephants are on the tip of an antique elephant tusk. Both pictures are slightly enlarged.

Jan Jonsson

In 1997-98, Jan Jonsson began making knives. Until that time he didn't show much interest in woodworking at all, but in these years he tried to make wooden boxes and birch bark craft. In the end, knifemaking was the most fascinating thing to him and he was hooked by it. Starting to make knives using antler has its roots in Jan's past. He was born and raised in a small village in northern Sweden, where he came in contact with the beautiful craft of the Laplanders.

Jan Jonsson uses only natural materials originating in Sweden. He searches for his wood in the forest, he buys caribou antler in northern Sweden, and for the hairy sheaths he uses leather, which he skins from moose and treats all by himself. Sometimes the material already indicates how the finished knife will look.

Jan does the horn engraving with a small cutting tool. It is based on three elements: line, bow, and triangle. These elements can be endlessly combined, but have to fit the design and color of the knife.

Jan Jonsson has already earned a lot of awards for his knives. He tells about the great camaraderie and engagement in the Swedish knifemakers' scene; in his opinion, this has greatly influenced him to improve the quality of his knives permanently.

Besides "crafting", as he calls it, his big satisfaction is to be outdoors in nature. Nature always gives new impressions and changes day by day and year by year.

Jan lives with his wife Anita in Vagnhaerad, sixty kilometers south of Stockholm. His workshop is located on the banks of the salmon river Trosa.

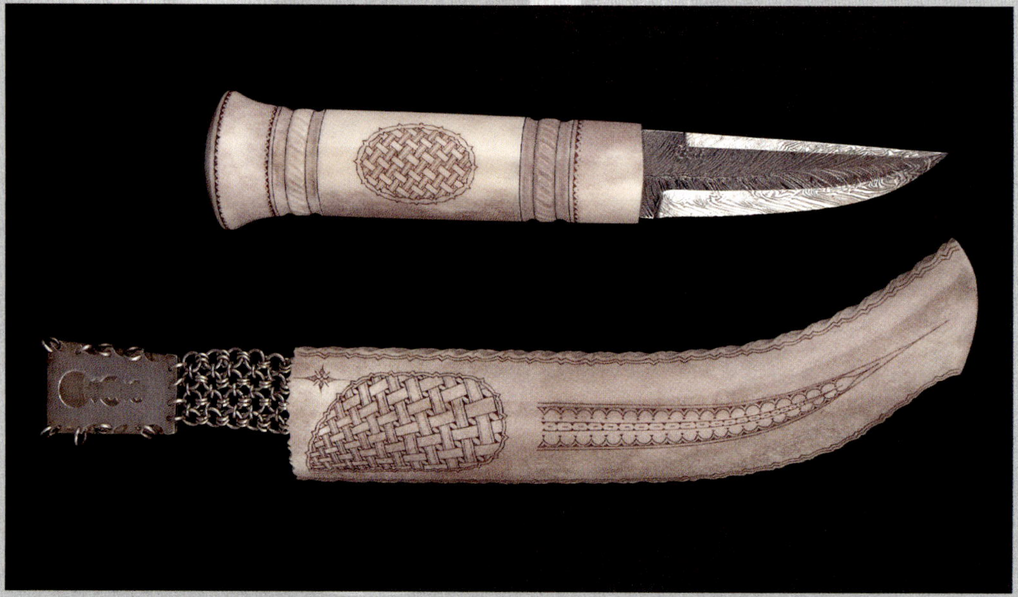

A small engraved pill container carved out of antler.

Below: Handle of a sword and the end piece of its sheath.

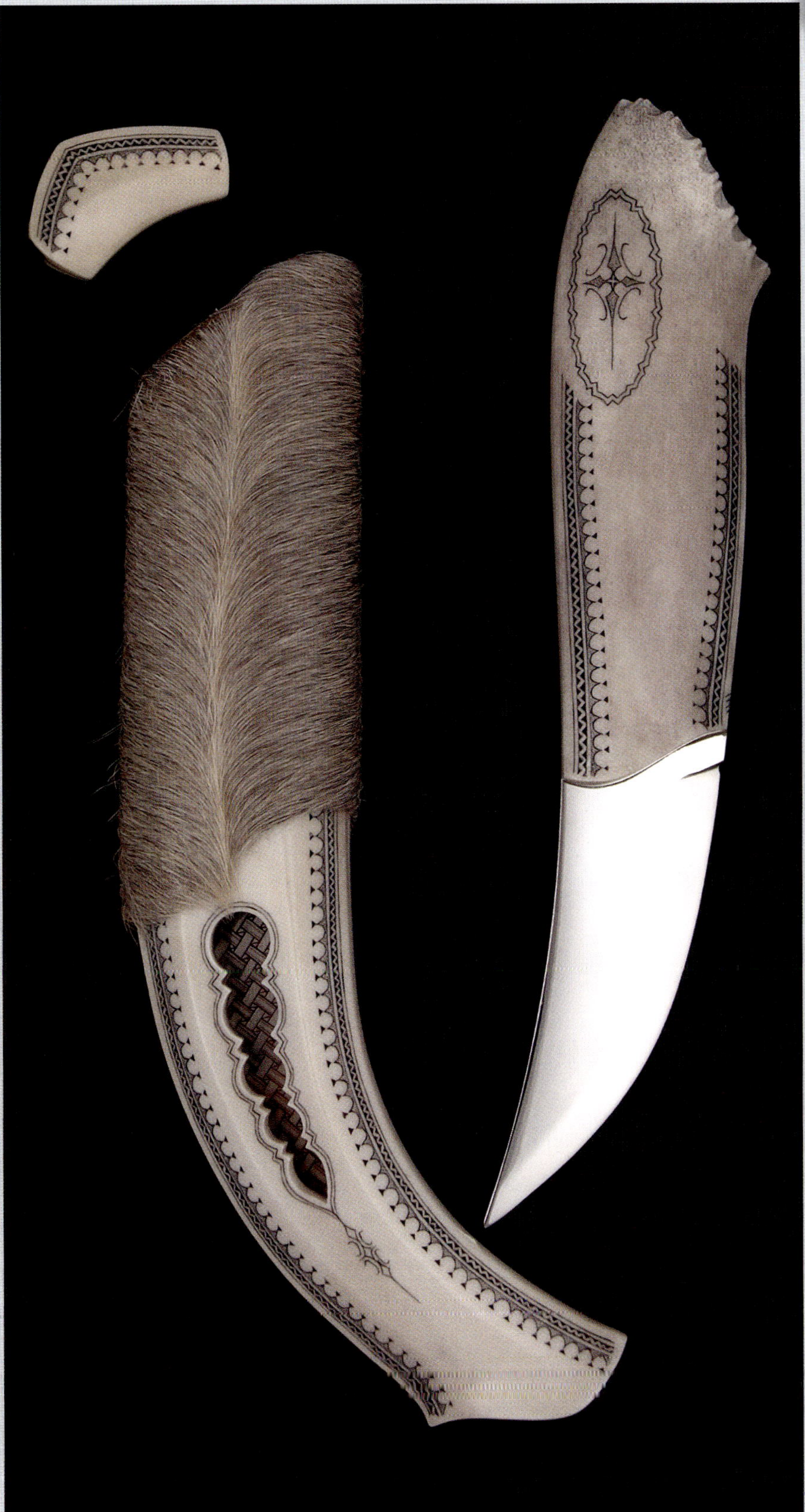

All of Jan's knives and sheaths are made of reindeer antler, all woods he uses are grown in Sweden and Lapland, and the leather is a typical traditional leather called "Same" leather or "Lapp" leather.

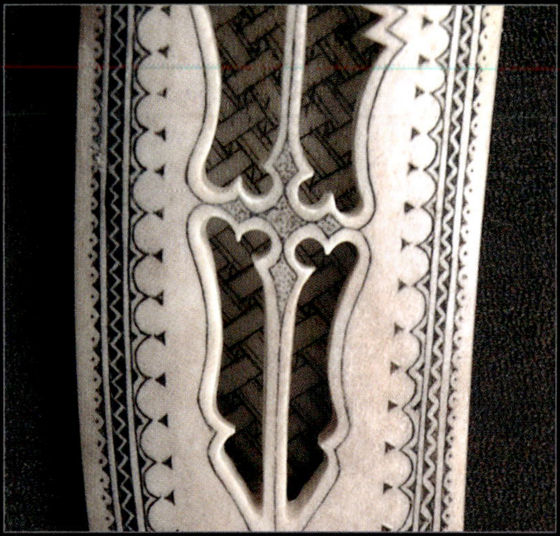

Top: Even the inside of the sheath is decorated with engravings.

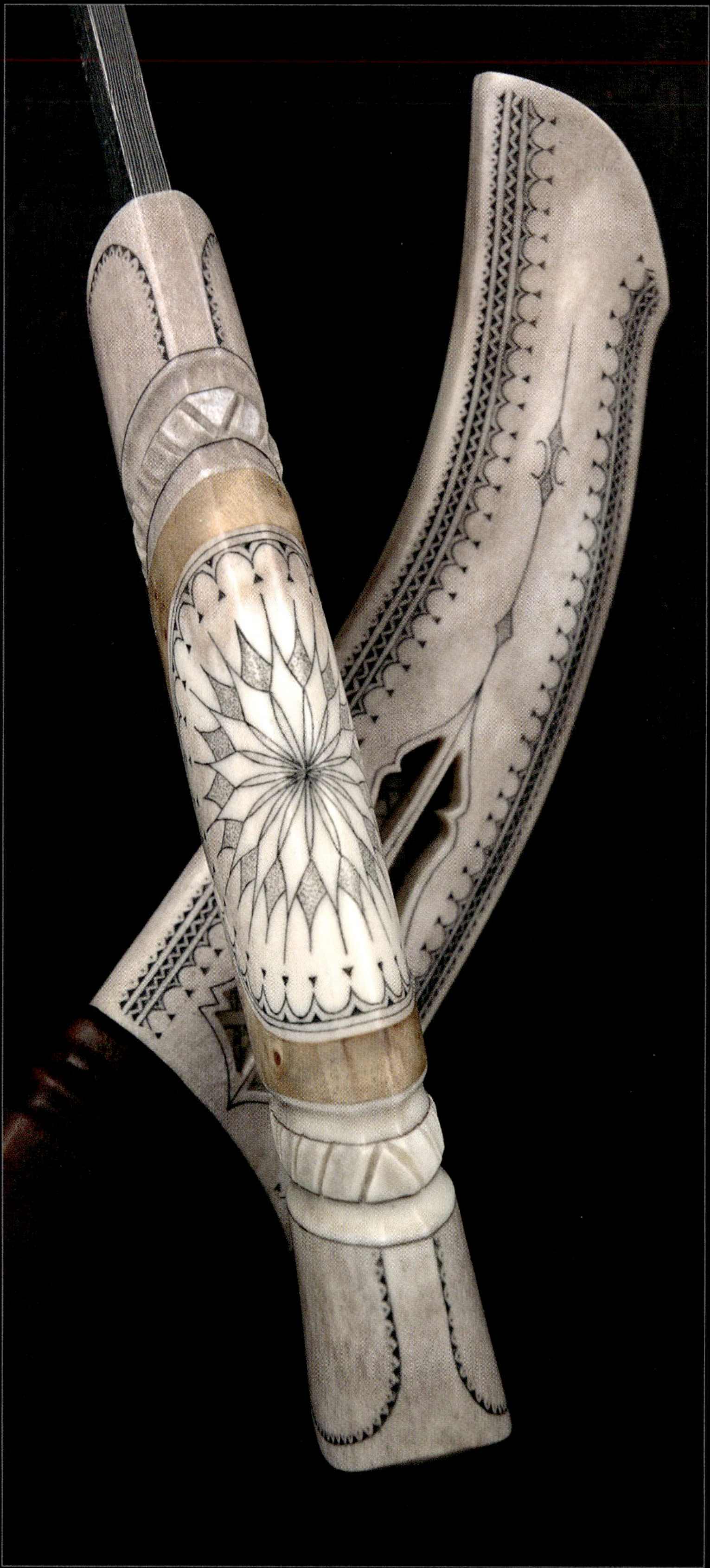

Beautiful traditional artwork. It is remarkable how precisely Jan engraves the lines and geometric patterns.

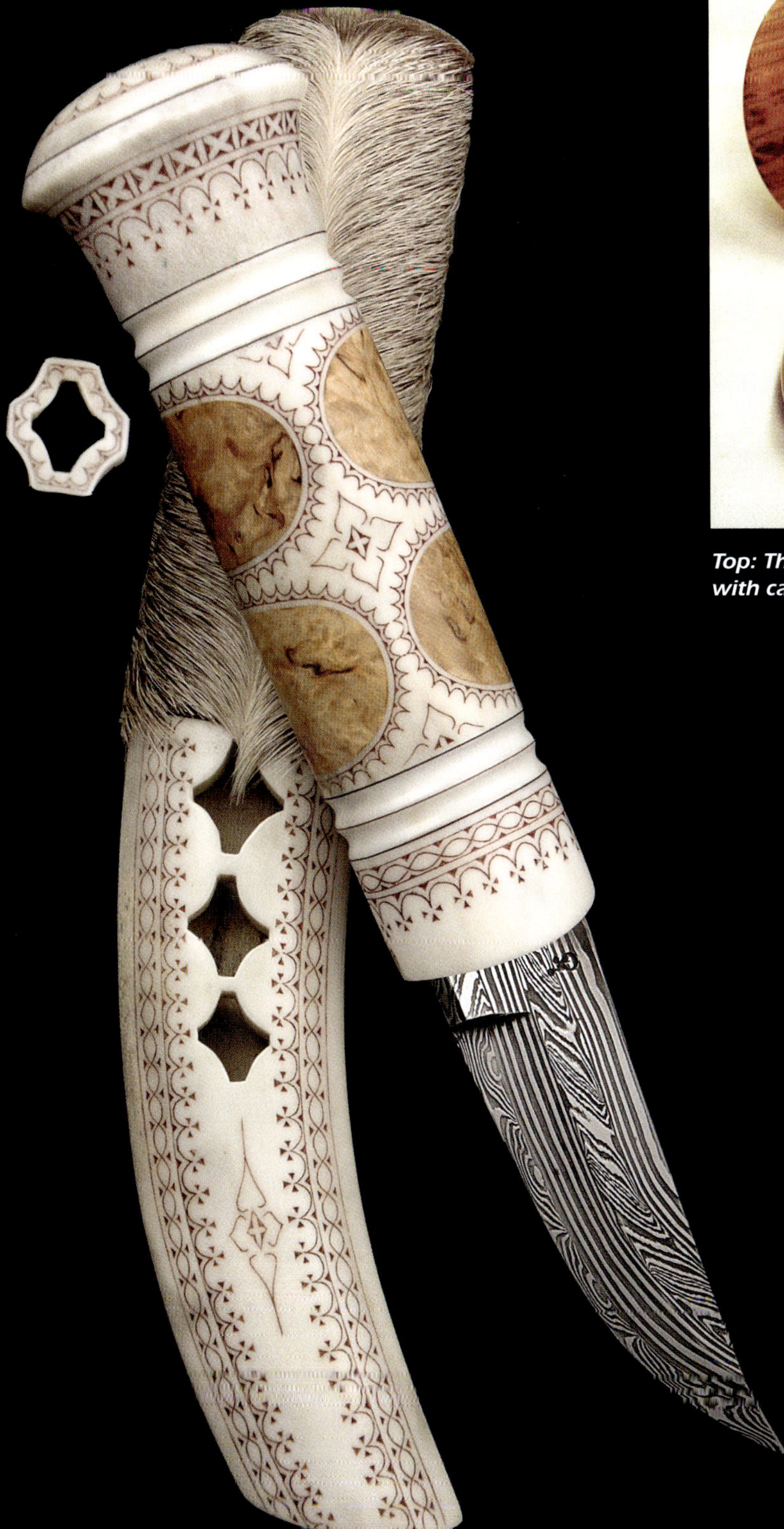

Top: This small knife has its place in a nice wooden box with carved decorations made of antler.

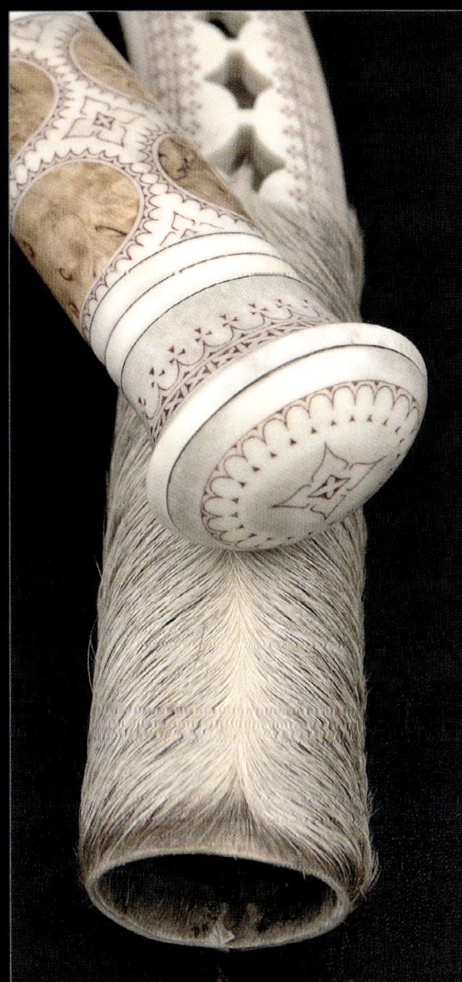

Nkosi Jubane

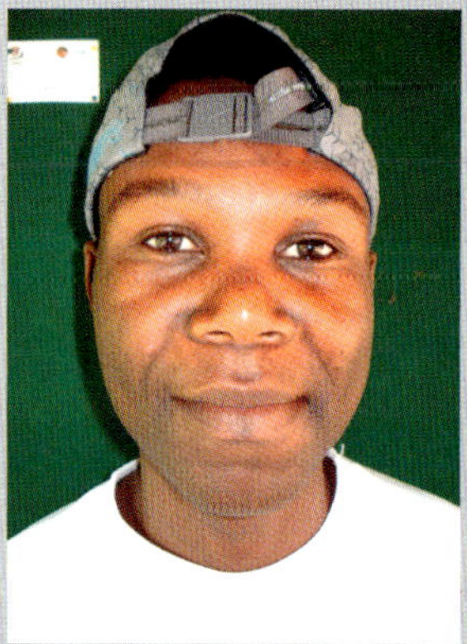

Nkosi Jubane comes from Phalaborwa, a small town north of Johannesburg in South Africa. At the age of seven he had already discovered his love for art, inherited from his mother, whose hobby was drawing.

In 1993, Nkosi had the opportunity to watch an artist create scrimshaw on black serpentine stone. When he saw that, he immediately felt the desire to try this technique himself. The result was that his first work was successful. From then on, Nkosi could no longer leave it alone. Since 1996 he has lived mainly from his scrimshaw work in Johannesburg, Hoedspruit, and Phalaborwa.

As his "canvas," as Nkosi calls it, he uses legal elephant ivory, hippopotamus teeth, and imitation ivory. He scrims both in line and point techniques, and is as happy working in color as in black and white. Nkosi has already created scrimshaw work for knife makers such as S. Mackrill, Mike Barnes, and the master knifesmith of South Africa, Kevin Harvey. Although he is also a gifted wood- and ivory carver, his first loves remain scrimshaw and painting.

Nkosi is also interested in wall painting. His paintings decorate the walls of the Phalaborwa and Zuma Zuma Game Lodge, a private home in Moditio, the Phalaborwa Foundation Gallery in Namagale, and the house of the Premier in Polokwane. Nkosi's works have also been displayed in 2007 in Polokwane and the monsoon Art Gallery in South Africa.

African themes on African material, like this filigree work on hippopotamus teeth or the African woman on elephant ivory, are a harmonious combination.

African wildlife ranks among Nkosi's favorite motifs. He handles their portrayal just as well as those of people.

Linda Karst

Linda began her scrimshaw training at the age of fifteen, learning the basic techniques at her first job. After high school, she continued to scrim and was trained in fine art at the University of Toledo and the Toledo Museum of Art. Her studies in anatomy, figure drawing, and design are reflected in her work today. Deciding to remain focused on scrimshaw, she has worked in this field for over twenty years.

Using only hand tools, Linda's style of scrimshaw combines several engraving techniques. She scrims primarily on ivory, which possesses a warmth and personality that often suggests a particular subject or composition. She is known for her ability to incorporate all of these elements into a finished work of art. Her realistic style has a depth and sculptural quality that brings her subjects to life.

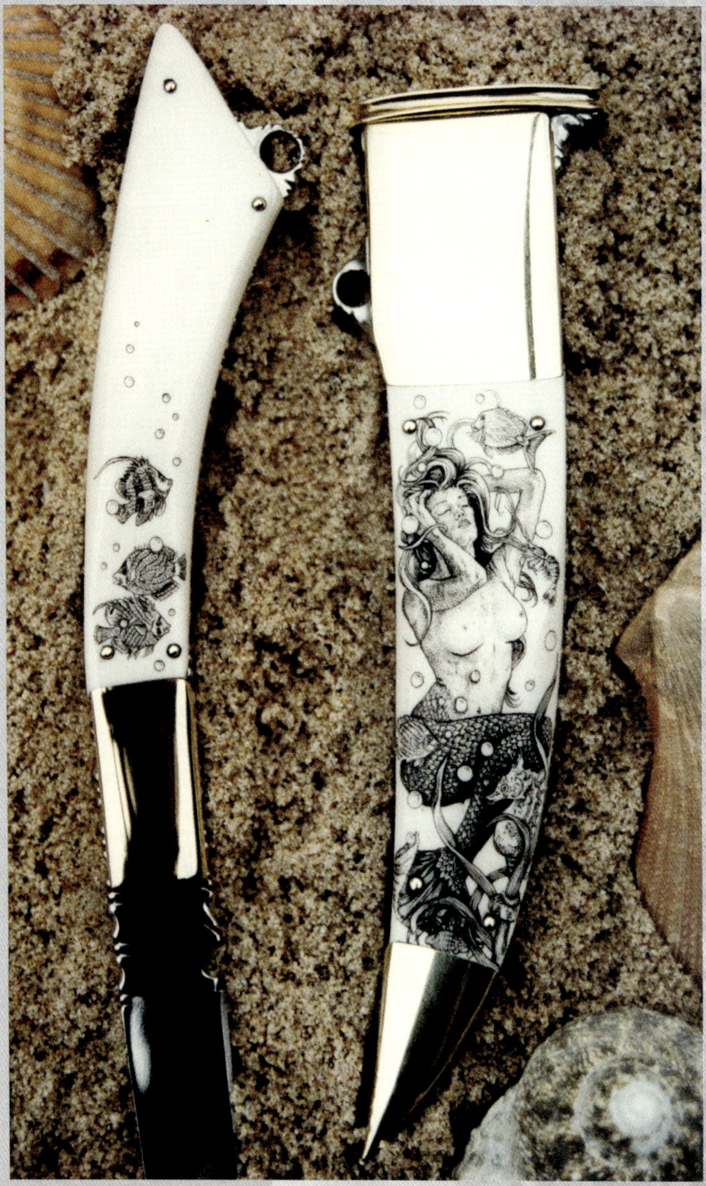

Linda is an avid traveler and photographer and draws on these experiences to design pieces that are part of her life. She enjoys meeting collectors and bringing their experiences, memories, and ideas together with her own talents to design a piece of art special to each client.

Linda resides in the Texas hill country with her husband Mark Stone. She exhibits at selected shows and enjoys collaboration with knifemakers worldwide. Individual collectors throughout the world commission most of her work.

Work by Linda in black-and-white on a knife grip and sheath. The material is elephant ivory. Knife made by Ed Lary.

Top: "Jungle Jaguar" on a knife grip and sheath by Ed Lary.

The knife with the lion is by Loyd McConnell and is a fine example of how free space can be used in the design. (Photo: Weyer of Toledo.)

A folding knife with a scene bordered by classical ornamentation.

Linda Karst

The American eagle is displayed here on a splendid knife by Loyd McConnell. The Damascus steel is gilded with 14-carat gold.

Two old billiard balls done as globes. The theme on the left is the world of animals, Africa with an elephant and giraffe, a jaguar in South America, with a gray whale beneath. On the right, the Swedish ship "Vasa" and the whaling ship "Charles Morgan" are scrimmed on a maritime globe.

The wolves are scrimmed on the naturally hollow end of a big walrus tooth.

"Temple Tiger", a knife by Dennis Friedly. Grip and sheath are of fossil walrus ivory and Damascus steel.

Another beautiful sheath with daisies and Indian paintbrush flowers. Knife by Dennis Friedly.

An Asiatic dragon on a knife by Gill Hibbon. Size of scrimshaw: 6 cm.

Gary Kiracofe

Gary Kiracofe has been quite fortunate. His older brother introduced him to scrimshaw in his early twenties. The two brothers had similar God-given artistic talents, and enjoyed lots of detail. This pushed them toward realism, and being nearsighted helped. Gary's brother recognized that scrimshaw would be an ideal art form for talents that had been somewhat frustrated by other artistic media. When his brother first demonstrated the art to Gary he was hooked for life.

Gary says, "This art form may demand discipline, the ability to concentrate and to sit still for a while, yet it calms the soul. This is why I do not like being interrupted when I work. Instead, I listen to recorded books and have probably listened to over a 1000 books already. It is wonderful for the mind."

During his career as a scrimshander, Gary has learned a lot about sailing and about drawing ships, lighthouses, and other related things accurately to avoid embarrassment. There mustn't be any errors in nautical motifs. There are too many knowledgeable people out there, and someone will immediately notice any mistake.

It was a challenge for Gary to scrim an accurate sailing ship on a disk one quarter the size of an aspirin. Such disks go on top of small twenty-four carat gold Nantucket Baskets the size of a nickel.

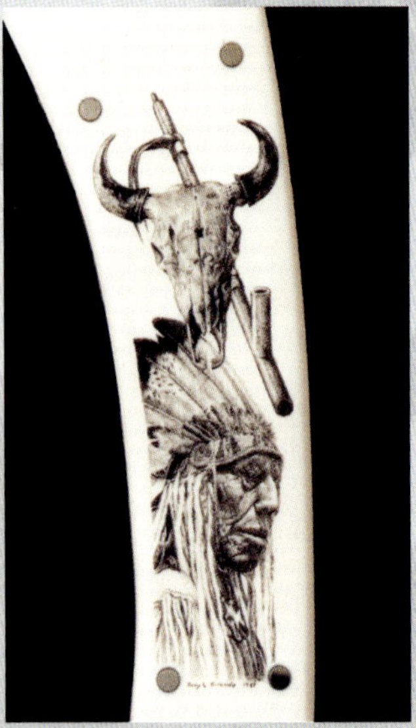

Gary regrets that he has not yet taken the time to enter any art shows or contests during his 25 years as a full-time scrimshaw artist, though he has been quite fortunate. His wife, Dawn Sandusky, deserves the praise for the financial success they have had in selling and promoting Gary's artwork. They own two retail stores in the Midwestern region of the United States and are partners with Gary's youngest brother, Brian, in a third store in Boston. Dawn's management and organizational skills, sales techniques, and beautiful displays have been the formula for success at their stores. Gary's problem has been keeping up with the demand that she and her staff have created. Their stores represent works by many of the top scrimshanders in the United States.

"Prayer to the Mystery", a finely detailed work on a knife grip of elephant ivory. The grip is 10 cm long and 2.5 cm wide.

One of the plaques as it looks attached to the typical Nantucket Basket.
Commissioned by the owners of the cottage.
Elephant ivory, 6.3 x 10.5 cm.

"Lady Liberty" on a sperm whale tooth.

The frigate "Essex" under full sail. One can really feel the fresh wind and hear the waves break on this lively scrimshaw.

All ovals are plaques that were mounted on Nantucket Baskets. The size of this schooner scene is only 5.5 x 8 cm.

"Trilliums" are Gary's favorite wildflowers; they are abundant in the northern Midwest forests in May.
Elephant ivory, 7 x 11 cm.

Below left: A lighthouse on one of the smallest plaques, measuring 5.5 x 8 cm.
Below right: The "Eagle & Flag" knife handle is elephant ivory and measures 10 x 2.8 cm. Gary did this knife in September 2002 as a tribute to the anniversary of 9-11-01.

This beautiful Oriental Lilly was commissioned work and was scrimmed on the model of the real flower outside Gary's garden.

These mallards are on the largest plaque, measuring 7 x 9.5 cm. Generally these plaques are elephant ivory, but occasionally mammoth ivory is crack-free enough to cut this large of an oval. Shown more than 1.5 times the original size.

Mirela Mack

Mirela Mack grew up in the city of Gdansk (Danzig) in northern Poland. There she finished her study of architecture and worked as an architect until she moved to Hamburg in 1987. Part of her program in architectural studies included artistic training in drawing, painting, and sculpting.

Her interest in the arts and her activity in various artistic techniques actually began much earlier, and have continued with small interruptions to the present day. In Germany, Mirela specialized in three-dimensional computer-generated architectural design. A few years ago, though, she turned her back on architecture, and she is now experimenting happily with ornamentation made of various materials.

The scrimshaw adventure began for Mirela Mack about three years ago. She calls it an adventure because for her it was like discovering a new land. It was a lucky chance: On a bookstore shelf she encountered the book *Modernes Scrimshaw* by Eva Halat.

After a close look at the pictures, she was fascinated at once by this beautiful world of handcrafted knives decorated with scrimshaw.

Mirela's was greatly astonished at her reaction, since she was now confronted by a realm of applied art that had been completely unknown to her up to that point. It was a real "aha experience," and suddenly it became clear to her that she wanted to learn this type of fine engraving.

At the start, Mirela had a hard time finding a material on which to practice the first steps of this technique. In her search for advice, she found the website of Lori Ristinen, on which the artist reported on her first ventures with plastic spoons. That was a good solution, and remarkably fine work was done on plastic spoons. Mirela works with magnifying glasses, and as a control she uses a jeweler's loupe with sevenfold magnification. At this time she prefers to use highly pigmented oil paint for coloring.

Meanwhile, Mirela has also come to know that scrimshaw is not for those who quickly become impatient as they work. It requires great concentration, much patience, and a lot of time for one's own development. It can become a faster process only through experience gained over time, but only within certain limits. It is the true discovery of tedium.

This finely worked jaguar shows how well Elforyn can be scrimmed. Design dimensions ca. 4.5 x 1.8 cm.

These are Mirela's two study projects (l) on plastic cooking spoons, in which artistic ability can already be seen. Each scrimshaw motif is ca. 6 cm wide.

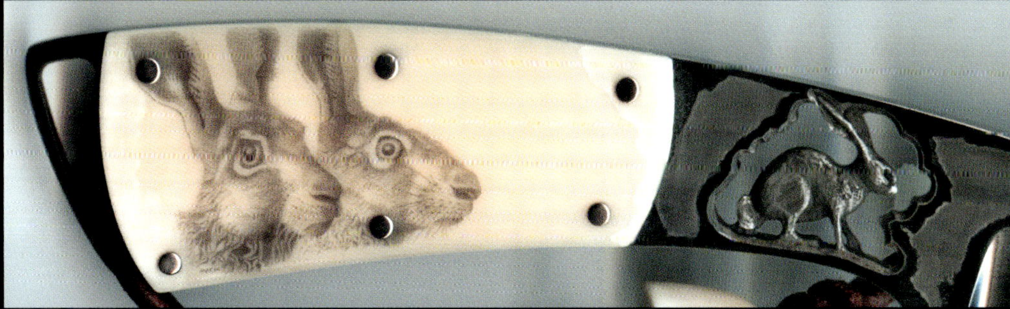

The two rabbit portraits blend with the engraved rabbit on this knife of Jesper B. Nielsen. The handle is made of sperm-whale tooth. The scrimshaw measures ca. 4.5 x 3 cm.

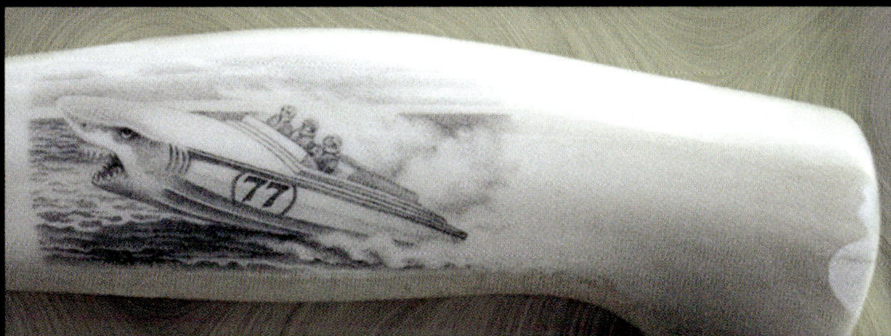

This motif was a customer's personal wish. Along with other details, Mirela was supposed to portray a speedboat with a shark's head.

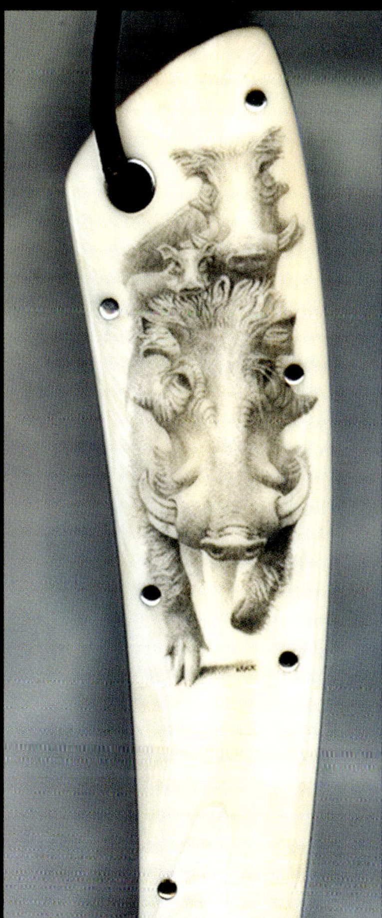

These feminine figures are carved on Micarta panels on both sides of this jackknife. Dimensions ca. 6 x 2.3 cm and 4.7 x 2. cm.

Left: A suitable motif: Warthogs on a handle made of wart-hog tusk. The knife is made by Jesper B. Nielsen. Scrimshaw dimensions ca. 6.5 x 2.3 cm.

A living background, out of which the Jaguar steps, on the mammoth ivory of this lovely knife handle.

Richard "Ritchi" Maier

Richard Maier was born in Austria in 1965. This Villach native started drawing and painting in early childhood. Later, as his talent became increasingly obvious, his parents made it possible for him to attend the HTBL (Advanced Technical Institute) at Ferlach in the field of artistic metalwork, where he was trained as an engraver in 1980.

His first year, he worked at a company in the Black Forest that also made knives. The engraving of knives was completely new territory for him and the idea of "scrimshaw" something completely foreign. Richard had his first exposure to scrimshaw at this time, and selected the name "Ritchi" to sign his art. This was the period when European fairs and shows specifically for knives and hunting equipment were first organized, and his work was exhibited at these shows.

A search for new challenges then brought him to Boeblingen near Stuttgart, where he worked for a well-known design studio in the automotive field. He rapidly found his feet in his new job as a design model builder and worked on a number of projects and model studies for the company's international automobile department.

At the end of 1991, he decided to work independently. He founded a joint venture with the knife maker Egon Trompeter, "Trompeter & Ritchi", located in Sindelfingen near Stuttgart. The firm produces handmade knives, scrimshaw, and engravings of the highest quality.

Ritchi has been producing new scrimshaw collections annually since 1991. Mostly he works on wildlife and animal themes, and sometimes he will produce a small collection of various subjects within a single theme.

Ritchi prefers to scrim on fossil mammoth ivory and always works simultaneously on several pieces at once. Sometimes this process can take several months, with interruptions. Individual commissions from clients are also accepted, and their particular requests and ideas are given careful consideration.

"Zebra Magic": zebras at first sight, even if you discover the details later. The folding knife is by Egon Trompeter. Richard scrimmed the zebras on stabilized mammoth ivory, which keeps the exactly fitted scales absolutely in shape. The knife's handle is titanium, and the stainless Damascus steel is called "Odin's Eye". JTMB2, length of the blade: 8.5 cm.

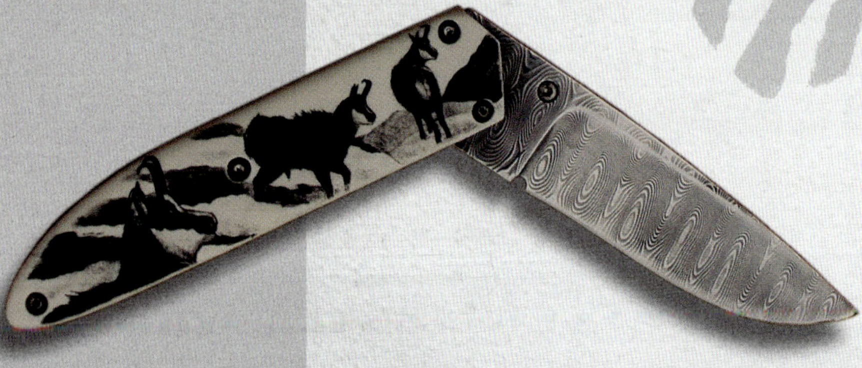

High alpine scenes with chamois scrimmed on both sides of a knife by Egon Trompeter. Grip scales of mammoth ivory. Damascus blade by F. Schneider. Grip length: ca. 9.5 cm.

Richard "Ritchi" Maier

Majestic look on mammoth ivory. The size of this lion portrait including stand is 12.3 cm.

The magical wolf face looks out of a piece of mammoth ivory.

The size of the bear scrimshaw with the interesting light effect on mammoth ivory is ca. 20 cm.

"Okavango Thunder", a splendid rifle with scrimshaw and bullino engraving by Ritchi. The two techniques work together harmoniously. The nosecap on the forearm and the ball of the bolt handle are of mammoth ivory and covered with scrimmed "elephant skin". The end of the forearm is decorated with two elephant heads, one on the left side, the other on the right.
Opposite right: An elegant overall effect. The cap on the pistol grip is also of mammoth ivory. The light etching of the ivory blends it harmoniously with the color of the wood.

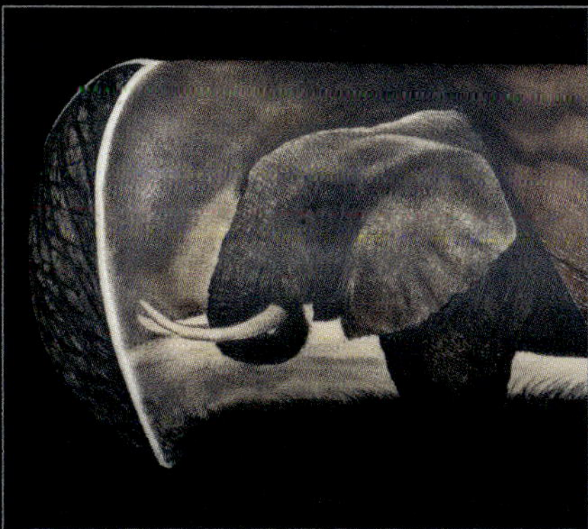

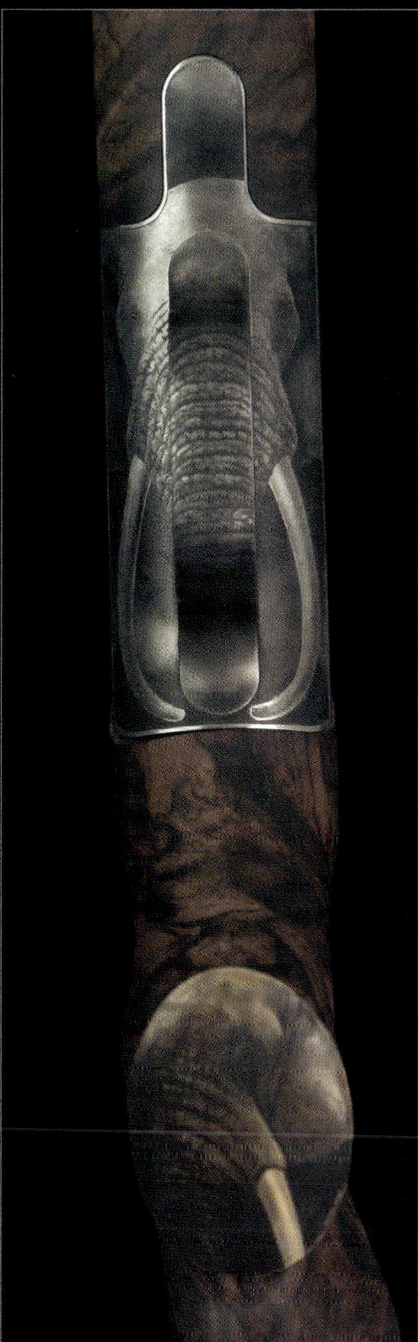

Another folding knife by Egon Trompeter, beautifully scrimmed with one of Richard's favorite animals, the elephant. JTMB2, size and material like the "Zebra" folder, the Damascus steel is called Mohamad's Ladder.

Below: The original size of the elephant scrimshaw is 7 x 6.5 cm.

Faustina Mead

Over the last 35 years, Faustina has been active in a number of artistic fields, includ-ing oil painting (portraits, landscapes, animals, and many other subjects), pen-and-ink drawing, and wood burning.

She was introduced to scrimshaw and acid etching in 1987 by the knife maker Paul (Pappy) Chamberlaine. As many of her colleagues have also discovered, Faustina found that drawing was a good basis for this art. Pappy had seen her pen-and-ink work and was looking for someone to do scrimshaw on his knives, so he gave Faustina her first tools and lessons in scrimshaw and engraving.

Since then, she has developed her technique in both media to produce some really fine works of art. She decorates knives, blades, belt buckles, necklaces, bolos, tie clips, and even money clips with fine, freehand artwork. She uses all kinds of natural materials, such as bone, ivory (various types), horn, water buffalo, and many artificial materials such as paper Micarta™ and artificial ivory as well.

Her work with acid etching is as impressive as her scrimshaw, and she works on many types of metals, including stainless and carbon steels.

Faustina can create works of art on many items, strictly by hand, whatever the object. The customer selects the subject to be portrayed. Each piece is unique and individual.

Faustina normally works in color. In the original, this piece is done in warm brown tones scrimmed on a Micarta™ knife grip.

Bears on ivory on a folding knife by Rodney Rogers.

The two bald eagle heads are also scrimmed on ivory on a knife by Rodney Rogers.

"Lady of the Evening". Scrimshaw on ivory on a knife by Joe Hytovich.

These yellow roses with the song from Texas were displayed in the 2002 issue of Knives Illustrated.

Top: Beautiful wolf's eyes.
In the middle: A pendant of ivory with a pair of cranes.
Bottom: A bass on a folding knife.

The "Inseparables" on ivory. Knife by Don Lozier.

A belt buckle with an eagle's head on ivory.

Indian on water buffalo horn. Knife by Reece Weiland

Another Indian on ivory. Knife by Dick Atkinson.

The knight is scrimmed on ivory.

Gerd Ohnesorge

Gerd Ohnesorge was born in 1940 in Altranft in the Oderbruch region in Germany and spent his childhood there surrounded by nature. After finishing school and completing his studies in art with a diploma in graphic design, he worked as a scientific illustrator in the field of anatomy for the Magdeburg Medical School (former GDR) from 1963 until 1977. After that he worked as a freelance illustrator, mostly for book publishers.

Gerd Ohnesorge became well known as an illustrator and co-author of numerous books on nature for both children and adults. Many of his books received awards, and some of his work may be found in the Buchkunstmuseum (Book Art Museum) in Leipzig.

Since 1991, he lived and worked in Halle an der Saale. Although knives fascinated him ever since he was a child, and he made some of his own, his enthusiasm for collecting was only awakened by the new opportunities made possible by the reunification of Germany in 1990. That is when he almost inevitably developed an interest in making knives; after that, he made several at irregular intervals.

He was especially interested in making knife grips and so was increasingly attracted to scrimshaw. Because of his long experience as a draftsman, he preferred a draftsman's style for his scrimshaw.

Gerd Ohnesorge died in 2005.

The knife on top has a grip and a carving of elephant ivory on the ebony sheath. The other knife is decorated with a dinosaur skeleton. The original skeleton is displayed at the Naturkunde Museum in Berlin. The grip is made of walrus ivory.

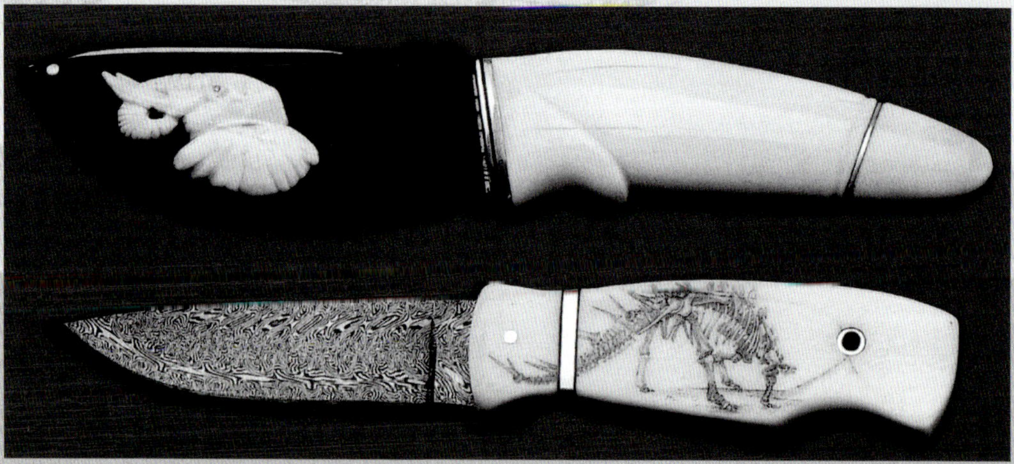

Two knives by Gerd Ohnesorge with grips of mammoth ivory.

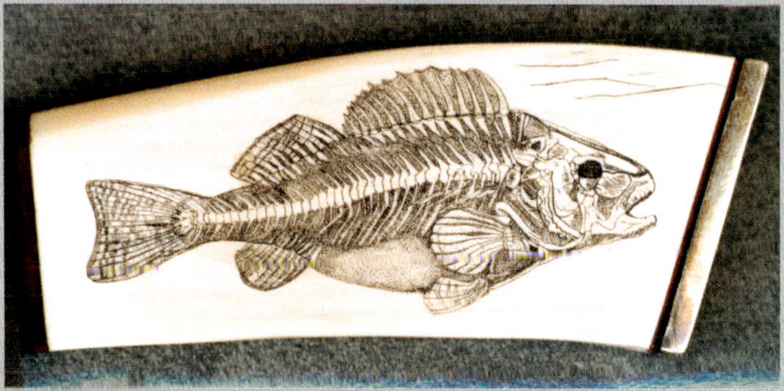

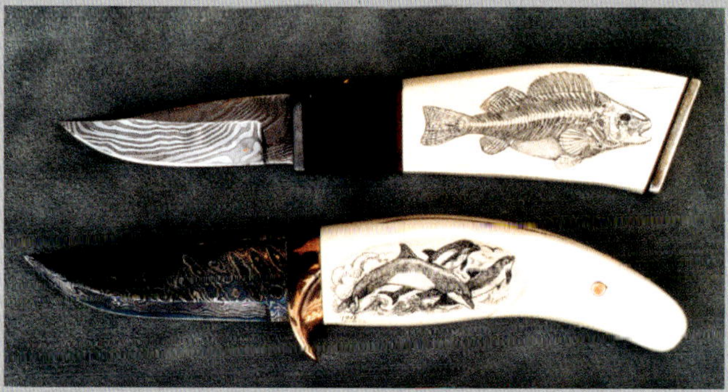

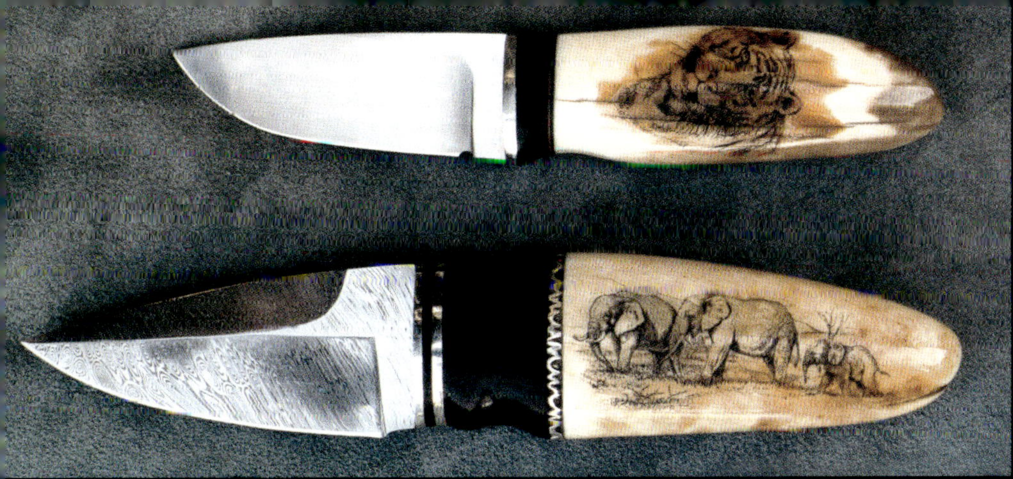

The tiger is placed to take advantage of the yellow-brown shadowing in the fossilized walrus tooth for the coloring of the fur. The knife grip with the elephant theme is made of ebony and the tip of an elephant tusk.

The elephant tusk is 45 cm long and scrimmed with a typical African scene.

The beautiful colors in these pieces of mammoth ivory seem to have been made expressly for the portraits of the cats on these bolo ties.

John van Opstal

John van Opstal lives near Horta on the island of Faial in the Azores. His studio often appears in films, and his house is a Mecca for tourists and collectors who spend their vacations on the Azores. Many of them come especially to this island for whale watching.

After studying art in Holland at the Rotterdam Academy, he worked for more than 25 years as a subcontractor to advertising agents and founded a large advertising agency himself. But after this long period, John says, he became homesick for art. He no longer felt that he was an artist, in spite of his work in a creative business.

Because of their love for islands, John and his wife, Joke, decided one day to look for an island where they could spend the rest of their lives. An article on the Azores in a Dutch newspaper aroused their curiosity, and when they finally traveled there, they felt immediately at home. They built a house in the Praia do Almoxarife Valley near the port of Horta. John has his studio and shop there today.

When they first moved to the Azores, John had intended to paint and draw landscapes, windmills, flowers, and boats on canvas as he always had. When he was asked one day in 1995 whether he could work on ivory, he began to paint landscapes in color on whale teeth as if they were canvas. Today, John himself laughs about it, and claims that earlier he didn't even know that whales had teeth.

His technique developed, however, and he studied old books with engravings of whaling ships and other scrimshaw subjects. Today, John does classical scrimshaw and continues to scrim traditional themes. He scrims ships, the sea, whales, and families back home. He mainly scrims scenes of the Azores, where the whalers were very active.

First, John puts a little wax on the prepared surface of a whale's tooth and then colors it with black ink. Then he scrims the scene, which first appears in negative, white on a black surface. Then he inks the surface again, giving the scrimmed lines their color. John then removes the black background with a wet cotton swab.

When John began scrimshaw, there were still plenty of whale's teeth on the Azores. They were recovered from the sea by divers searching for them near the old whaling stations at Pico and at Madeira. Since then, it has become harder to get enough of these teeth. So John is experimenting with other techniques, for example, engraving on glass, so that he can continue to work with his engraving techniques, should he finally be unable to obtain whale's teeth.

Two classical scenes from the whaling era scrimmed on whales' teeth: Seamen whaling and, right next to this scene, a wife or mother at home praying for her loved ones to make it safely back from the dangerous whaling voyage.

A portrait of a typical seaman with a whaling scene in the background.

Of course one of the most common scenes in traditional scrimshaw has always been the most dangerous moment in the life of a whaler, the harpooning and death of the whale.

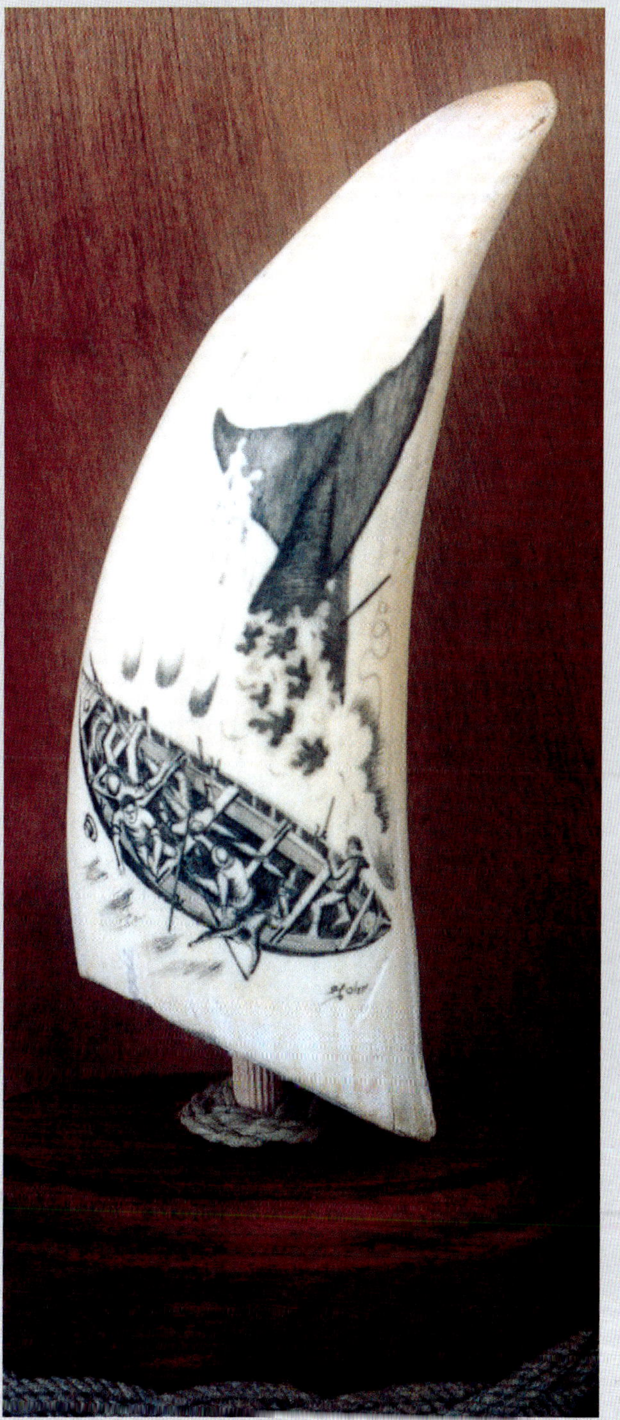

Mirella Pachi

Mirella Pachi worked as the art director for a large advertising agency in Italy, where she met Francesco Pachi, an advertising and nature photographer who later became her husband. At that time, Francesco hadn't started working with knives; and later, when he began, he produced only blank and undecorated knives. At about the same time Francesco displayed his first knife publicly, Mirella discovered the art of scrimshaw in European knife magazines and exhibitions.

As an artist, Mirella was delighted by this art form and avidly studied the meager literature available on scrimshaw. She made her first attempts on small pieces of Sambar stag antler, then finally got up the courage to work on one of her husband's knives. That was in 1995, when Francesco was still making knives only as a sideline.

That year, the couple flew to New York to learn and to participate in the "East Coast Show" there. Mirella met Rick Fields (a world-famous scrimshaw artist) at that show, and he taught her more about scrimshaw than she had ever hoped to learn.

While staying with Steve R. Johnson (Utah) and D'Alton Holder (Arizona), Mirella and her husband picked up even more valuable knowledge. Mirella was astonished to see that Pat Holder engraved knives. Until then she had thought that only men engraved knives. Mirella was given the much-coveted book *Scrimshaw Connection* by Bob Engnath as a gift, and this was the high point of her trip.

Mirella works exclusively by hand, stippling with hardened needles, in a com fortable workshop at home. She not only uses her technique to decorate her husband's knives, she also accepts commissions from other knife makers and continues to make small art objects and pendants.

This lynx is scrimmed on an inlay of an archery bow's handle.

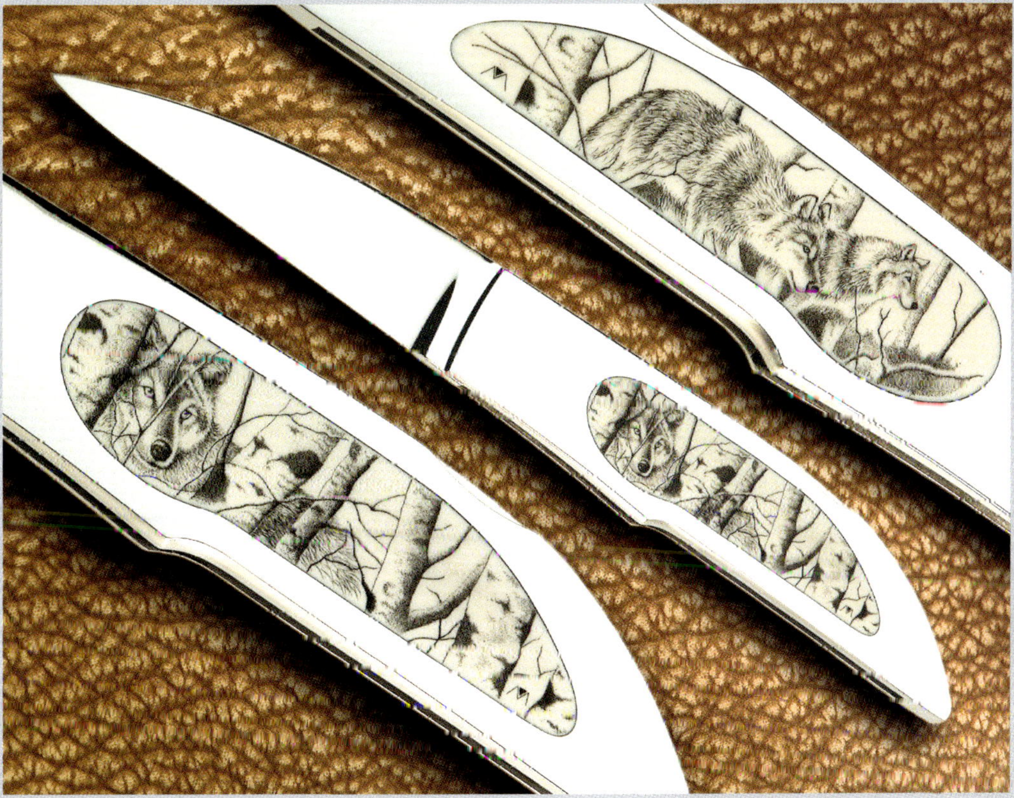

A knife called "Ant's Dream". Here you will love even ants. They are not only scrimmed but also engraved on the blade of this extraordinairy folding knife.

Mirella Pachi

A knife by Francesco Pachi. The shape of an eagle's head fits quite well on a knife grip.

Below: The leopard is accented in color in only a couple of places. That can have an interesting effect when it harmonizes with the surrounding color.

Shining eyes are inlayed on this folding knife.

This knife with the picture of a crane has grip scales of fossil walrus ivory.

Despite our most careful plans, in general good things happen to us simply by chance!

Hilton Purvis' interest in the art of scrimshaw came about through a chance encounter with pioneering custom knifemaker Des Horn, when Des was visiting Hilton's local sports club to talk about shooting sports. A friendship quickly developed that extended beyond the shooting range and into the knifemaking workshop.

Hilton was unable to participate in knifemaking, so Des suggested that he try his hand at "scrimshaw" and gave him some ivory samples and a sharpened dentist's probe. Hilton's first scratchings showed potential and the ivory samples were used for knives. At that time, Ettore Gianferrari was a regular visitor at Des' workshop, learning the knifemaking ropes. Ettore rapidly became one of the most talented makers in the Southern Hemisphere. He regarded ivory as the finest choice for a handle material and began to commission work from Hilton.

Hilton was not a complete stranger to custom knifemaking. The first seed had been planted four years earlier when he had been given an Owen Wood spring-blade folder on his twenty-first birthday. Little did he know that he would meet Owen years later as a fellow exhibitor at a knife show.

Des, Ettore, and Hilton decided to exhibit their work at the local Durban Easter Knife Show in 1986. Hilton met Owen Wood, Chris Reeve, and Andrew Frankland for the first time at this show. Frankland gave Hilton a prized tanto to scrim for him. Among the visitors testing the knifemaking waters at that show were Mike Skellern and his wife, Toi, who later became an accomplished knifemaker/scrimshander husband and wife team.

"Hunting Spaniels" scrimmed on a folding knife by Owen Wood.

So 1986 was a fateful year; Hilton started off very much as a fledgling scrimshander and was receiving commissions by the year's end. Many of the knifemakers he met that year have become his firm friends and have had great influence on his work. The logical next step came in 1987, when he became the first scrimshander to gain admittance to the Knifemakers Guild of Southern Africa.

Although scrimshaw was virtually unknown in South Africa fifteen years ago, it has rapidly developed into a recognized art form, especially by collectors of hand-made knives. Designs showing the Big Five (elephant, Cape buffalo, rhino, lion, and leopard) feature prominently, along with various other African game species, reptiles, fish, and bird life. This growth in demand brought talent out of the proverbial woodwork, and artists like Bruce Van Blerk, Toi Skellern, and Sharon Burger have discovered scrimshaw.

All this time, Hilton was fine-tuning his scrimshaw technique. He moved from his early line work to concentrate solely on the stipple method. The subtle challenges of monochrome tones have always been a part of Hilton's artwork. Even when he doodled on a piece of paper by the telephone, it was invariably in pencil and in tones. His basic tools include a lightweight aluminum pin vice, a paintbrush, ink, an Almore headband magnifier, and a fluorescent desk lamp.

Hilton has spinal muscular atrophy, and he has been in a wheelchair for the last 27 years. His physical limitations push completion times out to 70+ hours, but allow him to focus on detail. He makes exclusive use of the stipple method, working only in monochrome on freestanding items or handmade knives. With his limited hand strength and dexterity, scrimshaw machines, which can speed up the stippling process, are not practical. The average time he requires to complete a design is 70 –100 hours, which at present translates into a delivery time of approximately 12 –18 months.

The next big step forward in Hilton's scrimshaw came in 1989, when Owen Wood invited Hilton to join him at the New York Custom Knife Show. This gave Hilton an opportunity to examine world-class scrimshaw at first hand, and he was able to meet and discuss the finer points of the art with Rick Fields, probably the finest scrimshander of our time.

Hilton's work is represented in collections worldwide and has been published in a number of books and magazines dealing with the collection of handmade knives. He specializes in portrait work and African game, with emphasis on tone, shading, and fine detail. The 19th-century photography by Curtis has had a great influence on his work, as has the way Rick Fields gave Native American portraits new life in many of his '90s pieces. Hilton would like to create a similar portfolio of native African faces in the medium of scrimshaw.

Hilton's greatest triumph? ... the wonderful group of friends he has made through scrimshaw and custom knifemaking. Hilton lives with his wife Loretta in a house overlooking the Atlantic Ocean, surrounded by a garden filled with wild birds.

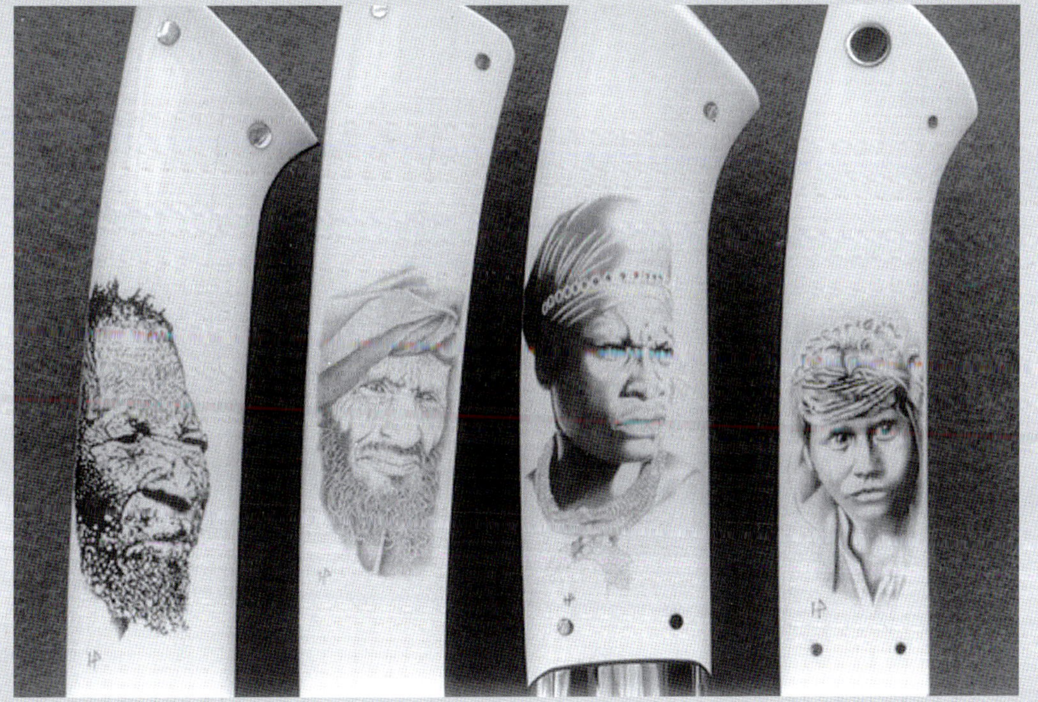

"Four Faces", portraits of Africans, done on knives by Rob Brown and Ettore Gianferrari.

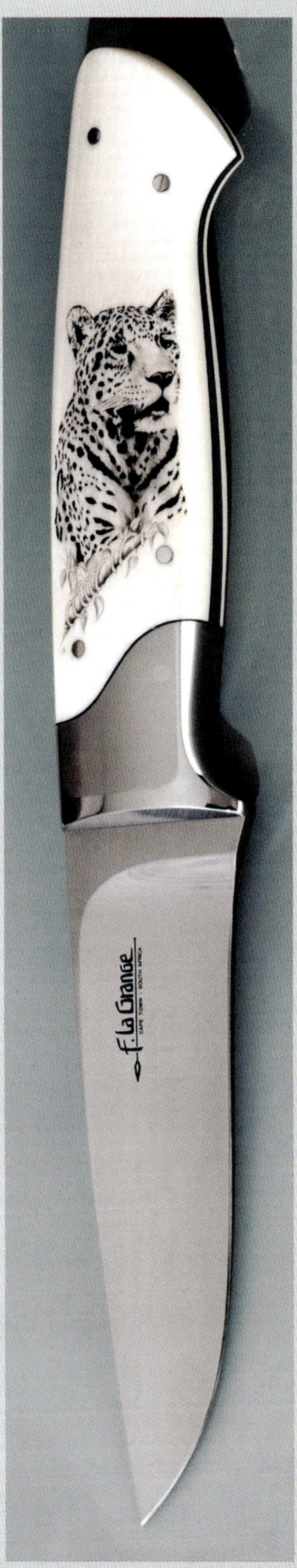
F. la Grange

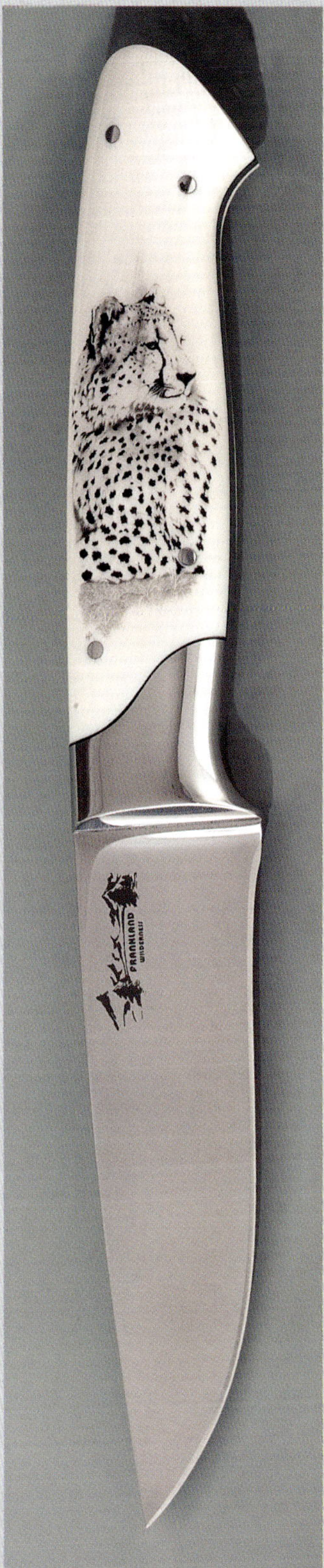

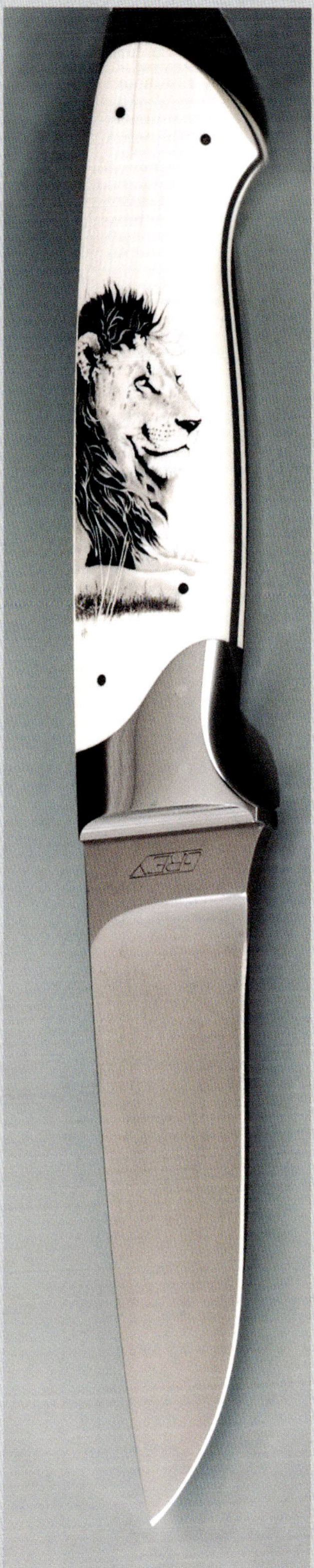

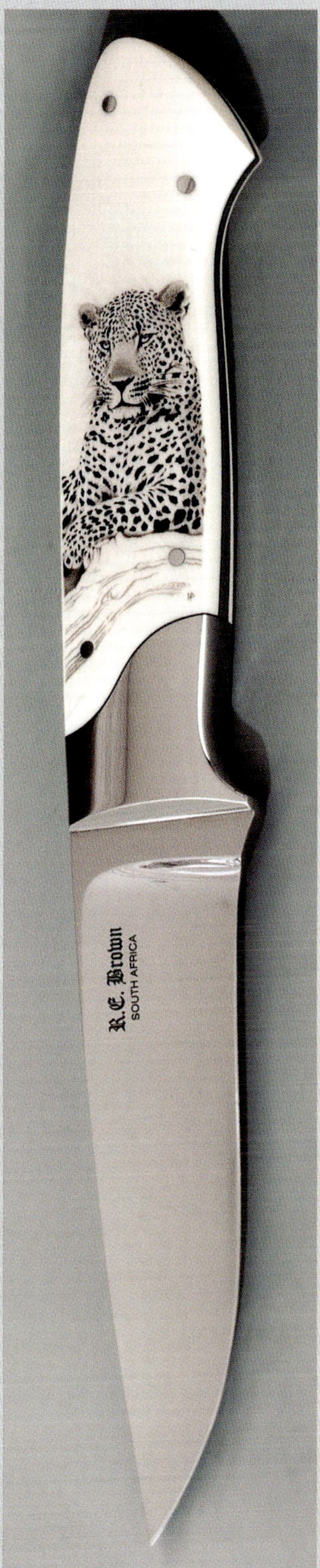
R.C. Brown
SOUTH AFRICA

The bald eagle is on a grip scale for a knife by Mick Russell and is part of a raptor set. This scrimshaw is on mammoth ivory; all of the other work was done on elephant ivory.

"5 Big Cats" This set of five knives by five different makers was assembled for a collector, all with scrimshaw by Hilton. Jaguar by Fanie LaGrange; Cheetah by Andrew Frankland; Lion by Piet Grey; Leopard by Rob Brown; Tiger by Owen Wood.

"Old Man", another impressive portrait, was scrimmed on a folding knife by Des Horn. Blade of Damascus steel with Gibeon meteorite backing.

Karen and Wayne Reno

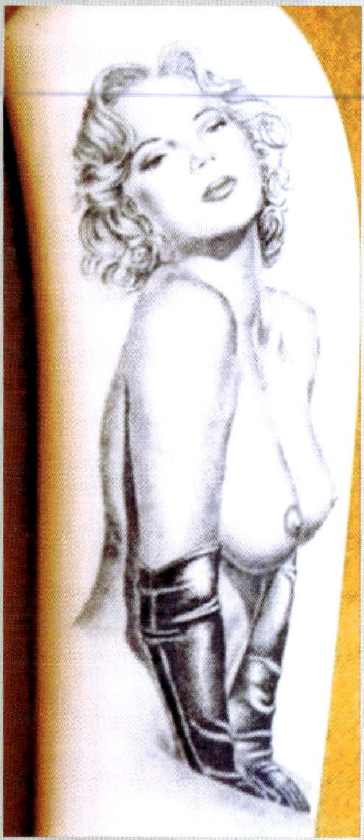

Karen and Wayne Reno work as a husband and wife team. They specialize in fine art knives, but they also do scrimshaw on a variety of ivories, which are usually mounted in silver and exotic woods. Both Wayne and Karen are scrimmers, but Karen usually does the scrimshaw, while Wayne makes the knives and stands and does the engraving.

Wayne has been doing scrimshaw and engraving for more than 35 years and likes an X-acto™ knife for the line scrimming he normally does. Before he starts, he polishes the surface to a high shine. He sketches the subject on the surface and then cuts what he has sketched.

Karen has been doing scrimshaw for about 18 years. She started scrimming herself because she wanted a piece for a necklace and Wayne was too busy with back-logged orders to do it for her. She watched him for a couple days and then sat down and started doing it herself.

Karen uses a sewing needle in a small pin vice and usually does stipple work. Her nudes are almost photographic. Wayne likes to draw the picture on the tooth or other ivory and then cut what he has drawn. After being cut, the piece is then polished lightly. Karen prefers to do an extremely high polish and then outline her picture with stippling. She does not draw anything on the ivory, but rather stipples in the outline. After the piece is completely scrimmed, she inks it, washes off the excess ink, and seals it.

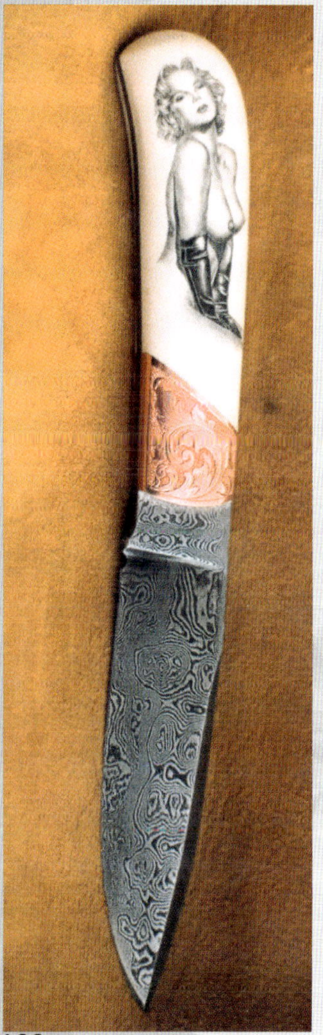

Karen originally did the nude as a piece of display art. However, the format was so suitable for a knife grip that it was finally made into one. Wayne made the knife out of L-6 and 5/60 steel, with copper backing.

This rifle was a very special commission. Wayne did the ivory inlays and Karen scrimmed the mountain sheep.

Two belt buckles and a bolo tie. They were made by Wayne and scrimmed by Karen

The Indian is worked on elephant ivory.
Dimensions 24.5 x 12 cm.

Karen and Wayne Reno

"The Pilgrim", scrimmed by Wayne on a whale tooth.

The bald eagle was done by Karen on elephant ivory. Dimensions: 24.5 x 12 cm.

Scrimshaw on elephant ivory using line technique. Scrimmed by Wayne.

Karen scrimmed this three-master on a piece of elephant ivory. 12.5 x 9.5 cm.

Another belt buckle, which Wayne made for Karen to scrimshaw.

The "Charles W. Morgan", the best-known ship in America's maritime history. Done by Karen on mastodon ivory. Dimensions: ca. 12 x 8.5 cm.

A great idea is scrimshaw on the ivory back of antique hairbrushes, here with a motif related to the time when the brush was made.

Lori Ristinen

Lori Ristinen started scrimshaw part-time in 1993 and has been a full-time professional scrimshander since 1995. Scrimming has been a constant learning process for her. The more she scrims, the more she improves, finding easier ways of doing things, whether with the materials she scrims, or her tools, or the inks and paints she uses.

She works out of her home in rural Minnesota, and she does not have a shop for her customers to visit. She sells her scrimshaw through her website and at gun and/or knife shows in the United States.

All of her scrimshaw is done by hand, one piece at a time. She does not use a machine or a pattern. She scrims in full color as well as in the more traditional black-and-white. She has scrimmed a wide variety of subjects from wildlife and scenic pictures to people and from portraits to still lives, on many different materials.

King Arthur on an ivory and Damascus steel knife by Doc Hagen.

At a client's request, these black and white tigers only have some subtle color at the nose and eyes and are scrimmed on mammoth ivory. The Damascus folder was made by Frank Centofante.

A crazy design on a knife by Ed Lary. The eyes with the tiger stripes are an especially effective way to take advantage of the overall shape. The Bengal tiger is scrimmed on ivory.

Lori Ristinen

A 60-cm elephant tusk decorated with an African elephant scene.

This snowy owl pendant is made of mammoth ivory and scrimmed with black ink. Size: 5 cm.

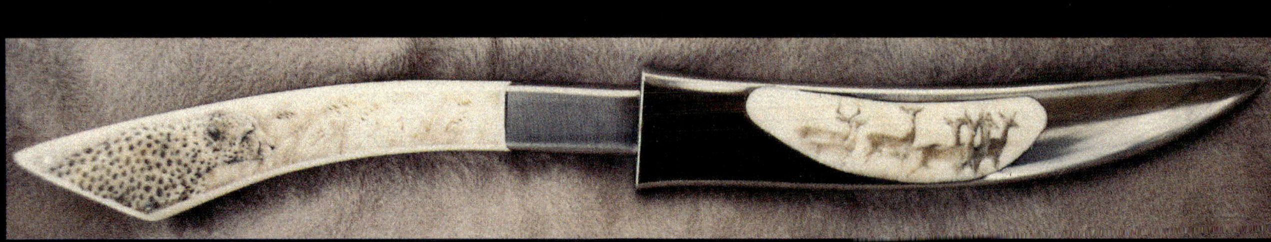

A cheetah theme on ivory decorates this Damascus steel knife by Ed Lary.

A pair of wolf's eyes on a knife by Dan Kendrick. Ivory grip

"Morning Glory". Delicate flowers entwine on both sides of this folding knife.

The knife with the parrot is by Kirk Rexroat.

Black Micarta™ can also be worked with fine, colored scrimshaw, as proven by this flower and the pink flamingo.

Heidi Robichaud

Heidi Robichaud has been creating scrimshaw since 1981. Her love of art spans her entire life, from her childhood passion for drawing horses and princesses to her current portraits of wildlife and native peoples. Although she has had no formal training or schooling in art, years of practice, study, and experimentation have honed her style.

Heidi moved to Alaska in 1979, where she fell in love with the land, wildlife, and culture. She has lived in several remote Alaskan "bush" areas and currently resides in the small isolated community of Gustavus, surrounded by Glacier Bay National Park.

Heidi became familiar with ivory while commercial fishing in Kodiak, Alaska, in 1980. After purchasing an ancient walrus tusk in a bar, she dedicated herself to finding an artist who could instruct her in the art of scrimshaw. Traveling across the United States in search of ivory art, she discovered the work of Diane Jacobs Thompson. Heidi spent one summer as an apprentice with Diane in Seward, Alaska, during which she learned the basic techniques and some of the finer aspects of the craft.

Heidi creates jewelry, knives, and custom display pieces on ancient walrus and mammoth ivories and on North American antler. She is known worldwide among scrimshaw collectors and enthusiasts for her fine wildlife and portrait work. She has recently finished a two-year masterpiece, an extremely rare fully scrimshawed mammoth tusk.

Heidi raised her two children surrounded by the wilds of Alaska. Currently living in the home she built on the banks of the Salmon River in Gustavus, Alaska, she enjoys gardening, hiking, fishing, and kayaking.

Two wolves on mammoth ivory. Originally scrimmed in color. Dimensions: 18 x 8 cm

This Inupiak family is scrimmed on ancient walrus tusk ivory.
Dimensions: 5 x 30 x 7.5 cm

"The fisherman". Scrimshaw on walrus tusk ivory artifact on a stand by Ken Fredericks.
Dimensions: 7.5 x 25 x 5 cm

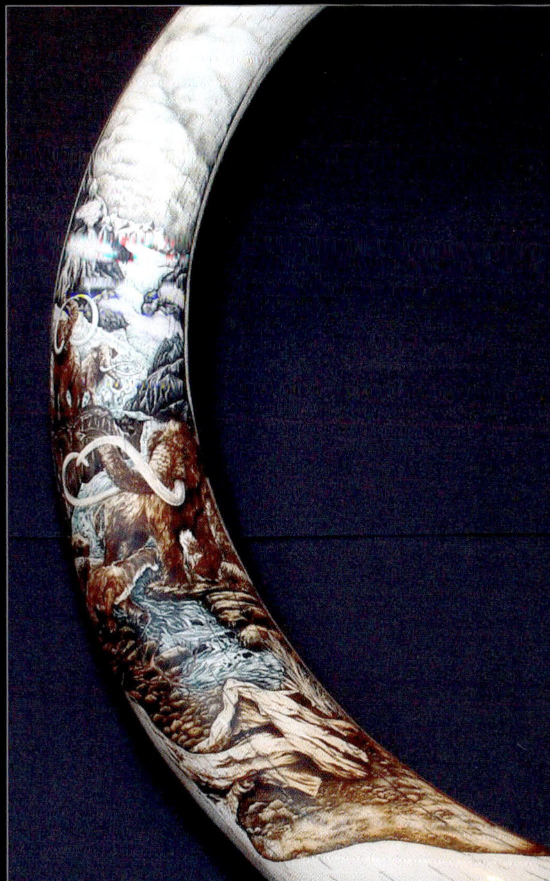

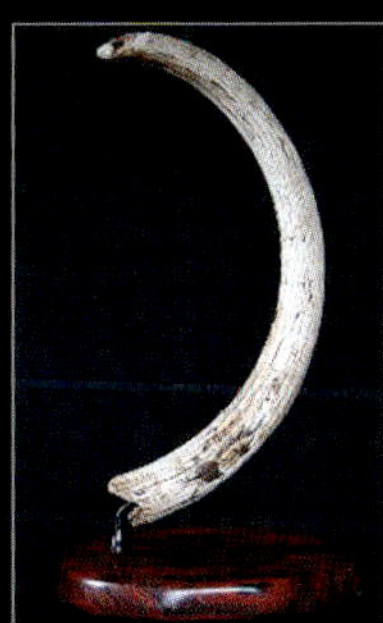

rear view

"Ancient Ivories, a Pleistocene Encounter", an outstanding collector's piece on which Heidi Robichaud worked for two years.
The mammoth tusk weighs 25 pounds and measures about three feet (about 90 cm) when displayed vertically.

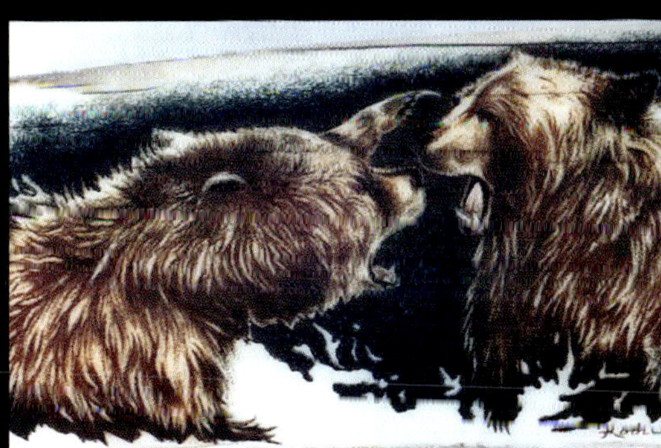

These two bears are scrimmed on a fossilized walrus ivory artifact, a net weight.
Dimensions: 10 x 6 x 5 cm, stand by Ken Fredericks

Howard Rosenfeld

Howard Rosenfeld was born in New Haven, Connecticut. Majoring in zoology, he graduated from the University of Connecticut. He served in the Peace Corps doing malaria eradication in Thailand, and worked in public health in San Francisco and around the United States. Sausalito, California, became his home port for almost ten years of living aboard ship and sailing the West Coast. "Becoming an artist was not even remotely on my career choice list. It just happened."

Howard learned scrimshaw the old-fashioned way: out at sea, sailing aboard tall ships, schooners and sloops, learning the details of hull, rig, and sail. These years of sailing led to an all-encompassing interest in the construction, maintenance, and handling of traditional sailing vessels. Sailing a replica whaler led to the study of whales and participation in whale research. He has since established credentials as a sea life artist and for accurate, historic ship portraits in scrimshaw, pen & ink, drypoint engraving, and carving. Howard has also been director of The Whale Museum and the Friday Harbor fire chief.

When Howard first started doing scrimshaw in 1969, sperm whale teeth had little value and were even being given away. So it seemed right to decorate these maggnificent teeth with engraving. He has been doing custom scrimshaw for over 35 years. Howard specializes in ship/sailboat portraits, but he has done everything from people to horses to helicopters as large presentation pieces, belt buckles, pendants, and plaques. Years later, when ivory became controversial, he discovered that he could "scrimshaw" a copper plate and make prints. This is drypoint engraving, a non-acid etching technique dating from 1400.

Howard's prints are sold in limited editions and the plates are "struck" with his initials and framed with the last print in the edition. Since he is also a professional picture framer, he sometimes frames a print with a scrimshaw "remarque" on a piano key (recycled ivory) or on larger mammoth ivory plaques.

Howard's awards include four Mystic Internationals, and he has been an artist member of the American Society of Marine Artists since 1982. His studio/gallery, Friday Harbor Art Studio, is in its 11th year.

Right: "Shenandoah", Scrimshaw on 15-cm sperm whale tooth, 2000. A famous Confederate raider that ravaged Yankee whalers and merchantmen in the Pacific during the Civil War but caused no loss of life. The end of the war terminated a plan to attack San Francisco.

"A Stroll Down the Dock", Scrimshaw on 27.5-cm fossil walrus artifact, Second Award Scrimshaw, Second Annual International Maritime Art Awards Show, 1981, Mystic Seaport, CT, USA.
A scene typical of New Bedford in the 1880s. From left: ship "Niger" is hove down for recoppering; schooner "Cameo" drying sails; bark "Sunbeam" at the wharf readying for sea with her whaleboats gathered off her stern; the recently returned "Charles W. Morgan" drying sails and being unloaded; bark "Tropic Bird" drying sails at anchor awaiting a berth. Purposely depicted are various rigs and hull types of the period.

"Jeff's Boat" on a sperm whale tooth.

"Scottish Fantasy II", Scrimshaw on 11.5-cm mammoth ivory set into a rosewood desk stand. About 1996.
This was a private commission for the owner from plans during construction.

Howard Rosenfeld

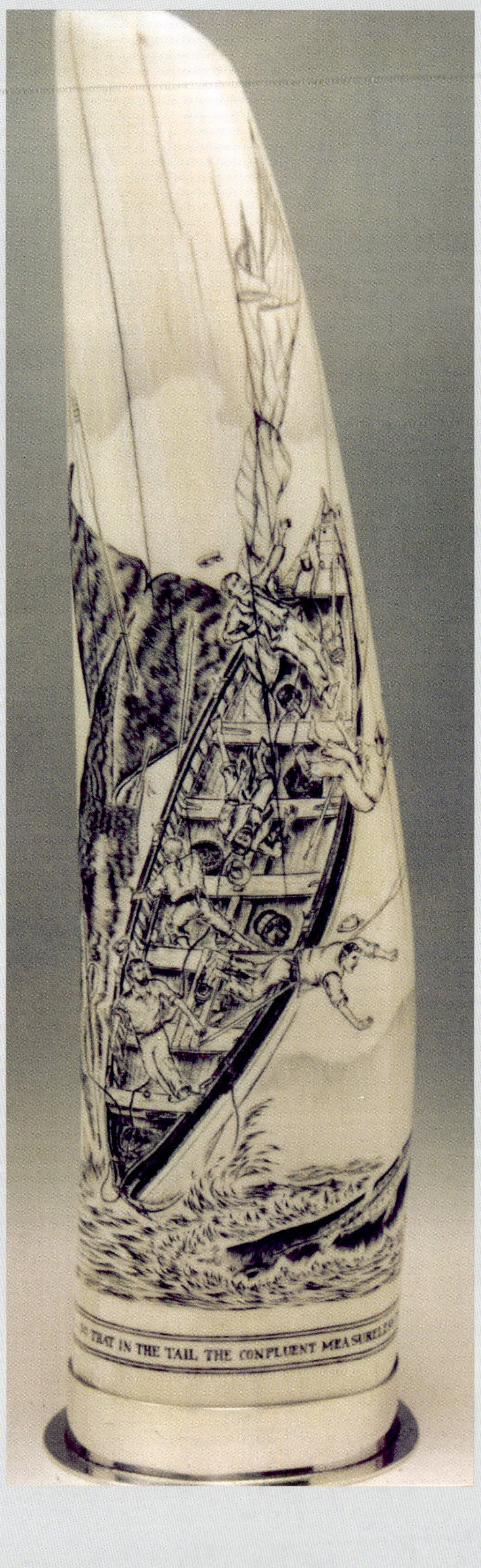

Top: "Essex", Scrimshaw on 17-cm sperm whale tooth with rosewood and brass base. Built by subscription of the citizens of Essex, MA. During the War of 1812, the frigate Essex was commanded by David Porter on a voyage of adventure into the South Pacific, destroying British whalers and taking possession of and participating in the tribal intrigues of the Marquesas. Captured at Valparaiso, Chile.

Right: "Upset Whaleboat", Scrimshaw on 30.5-cm tagged walrus tusk. Approximately 1984. Howard likes to show the whale winning. This did happen often, making whaling a very dangerous job. He's foreshortened the whale to get both the head and tail in the composition.

Howard Rosenfeld

"Morgan Tusk", Scrimshaw on a 68.5-cm tagged (legal) walrus tusk.
First Award Scrimshaw, Third Annual International Maritime Art Awards Show, 1982, Mystic Seaport, CT, USA
A somewhat idealized double portrait of Mystic Seaport's greatest treasure, the whaler "Charles W. Morgan", built in 1841, is shown as she appeared at two stages in her career. After her last working voyage in 1921, the "Morgan" was rerigged as she was thought to have appeared early in her career with ship rig, single topsails, and the painted faux gunports characteristic of merchantmen and whalers during much of the 19th century (left). The reverse (right) shows her as she looks today, a bark with split topsails and the plain topsides typical of whalers in the latter years of sailing whalers.

Mori Sacher

Mori Sacher comes from Argentina, where she studied art in her native city of Buenos Aires. In 1977, she and her husband, Alfredo Sacher, moved to the Tessin canton in Switzerland. Her husband has produced handmade knives since 1995, and his dearest wish was for his artistically talented wife to attempt the art of scrimshaw.

One day, at the urging of her husband, she finally decided to try it. And with each new piece, she became more and more enthusiastic about scrimshaw until finally it became her principal activity.

She works with both stippling and line technique. Sometimes she mixes them, depending on the subject she is working on at the time. Mori uses mainly black, but on occasion she also works in color.

The subjects she selects are mostly hunting scenes, animals, and drawings from American Indian culture. She doesn't work exclusively for her husband, but carries out commissions from different knife makers and other clients as well.

Mori's tools are simple. A sharply ground needle point, black ink, and plenty of patience.

Left: A knife with a black buffalo horn grip and Damascus steel blade.
The tiger below is scrimmed on walrus tusk. Both knives by Alfredo Sacher.

The elephant was scrimmed on mammoth ivory, all other knives on this page have a grip of antique elephant ivory and were made by Alfredo.

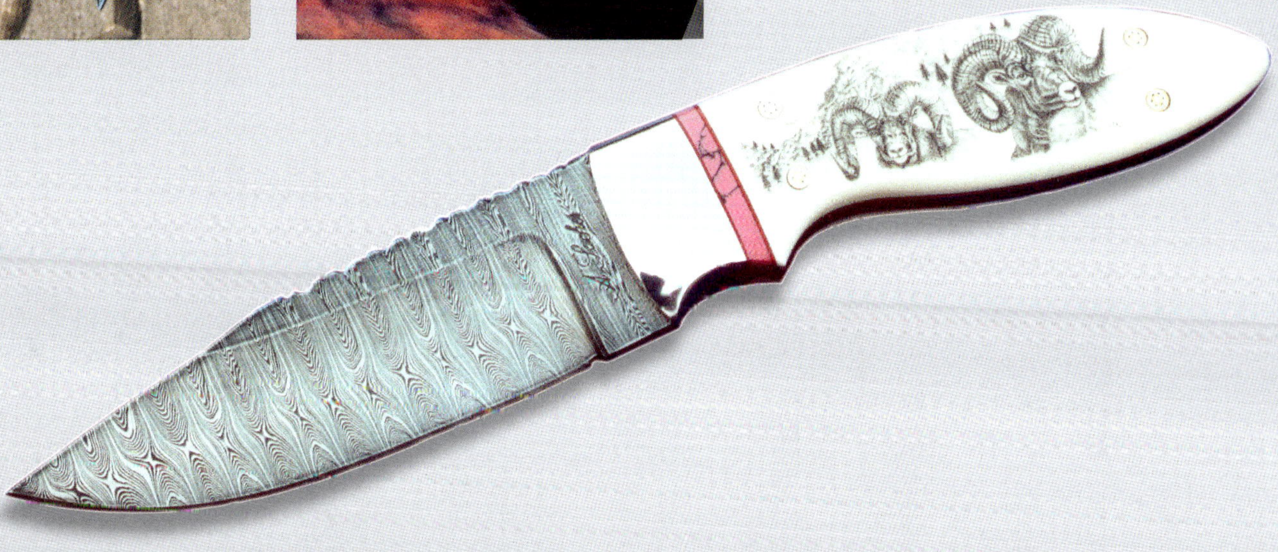

Mori Sacher

A hippo tooth was used to make this super pen. In accordance with the material, it is scrimmed with hippo scenes.

A knife by Juan Carlos Pereyra da Silva from Argentina. Its grip is antique elephant ivory, like the two others.

Penguins on mammoth ivory. The blade is "Superdancetwist"- Damascus steel by "Damasteel". All knives on this side by Alfredo Sacher.

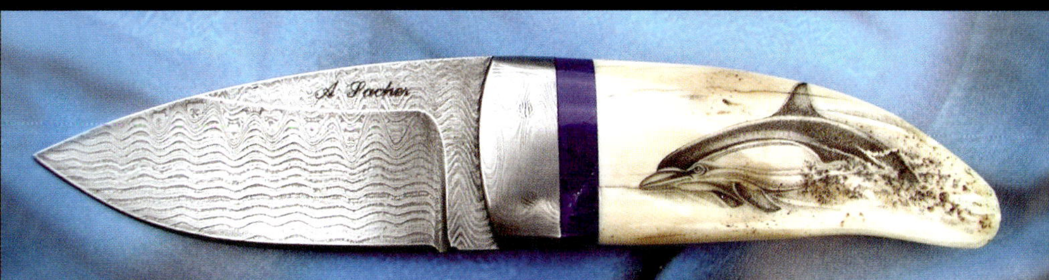

These knives show how beautiful the subtle shades of the material can look. The brown mammoth ivory bark can be included in the design, and rough material can be turned into splashing water, as in the dolphin motif on fossil walrus tusk, above.

Right: A knife with a black buffalo horn grip and Damascus steel blade. The tiger at left is scrimmed on walrus tusk. Both knives by Alfredo Sacher.

Viveca Sahlin

Viveca Sahlin began to do scrimshaw in 1996. She was attracted by the wonderful illustrations of scrimshaw by artists like Rick Fields and Gary "Garbo" Williams, which she found in American publications like *Knives Illustrated* and *Blade*. These two scrimshanders became and remain her idols in the field of scrimshaw.

An article on scrimshaw in one of these publications inspired her to try it herself. After considerable trial and error, using a variety of needles and colors, she discovered that stippling was her best technique. Today Viveca uses stippling about 90% of the time, but employs line technique for fur, hair, and similar textures. She also does negative scrimshaw on dark objects. She uses no machines, only needles and a pin vise.

Viveca is particularly pleased that you don't need any expensive machines to do scrimshaw and that you can create such fantastic pictures with such simple tools on suitable materials like mammoth ivory or buffalo horn.

Since 1998, Viveca has worked full-time as a scrimshander and has founded a small company called "ScrimArt". She does a great deal of scrimshaw worldwide for knife makers and collectors on commission. She is convinced that she will never lose her enthusiasm for scrimshaw.

After the Turkey Hunt. This scene is on the grip of a knife by Leif Reiersen.

Right: The Nordic god Thor, a very beautiful Scandinavian scene. Viveca shows the influence of her Swedish homeland in her work. Dimensions: 11 x 8.5 cm.

These three pairs of wolf eyes are scrimmed in black-and-white on the grip of a knife by Leif Solheim.

A living scene on a plate cut from a whale tooth.

A beautifully moving scene, as if from a storybook. On mammoth ivory. Dimensions: 10 x 7.5 cm.
Right: The sailing ship is worked on a whale tooth.

Viveca Sahlin

"Negative" work in color on a piece of water buffalo horn.

A fox-hunting scene on ivory on a knife by Alan Wood.

The bear is worked on a grip of mammoth ivory. The knife is by Leif Reiersen.

Right: A scene by the Swedish "national painter", Carl Larsson, on a folding knife by Johan Gustafsson. Inlay of mammoth ivory.

Display art on mammoth ivory. Lynx and lyon are approximately 15 x 10 cm.
The portrait of a tiger on a piece of mammoth ivory is about 16 cm high.

Harald Schlott

*Harald also does ivory carvings like this falcon with a rabbit in his talons.
It is the grip of a letter opener.*

Harald Schlott was born in 1957 in Suhl, Germany. Even as a young man, he participated actively in various drawing associations as an artist. After completing school, he apprenticed in Suhl as a firearms engraver, and because of his outstanding abilities, he finished early and was not required to take the examination.

He was assigned to the East German ministerial cabinet in Berlin, where, among other things, he was responsible for the production and distribution of gifts, particularly those associated with hunting, for presentation to the communist leadership and their guests.

He is qualified in a number of technical fields, including gunsmithing, and apart from his profession, he also received a degree in political science. Because he lacked political influence and connections, he was denied the opportunity to pursue advanced studies in any artistic field.

After the collapse of the East German political system, he had a hard time beginning again. He spent a few years as an engraver with a dealer in hunting supplies, and then came a period of unemployment when the dealer went bankrupt. In 1993, he passed the examination for master engraver, and in 1995 he began to work as a self-employed engraver, sculptor, and scrimshander.

Along with a large number of original creations, he also does creative work for goldsmiths, knife designers, gunsmiths, and private clients. Above all, professional recognition is important to him - far more than awards and trophies. In spite of his infrequent appearance in galleries and at exhibitions, his work has achieved special international recognition in the field of art knives. Knives by various international knife makers with his engravings have won many awards.

On the occasion of the 2000 International Knife Show in Munich, he became the first engraver to receive the Award "Best Art Work" for his overall creative contribution to the field of knifemaking. He saw scrimshaw for the first time in connection with knives. He taught himself that creative art, seeing possibilities in it as a significant supplement to his engravings. He does his scrimshaw exclusively in black-and-white, and he believes that this has the best optical effect (as in metal engraving). When necessary, this allows him to produce photo-quality scrimshaw in stippling and line technique, which he does partly under a stereomicroscope. His opinion concerning the precision of his work is based purely on economics: "As precise as necessary, not as precise as possible."

Harald Schlott

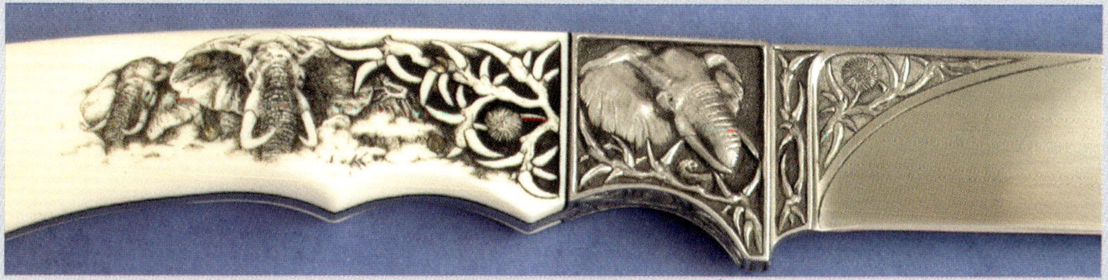

A beautiful combination: metal engraving and scrimshaw, both done by Harald on a knife by Joachim Faust.

Below: a whaling scene on mammoth ivory. Dimensions: 11.4 x 3.4 cm.

Two rings with scrimshaw motifs.

Elephant portrait in a silver stand with engraved African plants on a desk set.

Toi Skellern

Toi Skellern lives in South Africa. She was first introduced to the art of scrimshaw and the knifemaking scene 13 years ago by Hilton Purvis at the Durban Easter Knife Show.

For her subjects, she concentrates on African wildlife (big and small), which she scrims in full color, utilizing the stipple technique. Her favorite materials for scrimshaw are mammoth, elephant, hippo, and other fossil ivories and a variety of other animal teeth and horns.

In 2000, she exhibited in France at the Paris Knife Exhibition, where she was awarded the prize for the best scrimshaw. Toi has also exhibited her work at the Milan show in Italy, an uncommon accomplishment for a scrimmer from South Africa. Following the Milan exhibition, her work received a four-page spread in *Lame D' Autore*, an Italian knife magazine.

She is an Associate Member of the Knifemakers' Guild of Southern Africa.

A knife by Toi's husband, Mike.
The scorpion is set as a small vignette on the mammoth ivory knife handle.

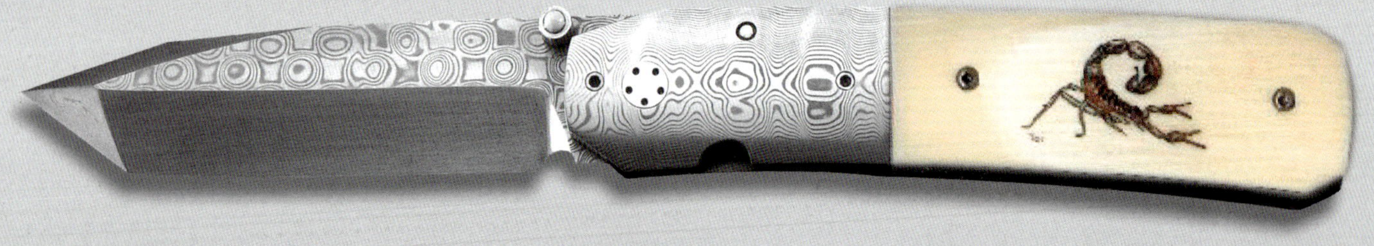

The knife with the bees is by Piet Grey. Grip of elephant ivory.

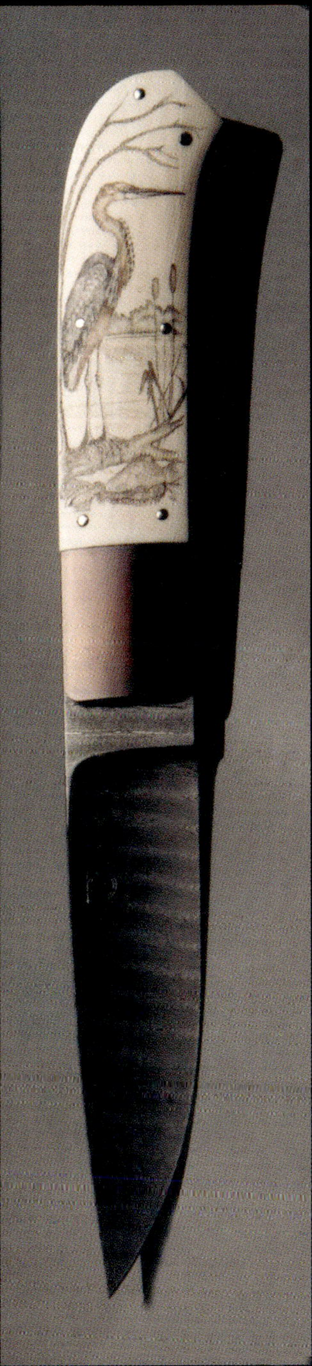

Left: A Goliath heron on mammoth ivory. Knife by Owen Wood.

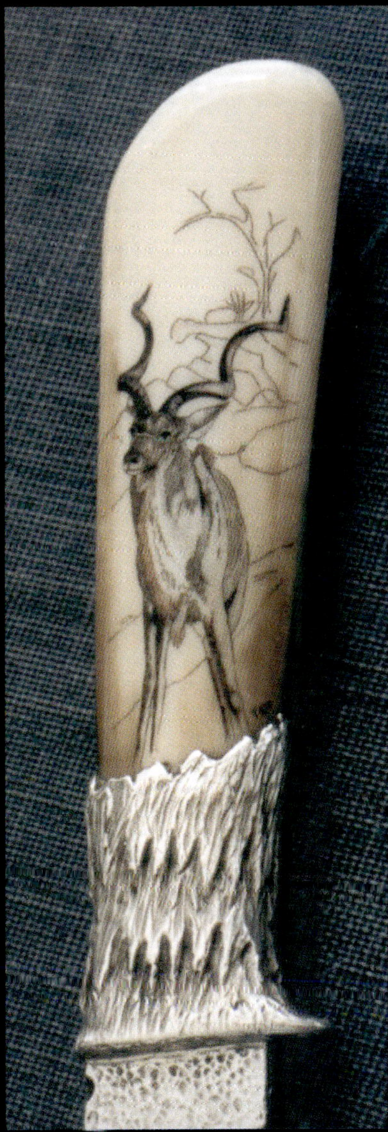

A special knife by Howard Hitchmough. The kudu is scrimmed on mammoth ivory.

Toi Skellern

These two folding knives
were also made by Toi's husband.

Reclining cheetah on mammoth ivory. Knife by Mike Skellern.

This sensitive sketch-like scrimshaw on mammoth ivory decorates a folding knife by Mike Skellern.

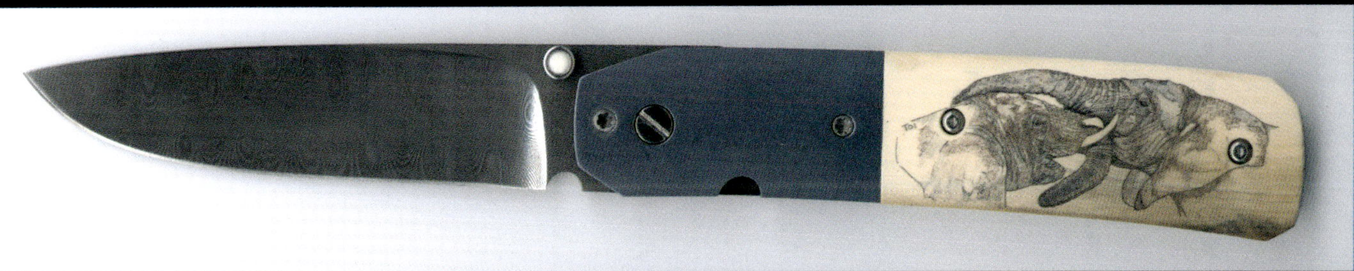

Another knife by Mike. An Egyptian theme on mammoth ivory.

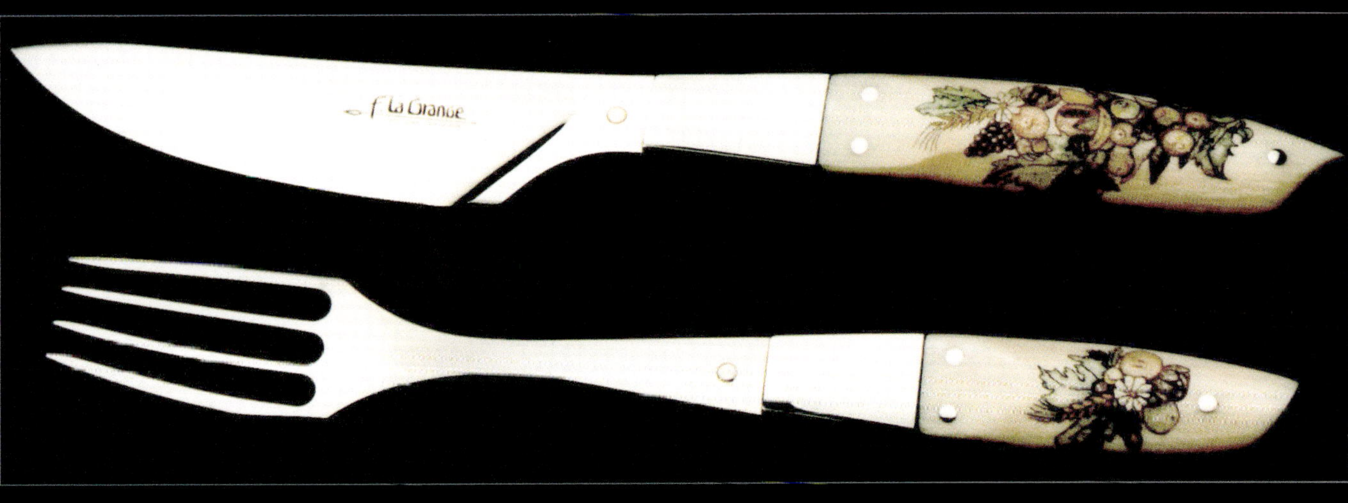

A place setting by Fanie LaGrange with blossom and fruit decor on elephant ivory.

Spending his life in Rhode Island, nearby New Bedford and Nantucket with their old whaling history motivated David Smith to launch into the art of scrimshaw.

Combined with his knowledge of sailing, this background has given David an emotional commitment to traditional nautical themes, which radiate from his scrimshaw work. Each piece is created with a deep personal understanding and appreciation of the subject he depicts.

David utilizes a stippling technique to achieve fully shaded themes on each piece he undertakes. His style of work has been described as uniquely distinct from other scrimshaw, possessing a soft strength.

He often makes use of photographs of wildlife or nautical scenes in conjunction with in-depth research to help create his themes. He works mainly on the ancient fossil ivories of mammoth, mastodon, and walrus and prefers to use the single colors of black or sepia in his engravings to complement the earthy brown hues often seen in these types of ivory.

Between 1998 and 2005 (the first publication of this book), David Smith has won ten 1st place awards at international scrimshaw and art exhibitions for his work.

David won the 1999 Rudolph J. Schaefer Maritime Heritage Award with the portrait "Around Alone: Capt. Joshua Slocum".
The size is 16 x 11.5 cm.

"Fastnet" was shown at the American Society of Marine Artists, 13th National Exhibition 2004.
Stand of antique ivory and cocobolo.
Size: 23.5 x 8.5 cm

"Emperors", an interesting black-and-white work. David Smith has placed white highlights over the ivory-colored background of this sensitively shadowed scrimshaw. It took first place at Wildlife Mystic Scrimshanders International Scrimshaw Competition.
Ivory / ebony stand, 22 x 8.5 cm

"HMS Leopard-USS Chesapeake"
an 8.5 x 11cm scrimshaw of a sea battle.
This work was honored with the Mystic Scrimshander's Nautical Award in 2002.

"Pride II" does honor to its name.
With this lion's profile, David won the first prize in the category "Wildlife" at the 2001 International Competition in Hawaii.

"Charles Darwin: Arrival at the Galapagos",
scrimmed on antique ivory on a stand made of ivory and cocobolo. Size: 29.5 x 19 cm.
Exhibited at Mystic International 2003.

"Vigilant", a portrait of a leopard, was also exhibited in Hawaii in 2001. Dimensions: 7.5 x 14.5 cm.

Kurt Sperry

"The special beauty of scrimshaw for me lies in its fundamental honesty. In a world of artspeak and mechanically reproduced prints, it is wonderful to hold an honestly made art object in your hand."

This quote by Kurt Sperry is a fine expression of the general fascination exerted by scrimshaw and the scrimshander's dedication to his work. Kurt has been expressing himself artistically since he was old enough to grasp a crayon. He began working as a scrimshander in 1976 at the Alaska Silver and Ivory Company in Bellingham, Washington. He enjoys working with a wide variety of motifs, from wildlife to nautical themes and other subjects. All of his work is done 100% by hand. To achieve the finest and most honest quality, he refuses to use any mechanical tools or machines.
At present, he works at his own studio in Bellingham. His work has been commissioned by numerous galleries in the United States.

The globe was scrimmed on an antique billiard ball. The size is evident from the ruler shown. (1 inch = ca. 2.5 cm)..

Inuit on mammoth ivory.
Original dimensions: 12 x 9 cm.

Below: The wolves are scrimmed
on a ca. 27 cm-wide fossil walrus tusk.

A sailing ship on a piece of an Inuit artifact of fossil walrus ivory. Height: ca. 15 cm.

More views of the globe, which is scrimmed in the classical style of an old world map.

An idyllic scene about 50 cm wide from the life of the Makah Indians of the northwest coast of the United States. Scrimmed on an antique walrus tusk.

A proud sailing ship on a voyage from England to America. Kurt scrimmed it on a ca. 33 cm-long fossil Inuit axe from St. Lawrence Island in the Bering Strait.

John Stahl

John has been a scrimshander since 1979. Prior to that, his hobbies were drawing in colored pencil and pen-and-ink. He read extensively to learn about the art and techniques of scrimshaw and conferred with other scrimmers, receiving a great deal of guidance from Bob Engnath and Rick Fields.

John's favorite medium is elephant ivory because of its consummate uniform density and neutrality of color. He also utilizes mammoth and fossil walrus ivories, bone, buffalo horn, Micarta™, and other synthetics. Most of his work is done using the stippling method.

John does much of his work on knife handles, but he also creates freestanding display pieces, each of which features a base fashioned from exotic hardwoods. In addition, he makes utilitarian pieces such as letter openers, shaped from ivory or ivory and wood, some with scrimmed images. On occasion, he will utilize stainless or Damascus steels for blades and ivory with scrimshaw for grip scales, producing what might be termed a "full-bore" letter opener.

John works on commission, but he also does pieces of his own choosing, which allows him to do subjects that appeal to him. His love of felines leads him to create frequent portraits of the big cats of the world. An inveterate birder, he is very fond of birds of prey, and they appear in many of his works. He will do an occasional dragon or figure study, but avoids nautical and maritime subjects.

John has received recognition of his work in the world of handmade knives through the publication of many of his pieces in annual knife journals and in knife magazines.

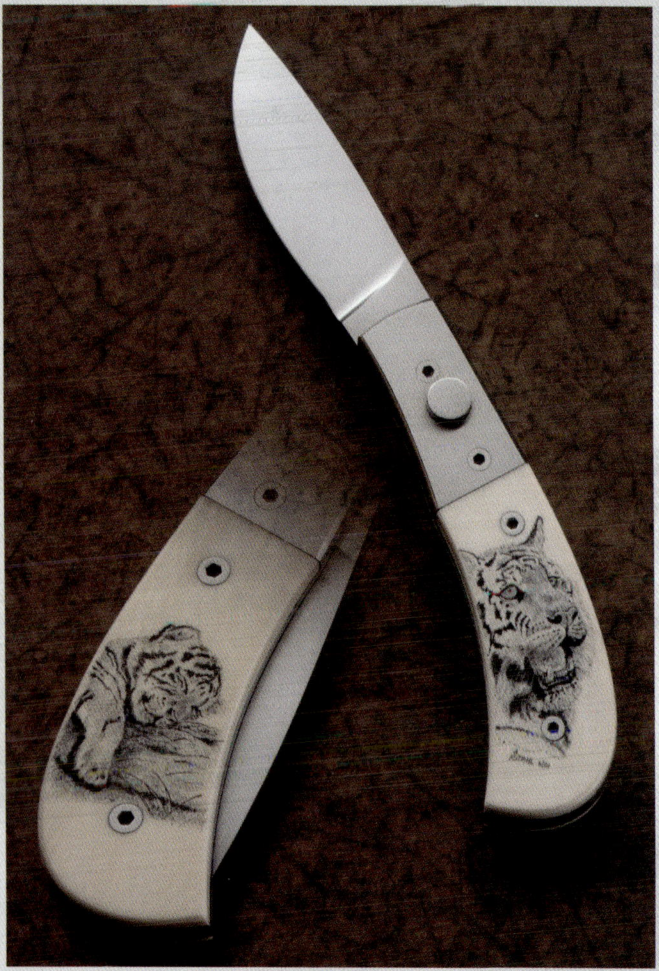

Button-lock folding knife by Ron Richards. The adult Siberian Tiger and the baby tiger are scrimmed on elephant ivory scales. Blade 7.5 cm, length closed 11.25 cm (Photo by PointSeven Studios)

A large woolly mammoth tusk display piece. Dall sheep in mountain setting. 40 x 8.75 cm. (Image - SharpByCoop.com)

Claw-shaped knife by Howard Hitchmough. Blade of stainless Damascus steel. Mammoth ivory scales. Golden eagle motifs on both sides. Overall length: 13.75 cm.

Folding knife by W. R. Carnes with elephant ivory scales and raccoons scrimmed on both sides. Overall length: 15 cm.

This large letter opener with a scrimmed merlin family has a blade of cocobolo and elephant ivory scales. 24.5 x 3.75 cm. (Photo by PointSeven Studios).

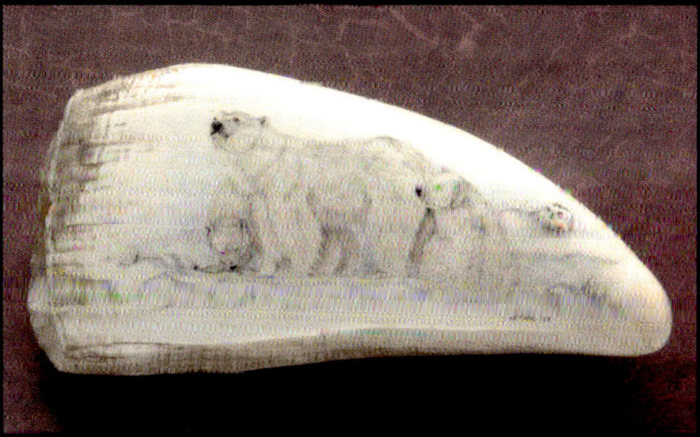

Mother polar bear and cubs with a snowy owl on a big sperm whale tooth. 17 x 8.75 cm.

Another polar scene scrimmed on ivory scales. Boot knife by Curt Erickson. 18.75 cm.

On elephant ivory: A goshawk in action and a head study scrimmed on this display piece. The base is made of bird's-eye maple, cocobolo, and ebony. 12 x 5.5 cm.

Siberian tigers on elephant ivory decorate this hunting knife by Fred Carter. 17.5 cm. (All photos on this page by PointSeven Studios).

Dorinel Stoica

Dorinel Stoica was born in Mediasch in Transylvania, Rumania. Because of that country's poor economic situation, he had few toys as a child. To make up for it, his parents bought him colored pencils and watercolors. So Dorinel painted all day long, first copying models but later giving his imagination free rein. He was so fascinated by painting that he went on to develop his abilities in that art.

However, his parents were determined that he should learn a "proper" trade. So he was trained as a furniture finisher. Of course, this trade gave Dorinel no room for creativity, so he changed jobs, becoming a decorative dish painter in an enamelware factory. After several years of working with enamel paints, he became interested in oil painting. In 1978, he began to paint for friends and acquaintances and later did a great deal of work on commission. His pictures have also been sold outside of Rumania.

When the Ceausescu regime fell in Rumania, it finally became possible for Dorinel Stoica to travel and visit friends in Germany. While there, he saw knife engraving for the first time. Fascinated by this technique, he began with scrimshaw in 1995 and rapidly developed considerable ability.

Dorinel has also been active in knife making and has made some good ones himself. Naturally, these are also furnished with scrimshaw. Some of his knife models have scrimshaw on buffalo horn, mammoth ivory, and even steel. Dorinel Stoica scrims his exclusive art work on knives, jewelry, letter openers, and many other things. He is happy to follow the personal wishes of his customers, and there are an increasing number of connoisseurs who collect his work.

Top: The owl and the dog are both worked on mammoth ivory. The owl, in particular, looks very beautiful against the steeply angled Schreger lines.

Right: A dwarf smith on mammoth ivory. Dimensions 20 x 15 cm.

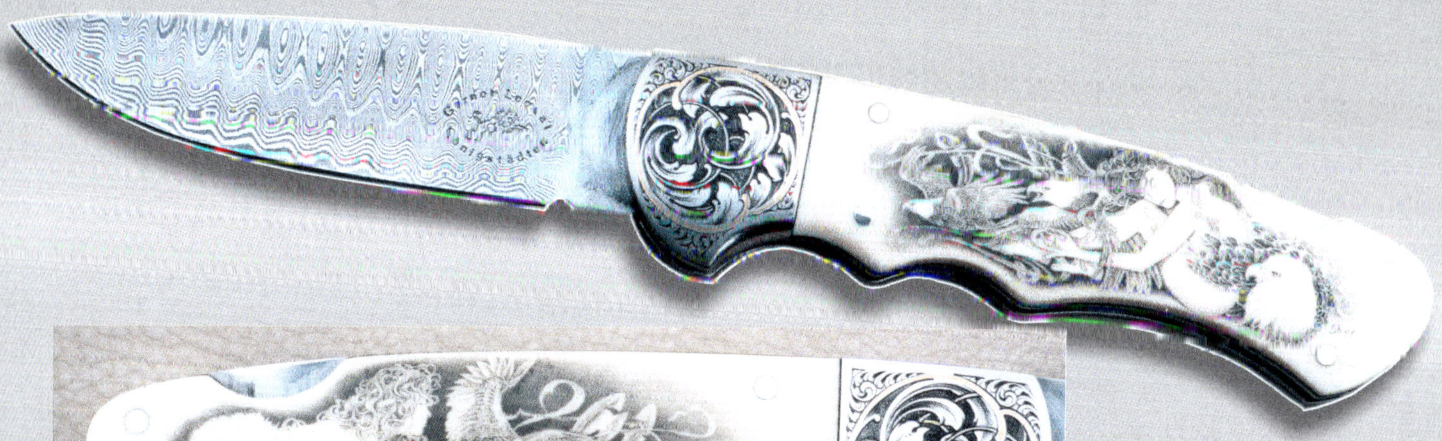

Finely worked scrimshaw on both sides of a knife by Gernot Loquai. Grip scales are of elephant ivory.

Another piece in Dorinel's style on a knife by Michael Staubach.

This pencil holder was made from the hollow end of an elephant tusk. And, like all curved surfaces, the curvature here causes additional problems, since only a small part of the subject is clearly in focus at any one time under a magnifier.

Dorinel Stoica

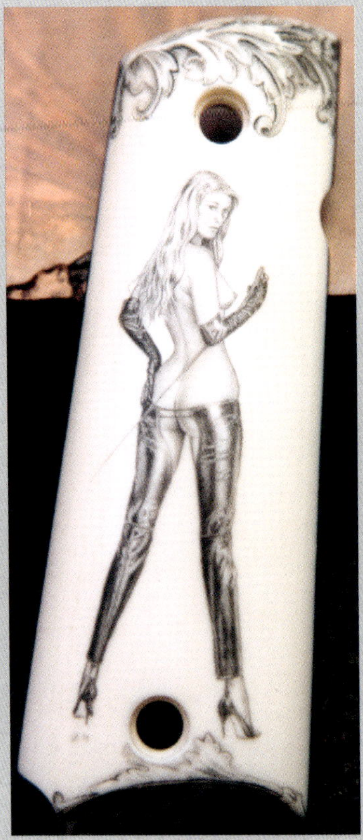

Dagger by Hansel with an elephant ivory grip.

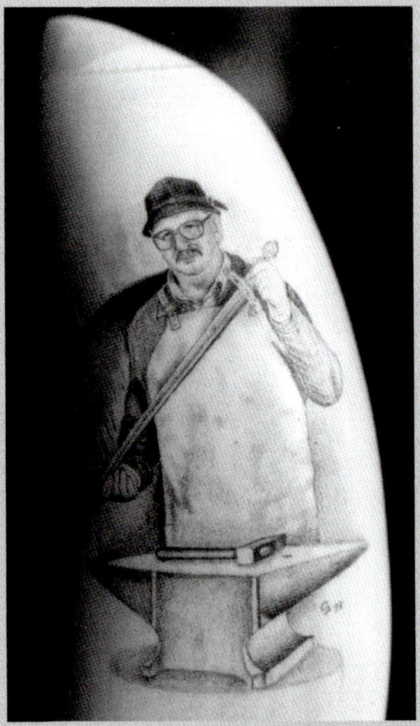

A sword by Manfred Sachse. The grip is a whale tooth with the scrimmed portrait of this well-known smith.

These pistol grip panels are of elephant ivory..

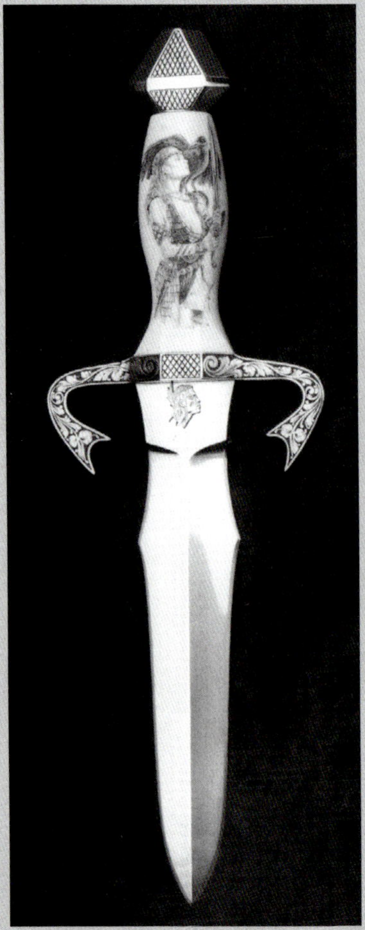

All three scenes – the bear in his cave, the comfortably dozing lion on a branch, and Chief Geronimo – were scrimmed on mammoth ivory.

Matt Stothart

Matt Stothart grew up in Santa Fe, New Mexico. He spent a great deal of time in his father's gallery and framing workshop, where he got to know many of the local artists. Since he had always been interested in drawing and painting himself, this inspired him to seriously consider a career in art. He moved to Bellingham in the northwest corner of Washington State in 1976 to attend art classes at Western Washington University. After a year or so of college, it became apparent that he needed a paying job more urgently than formal schooling. He was fortunate to see an ad in the paper from a local business needing artists. That business was the Alaskan Silver and Ivory Company (ASI), which produced handcrafted scrimshaw jewelry, and so he was introduced to the art of scrimshaw.

The work itself was tedious and production-oriented, but the circumstances were truly inspiring. The twenty or so artists working there, along with those who had come and gone since 1973, had created a kind of renaissance in scrimshaw. This environment served as an incubator for creativity and innovation. Much of what is considered characteristic of the West Coast style of scrimshaw was developed in this atmosphere: an emphasis on the use of color, an expanding range of subject matter, and a refinement of technique and craftsmanship to achieve realism through intricate detail.

In 1980, ASI closed down due to the poor economy, but there was a growing market for larger display pieces on fossil walrus and mammoth ivory. Many of the ASI artists joined other scrimshanders already working independently in the freelance market. Matt was again lucky and ended up sharing a studio with several of the finest. This gave him the opportunity to learn from them, refine his skills, and develop an individual style.

Today, most of the Bellingham artists have gone on to work in other media or to other careers entirely. Scrimshaw is a slow and difficult medium to work in, and it can be even harder to make a living doing it. Matt has been very fortunate to be able to continue doing something he loves for the past twenty-five years.

Though he does start with India ink to develop the blacks in a composition, he relies mostly on color (oil paint) to develop the detail and sense of space and depth in the scene, giving his work a painterly quality. He also occasionally likes to do a piece that is in keeping with the more traditional style, using only black ink. He is considered one of the more versatile contemporary scrimshanders because he likes working on a wide range of subjects, including nautical themes, wildlife, portraits and figures, historical subjects, and old world globes.

He works primarily on fossil walrus and mammoth ivory, but also does some work on legal whale teeth and antique elephant ivory. His scrimshaw can be found in a variety of galleries in the United States and Hawaii and in many private collections throughout the world. His pieces are signed "M. Stothart".

Whaling with the harpoon. A classical scene, scrimmed on a sperm whale tooth. Original size: ca. 6 x 13.5 cm.

"Breaking the Line", finest scrimshaw on fossil walrus ivory. Dimensions: 6.5 x 27 cm.

"The USS Monitor vs. the CSS Virginia", on fossil walrus ivory. Dimensions: 5 x 10 cm.

"The Golden Hind", also on fossil walrus ivory. Dimensions: ca. 6 x 30 cm.

Matt Stothart

"Endeavour Under Sail", on fossil walrus ivory.
Dimensions: 13 x 5 cm.

Matt Stothart very delicately scrimmed "The Old World" as a globe on this antique billiard ball.
Dimensions: 10.5 x 7.5 (Stand by Roger Cash).

The samurai is worked on mammoth ivory.
Dimensions: 11 x 7.5 cm.

Matt Stothart

Another depiction of the "Old World". The continents stand out here. The blue water and the dark contours put the white of the landmasses into the foreground. Diameter of the antique billiard ball: 5.2 cm.

Above: Whaling scene on fossil walrus ivory. Dimensions: 23 x 6.7 cm.

Right: A clipper on a sperm whale tooth. Dimensions: 14.5 x 6 cm.

Jane Tukarski

Jane Tukarski's goal as a scrimshander is to perpetuate the unique American maritime folk art of scrimshaw. Early on, she was captivated by the romance of the bygone tall ship era, and she knew that the sea was in her soul. She was especially enthralled by the story of the United States on the high seas and the history of the whaling industry, as documented by her predecessors, the early scrimshanders. She is working to revive and preserve this traditional craft, which is truly in danger of extinction!

Patience, a steady hand, and great eyesight are Jane's strengths as she pursues this demanding and intricate folk art. Although she is primarily a maritime artist, she likes to go beyond the traditional limits of the art form by incorporating themes such as wildlife, landscapes, and detailed portraits of faces with character, which are her forte. She has been challenged by unusual requests such as Harley Davidson motorcycles, airplanes, a Coast Guard icebreaker, and knife handles featuring dragons, mermaids, and boats.

Jane prefers to engrave on fossil mammoth and walrus ivories, although antique billiard balls and pre-ban sperm whale teeth are also intriguing surfaces for her. She is a purist using only a hand-held, finely-honed, metal engraving tool to achieve texture and line. Applying ink to the surface of the ivory, she then engraves through it, creating a white line against black. The final step – the moment of truth – is to remove the ink to reveal the positive image, as the ink stays in the line and wipes off the surface. The texture and hardness of each piece of ivory is different, making it a matter of feel to achieve the correct result.

After obtaining a BS degree in textile design at the University of California, Jane was working on a masters degree at the University of Washington when she answered an ad for an artist in a Seattle newspaper. This resulted in a two-year apprenticeship as a scrimshander! She was immediately intrigued and challenged by the art and still is today.

As an artist member of the American Society of Marine Artists, Jane has exhibited scrimshaw at several museums including the Mystic Maritime Gallery and the Cape Museum in Dennis, Massachusetts, and in juried maritime art shows in the mid-Atlantic region of the United States. She has also won awards at the Mystic Scrimshanders International Scrimshaw Competition.

Jane and her family now reside near Chesapeake Bay in Maryland.

They call it "Nantucket Sleigh Ride" when the boat was pulled by the whale during the most dangerous of hunts. Scrimmed on a 15-cm sperm whale tooth.

The "James Corner Knife". Knife handle of sperm whale tooth.

Top: "The Hunt" a classic whaling scene wrapped around a 20-cm bull sperm whale tooth.

Maritime life at its most mysterious: Seahorses. Scrimshaw on pre-banned elephant ivory on a base of ebony surrounded by coral.

Jane Tukarski

"Harmony". Scrimshaw of mother and baby humpback whales on woolly mammoth ivory. 20 x 15 cm

"Raven Blanket", Nez Perce Indian.

"Hermann Melville Tooth", Portrait of the author with the ship Pequod and Moby Dick in the background. Engraved on 15-cm sperm whale tooth.

One of several billiard balls that Jane has turned into globes with old maps and maritime themes.

On a slab of ancient mammoth tusk: the weathered face of an "old salt" waterman and pound net fisherman from Chesapeake Bay.

On mammoth ivory, 25 x 15 cm: Commodore Edward Preble and one of the first US warships, the USS Constitution, which is still in existence today in Boston harbor. Also called "Old Ironsides" because so many British cannonballs bounced harmlessly off her thick sides.

Robert Weiss

A native New Englander and a 1978 graduate of Pratt Institute, Bob is one of only two marine artists to have won the prestigious Rudolph J. Schaefer Maritime Heritage Award three times. This is the top award given each year at the Mystic International Marine Art Exhibition, recognizing the one work in the show that "best documents our maritime heritage, past or present, for generations of the future".

After graduation from Pratt Institute, Bob pursued a career as an art director/graphic designer in Manhattan. In 1985, a friend living on Nantucket sent him a scrimshaw kit for Christmas, and this proved to be the major turning point in his career. He fell in love with the art form and, after several years of working by day as an art director and by night on scrimshaw, Bob finally quit his "day job" and went into scrimshaw and marine art as a full-time career. Since then, his unique approach and reverence for the traditions of scrimshaw have won him accolades from collectors, gallery directors, and artists alike.

At the beginning of his scrimshaw career, he began an intensive and continuing study of whaling ships, whales, and whaling history. This in turn has led into many other areas of marine research. Bob spent 1993-96 studying classical realism, with a particular focus on portrait painting, at the Riley League of Artists in White Plains, New York. This gave him the picture-making skills needed to push the art of scrimshaw to new and higher levels.

His work in contemporary marine art now stands on a par with the best in the world. It is set apart from the rest of contemporary scrimshaw by its high technical level, devotion to historical accuracy, and originality of concept. Bob has focused on creating original images through the melding of painstaking historical research and an almost painterly engraving technique.

"The Morgans", with a portrait on one side and the proud sailing ship on the other side of this antique sperm whale tooth. The stand was made out of cocobolo, ebony, and mammoth ivory and has "The Charles W. Morgan" written on it.
In 1996, this work was honored with the Award of Excellence at the International Ocean Voyager's Art Exhibition in Mystic.

"The Constitution Tooth". Robert Weiss received the 1998 Rudolph J. Schaefer Maritime Heritage Award in Mystic for this work on a sperm whale tooth. Dimensions of the tooth: 19.6 x 9.8 x 4.3 cm.

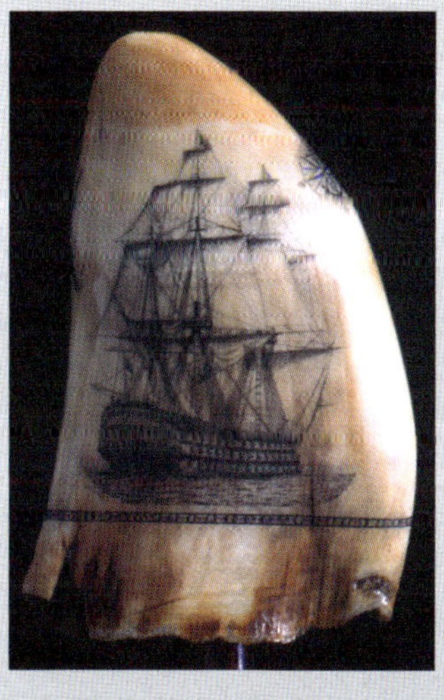

"Nelson and HMS Victory" on an antique sperm whale tooth. Placed on a stand made out of cocobolo, ebony, and mammoth ivory with abalone inlays. Dimensions of the tooth: 13.5 x 8.5 x 3.7 cm.

Robert Weiss

"Procession" is a sensitive and impressive work. A school of whales swims around an entire sperm whale tooth. All of Robert's work is presented on fine stands.
Dimensions of the tooth: 16 x 7.5 x 4.3 cm.

"Queequeg", known from the famous novel and film Moby Dick, on an antique sperm whale tooth.
Dimensions of the tooth: 15.3 x 6.7 x 4.3 cm.

Robert Weiss

"The Scrimshanders", a scene from the lives of the forerunners of the artists presented in this book. On fossil walrus ivory on a stand of rosewood, ebony, and mammoth ivory. Overall dimensions: 24.5 x 8 x 8 cm.

"Arctic Trio" on fossil walrus ivory. Mounted on a stand of cocobolo and fossil walrus ivory. Dimensions: 19.6 x 8.5 x 5.5 cm.

Gary "Garbo" Williams

Gary "Garbo" Williams has worked as an illustrator for the United States Army at Fort Knox, Kentucky, since 1976. He left his job at Fort Knox in October 2003 to work as a full-time scrimshander.

He first started scrimshaw in 1987 when Gene Baskett, a custom knife maker and member of the Knifemakers Guild in the United States, asked him to try some scrimshaw on one of Baskett's knives. Since that time, most of his art has been devoted to scrimshaw, but he has also created art in painting, sculpture, ceramics, wood carving, and illustrations for books, calendars, and record covers.

He has done work on knives, miniature knives, guns, duck calls, boxes, jewelry, walking canes, and display art pieces. He has done scrimshaw work for customers in the United States, Japan, Germany, Italy, Sweden, Canada, Bahrain, and other countries around the world. He displays his work at custom knife shows and at various art shows.

Gary prefers to work only on real ivory. His specialty in scrimshaw is close-up studies of people and animals. He was the first scrimshaw artist to show only the close-up of an animal's eyes on a knife.

He prices his work at an hourly rate for the time it takes to complete it. His work is signed "Garbo", which started as a nickname in college and developed into a pen name for his artwork.

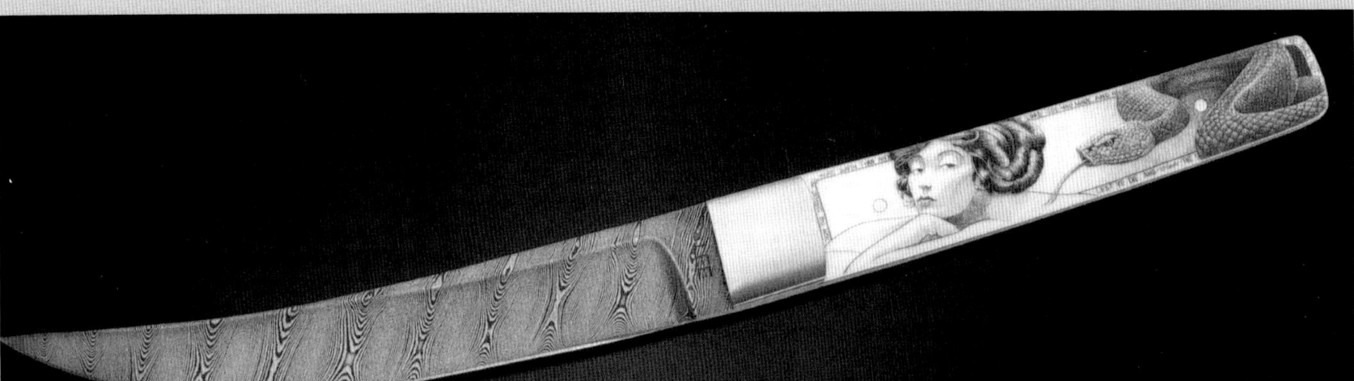

A work whose design and mood harmonizes well with this tanto. Grip of elephant ivory. Knife by Tommy Lee. Length: 19.5 cm.

Gary "Garbo" Williams

Delicate work on a miniature knife by Earl Witsamen. Grip of elephant ivory. Length: 7.5 cm.

The wolf's eyes stare from a folding knife by Frank Centofante. Grip of mammoth ivory. Length of the closed knife: 7.5 cm.

"Whaling Days", a piece on a sperm whale tooth in memory of the old times. Height of the tooth: 14.7 cm.

"Winter Pack". Display art on mammoth ivory. Height: 7.5 cm.

Gary "Garbo" Williams

A bald eagle worked on walrus ivory on a knife by Willie Rigney. Length of the knife: 19.5 cm.

A fine fillet knife with very detailed scrimshaw on a grip of mammoth ivory. Length of the knife: 22 cm.

Antique style scrimshaw on a Bowie knife by Keith Kilby. Total length: 29.5 cm

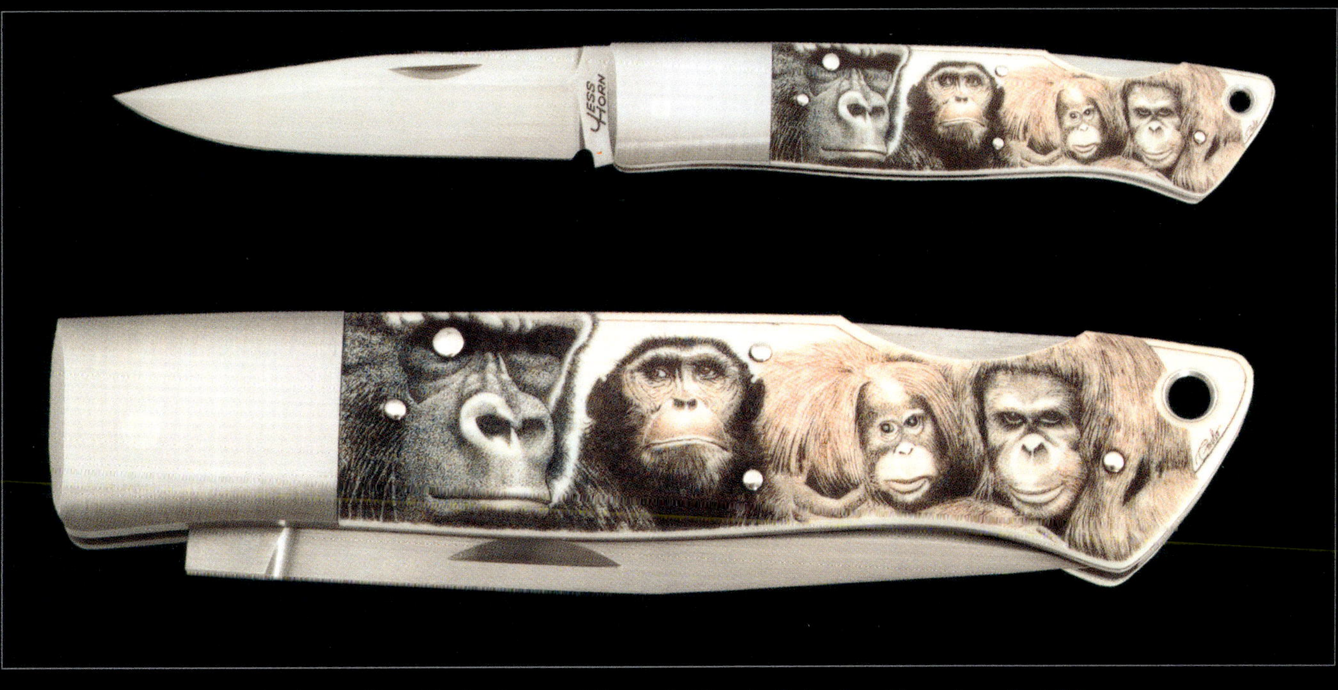

A bizarre scene, especially the gorilla with the "monocle" on a folding knife by Jess Horn. Length: 18.4 cm.

Melodie de Witt

Melodie de Witt became interested in scrimshaw in 1992, while she was living in Natal (South Africa), which is also the home of well-known scrimshander Toi Skellern. She went to see Toi who "showed her the ropes". Melodie was working at that time, so she didn't really have sufficient time to devote to the art, but her interest had been awakened.

About five years later she moved to Secunda and then decided that it was "now or never." She had no knives to work on, so she practiced on a few pieces of loose ivory. Then, about three years ago, she took the plunge, purchased an airline ticket, and flew down to Cape Town for a weekend with Hilton Purvis. He taught her a great deal, and it gave her sufficient encouragement to look for work with knifemakers who liked her art.

She became an Associate Member of the South African Knifemaker's Guild in September 2002.

Melodie really enjoys being a scrimshander. She has worked on elephant, hippo, and warthog ivory, but prefers well chosen and well prepared elephant ivory. Before starting work on a piece, she studies the picture of her model and other pictures of the same animal very carefully, because she wants her work to be the best she can do. When it's done, she wants it to look like a black and white photo of the model. She likes a lot of shading and detail and spends a great deal of time on one piece. She stipples and sometimes makes very light scratches. Then she puts in ink to make the picture. Her only tools are a sharpened needle, a magnifier, and a fluorescent table light.

She has many other interests, including interior decorating and pencil art on ostrich eggs. She is married and has two children, a son and a daughter, and she is happy that they are all avid supporters of her scrimshawing.

This knife was decorated with roses on elephant ivory.

Melodie de Witt

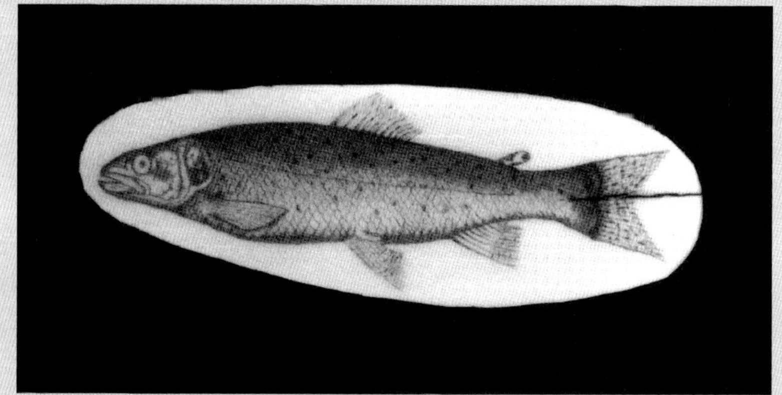

Melodie scrimmed the trout from a drawing onto a piece of elephant ivory. The size is 6.7 x 2,2 cm.

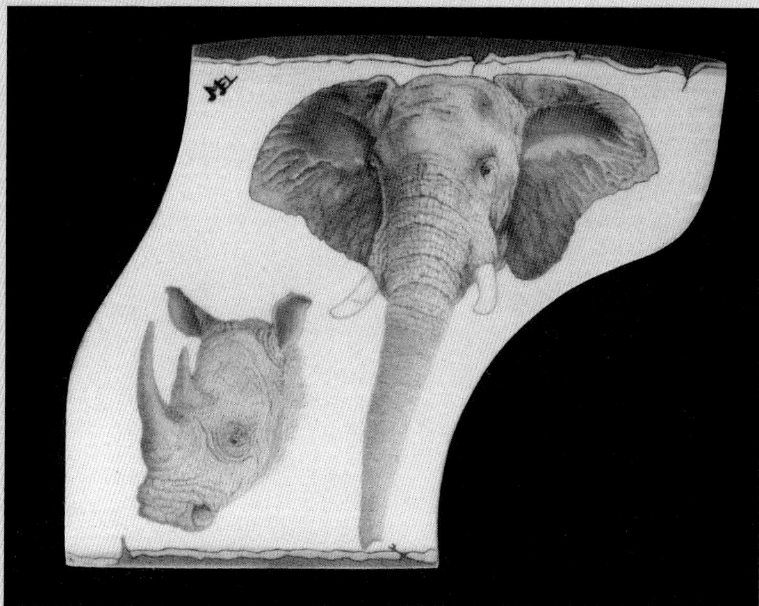

Delicate work. Elephant and rhinoceros on a piece of elephant ivory. 7.5 x 6 cm.

The beaver is worked on a grip of elephant ivory. The knife with the Damascus blade is by Carel Smith of South Africa.

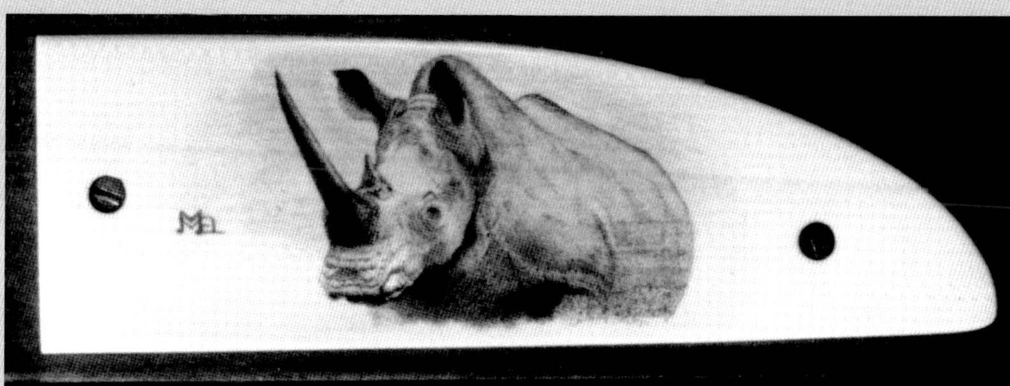

The rhino is worked on mammoth ivory in a mixture of stippling and fine scratch method.

Melodie de Witt

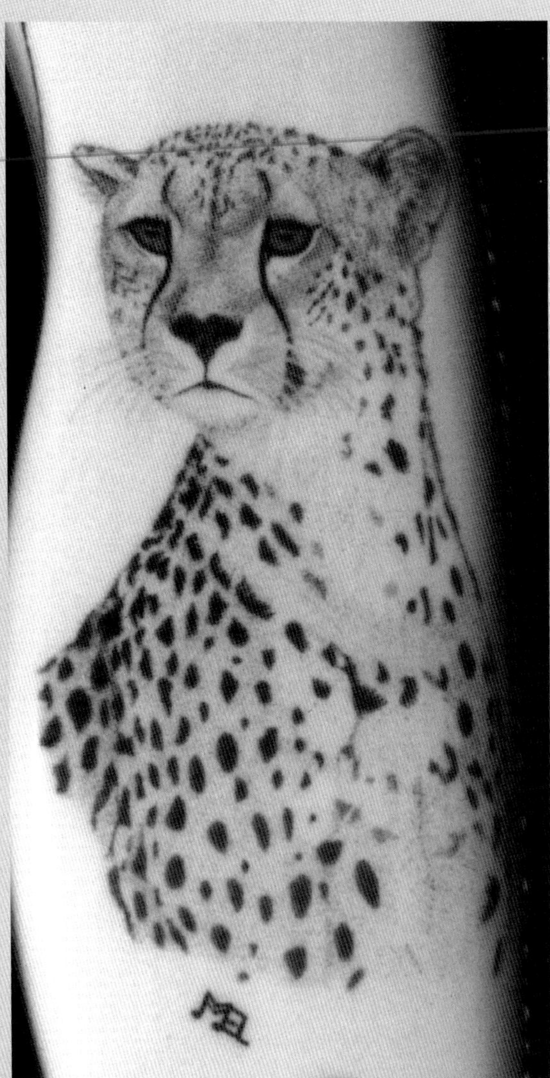

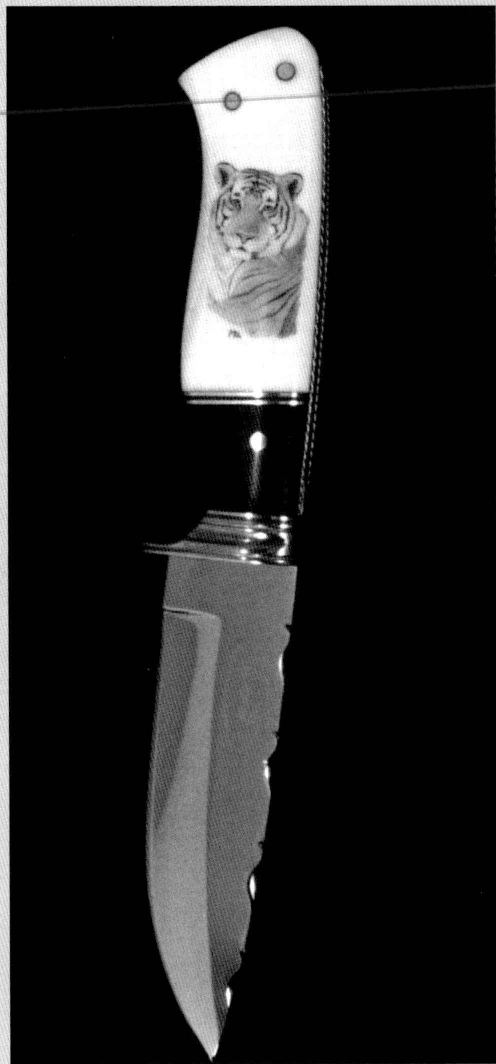

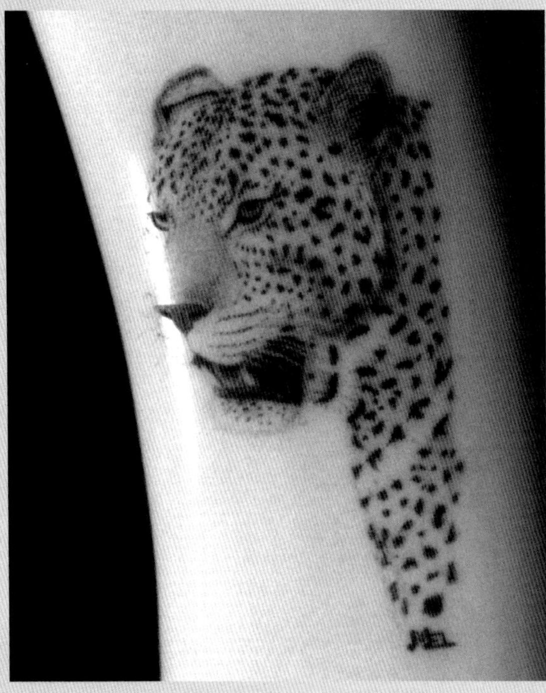

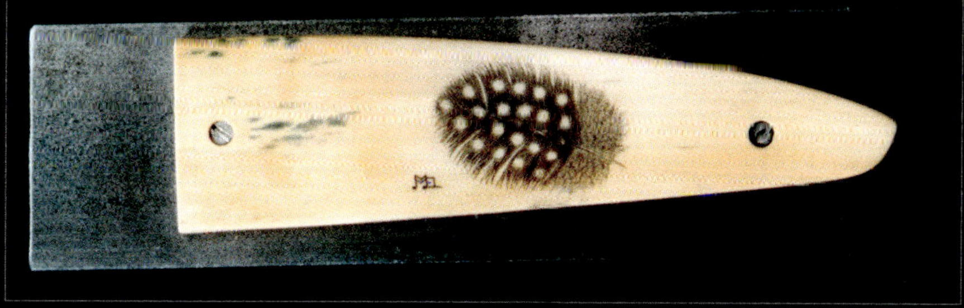

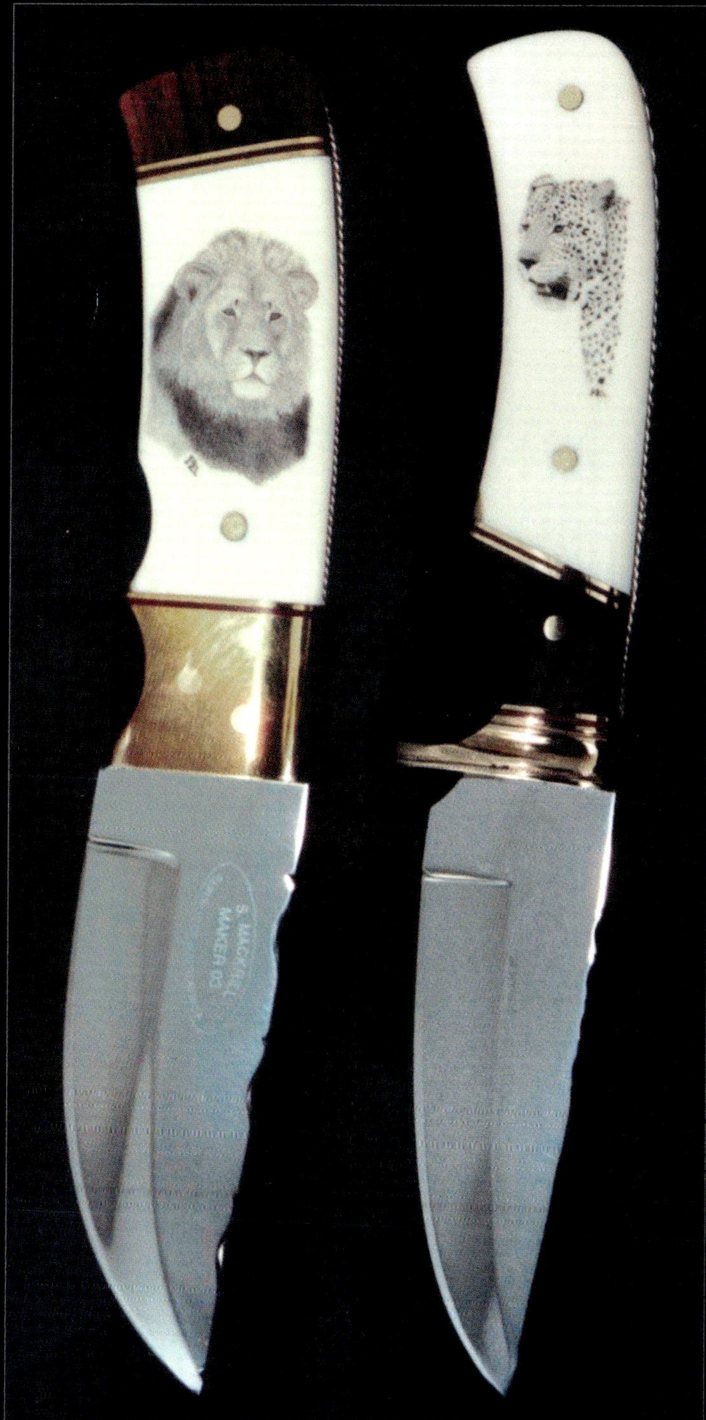

Melodie has scrimmed a cat series on five of Michele Mackrill's knives: cheetah, tiger, leopard, lion, and cougar. All are done on hippo ivory.

Richard Zirbes

Richard Zirbes was born in 1955 in Lieser at the Mosel river in Germany. He was trained as a machinist. In 1992, he took the master's examination in industrial metalworking. Since then he has worked in the area of product development and construction for a company producing plastics in his hometown.

Richard's hobby has been art (painting, sculpting) from infancy. Some years he has devoted his hobby entirely to portrait painting or to some other specific subject.

He became aware of knife making through an article on famous knife makers in a knife magazine. First he sketched a few knife patterns of his own design. His first handmade knife came from a desire to convert the drawing to reality. From the beginning, he has emphasized precise craftsmanship and his own style. Very soon he participated in well-known exhibitions, and for several years he has been a member of the German Knife Makers' Guild.

The next step, knives with fine scrimshaw, which he always enjoyed seeing at these exhibitions, brought Richard closer to doing scrimshaw himself. Since painting, and especially portrait painting, had already been his hobby, he succeeded in doing satisfactory scrimshaw on his first attempt. First he scrimmed an animal subject, a roe buck on a medallion-shaped piece of mammoth ivory. Then he did another on one of his handmade knives.

Richard's detailed, photorealistic scrimshaw of themes such as animal scenes, portraits, and nudes is produced by stippling technique under a stereomicroscope. His working tools are HSS needles, ground and polished to a fine point.

The material he uses for his scrimshaw is almost always the interior core of mammoth ivory. He uses the outer bark of the mammoth ivory for inlay work, for example in a knife guard. Because of the very long time required, he can only make a few pieces each year. His scrimshaw work is found almost exclusively on his own knives, but may also appear on medallions, broaches, earrings, and a variety of other objects.

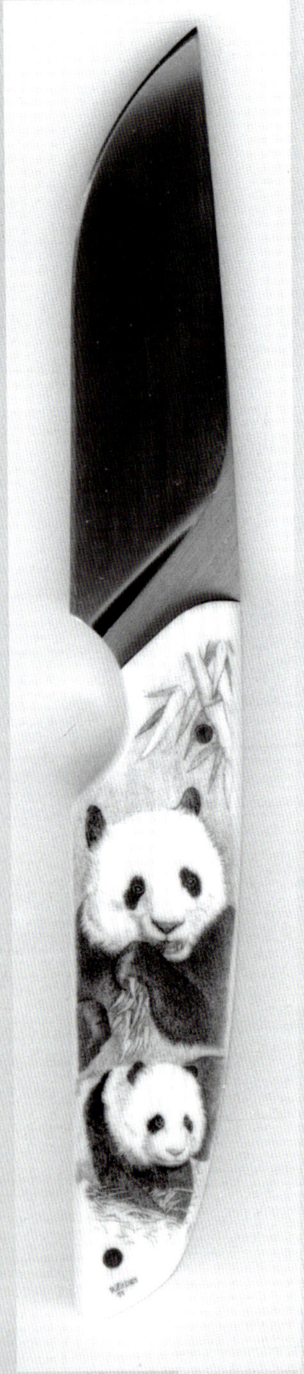

Richard Zirbes

The knife grip with the lynx is an exception, being of cow bone. A good example of how finely scrimshaw can be done on bone.

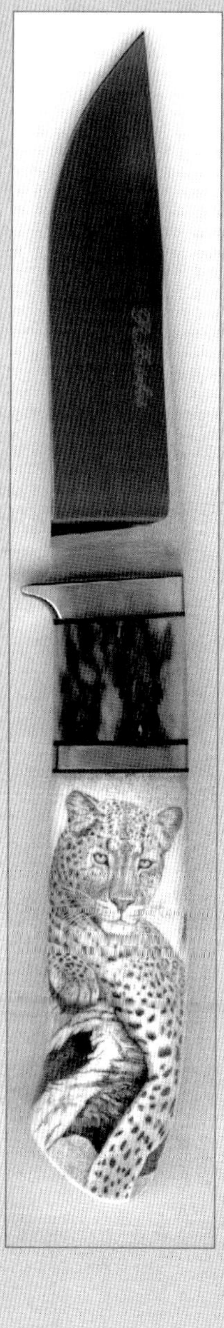

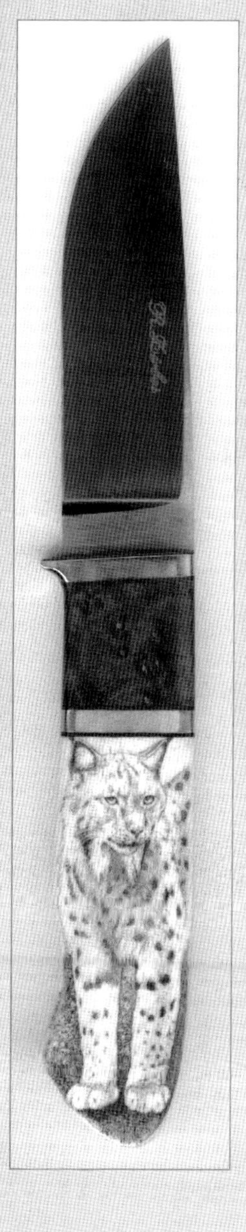

Richard Zirbes

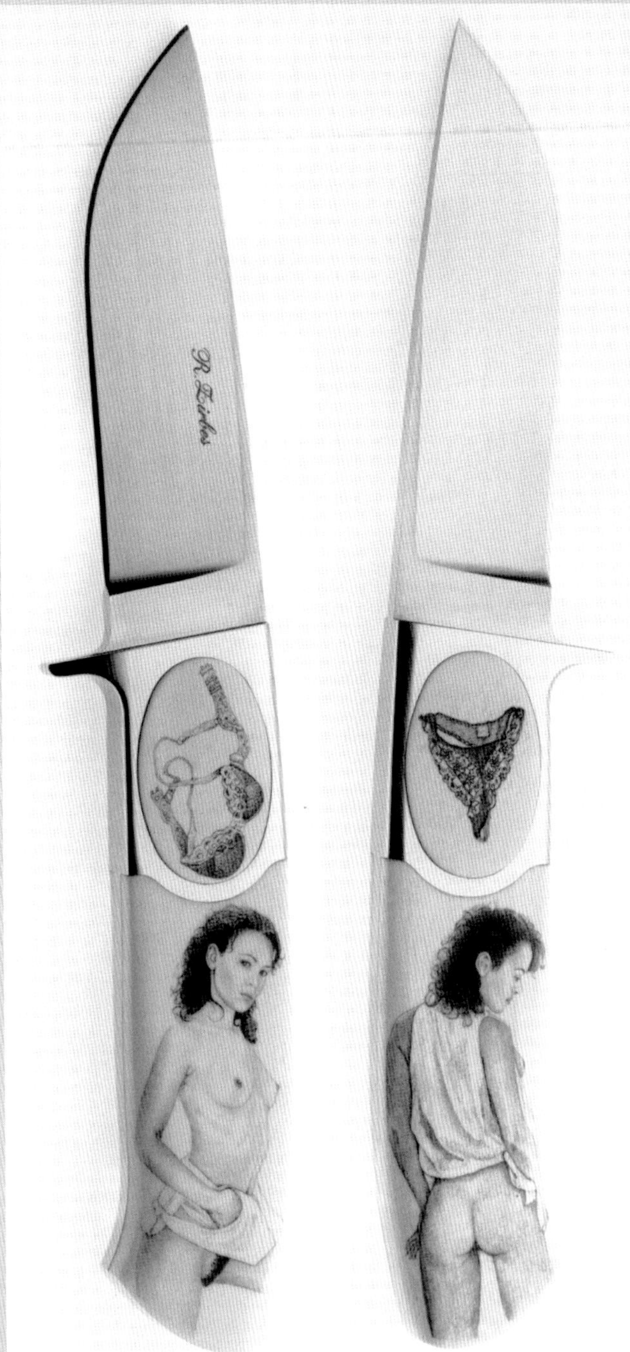

A stimulating idea. The underwear scrimmed in the inlay makes the nude look a little more dressed...

How finely Richard works to shape soft skin can be seen in the oversized detail of the mermaid.

The pattern of the steel harmonizes well with the pattern of the tiger's fur on the knive above.

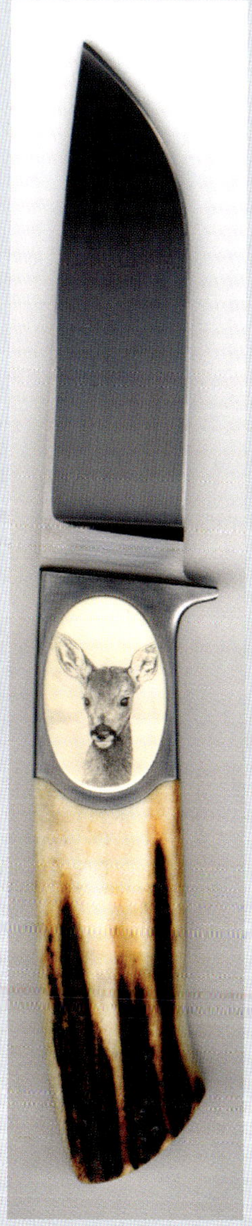

A fine hunting knife with a grip of antler.

Trade in protected natural materials is covered worldwide by the provisions of the Washington Species Protection Convention, (CITES = Convention on International Trade in Endangered Species of Wild Fauna and Flora). At this time, 165 countries are members and have agreed to bring their own legislation on species protection into agreement with the CITES provisions.

Regulations on trade and possession of the different natural materials suitable for scrimshaw are different in each of the member states. Although based on the CITES guidelines, the regulations still vary in detail from country to country. For example, import and trade in recent or "new" elephant ivory is entirely prohibited in the United States and Germany, but at this time, strictly controlled trade in elephant ivory from old stocks is possible in Germany. And German import of walrus ivory from Russia is forbidden, although it may be exported from Russia. On the other hand, walrus ivory from Greenland may be imported into Germany with appropriate permission.

From just these two examples, you can see that the legislation makes very fine distinctions and that the laws are very complex and involved, even regarding the age of the materials. There are differences between new, antique, and fossil materials, and sometimes there are distinctions between raw material and objects that have already been worked into art.

In every case, to avoid serious problems it is recommended that you get your information on the regulations that apply in each case directly from the responsible authorities in the countries concerned. It is easy to see that, although you may feel yourself lucky to find and openly purchase a certain rare material in one country, you may run into serious difficulties with customs when you try to import it on your return home.

I have listed a few addresses below where you can get information on current regulations by telephone or on the Internet. The CITES Secretariat homepage also provides a list of addresses for the responsible authorities in each of the 165 countries that are party to the convention.

Australia
Wildlife Permits and Enforcement
Environment Australia
G.P.O. Box 787
CANBERRA, ACT 2601
Phone: +61 (2) 62 74 19 00 (general/général); 62 74 22 70 (Director/directeur)
Fax: +61 (2) 62 74 19 21
Email: wildlifetrade@ea.gov.au
Web: http://www.ea.gov.au/biodiversity/trade-use/index.html

Austria
Bundesministerium für Land- und Forstwirtschaft,
Umwelt und Wasserwirtschaft
Abteilung für Natur- und Artenschutz
Stubenbastei 5
A-1010 WIEN
Phone: +43 - 1 - 51522 1401

Denmark (including Greenland and the Faeroe Islands)
Miljø- og Energiministeriet (Ministry of the Environment and Energy)
Skov- og Naturstyrelsen (Danish Forest and Nature Agency)
Haraldsgade 53
DK-2100 KØBENHAVN Ø
Phone: +45 - 39 47 20 00; - 39 47 24 27; - 39 47 24 28
Fax: +45 - 39 27 98 99; - 39 47 23 12
Email: cites@sns.dk
Web: http://www.cites.dk

France
Ministre de l'aménagement du territoire et de l'environnement
Direction de la nature et des paysages
Bureau des échanges internationaux d'espèces menacées
20, avenue de Ségur
F-75302 PARIS 07 SP
Phone: +33 - 1 - 42 19 19 03
Fax : +33 - 1 - 42 19 19 81
Email: sylvie.guillaume@environnement.gouv.fr (chef du bureau)
stephanie.jacquet@environnement.gouv.fr (adjointe)

Germany
Bundesamt für Naturschutz
Konstantinstr. 110
D- 53179 Bonn
Phone: +49 - 2 28 - 84 91 - 0
Fax: +49 - 2 28 - 84 91 - 200
Web: www.bfn.de
Specialist: Mr. Sterz
Phone.: +49 - 2 28 - 84 91 - 4 48
Email: sterzM@bfn.de

Great Britain (including a number of commonwealth countries)
Department for Environment, Food, and Rural Affairs (DEFRA)
Global Wildlife Division
1st Floor, Temple Quay House
2 The Square
Temple Quay
BRISTOL BS1 6EB
Phone: +44 - 117 - 372 80 17
Fax: +44 - 117 - 372 82 06
Email: cites.ukma@defra.gsi.gov.uk
Web: http://www.ukcites.gov.uk

South Africa
Department of Environmental Affairs and Tourism
Subdirectorate: Trade and Regulation
Private Bag x 447
PRETORIA 0001
Phone: +27 - 12 - 310 35 45; - 310 39 11; - 310 37 99
Tx: 320142 enom sa
Cable: OMGEWING PRETORIA
Fax: +27 - 12 - 320 70 26
Email: smeintjes@ozone.pwv.gov.za
Web: http://www.environment.gov.za

Switzerland
Bundesamt für Veterinärwesen
Liebefeld-Bern
Schwarzenburgstr.161
CH- 3003 BERN
Phone: +41 - 31 - 323 85 0 - 6 / - 8 / - 9

USA (and some dependencies)
US Fish and Wildlife Service
Division of Management Authority
4401 N. Fairfax Drive
Room 700
ARLINGTON, VA 22203
Phone: Chief and Operations Branch:
+1 - 703 358 20 93; 358 20 95
Branch of Permits:
800 toll-free within the United States; otherwise +1 - 703 358 21 04
Fax: Office of Chief, DMA: +1 - 703 358 22 80
Branch of CITES Operations: +1 - 703 358 22 98
Branch of Permits: +1 - 703 358 22 81
Email: managementauthority@fws.gov (general/général)
Web: http://international.fws.gov

You can get interesting information on the various materials from the following Internet address for "the only crime lab in the world dedicated entirely to wildlife. It serves both the national and international communities."

National Fish and Wildlife Forensics Laboratory
http://www.lab.fws.gov
1490 East Main St.
Ashland, Oregon 97520, USA
Phone: +l - 541 482 4191
Fax: +1 - 541 482 4989

Homepage for the CITES Secretariat: www.cites.org
And under http://www.cites.org/common/directy/e_directy.html
you can get a listing of all member nations.

Gaétan Beauchamp
125, de la Rivière
Stoneham, Que. Canada GOA 4P0
Phone: + I - 418 - 848 - 19 14
Fax: + I - 418 - 848 - 68 59
Email: knives@gbeauchamp.ca
www.beauchamp.cjb.net

Petra Bergoint
Almenweg 24
D-64747 Breuberg-Sandbach, Germany
Phone: +49 - 61 63 - 53 27
Fax: +49 - 61 63 - 91 36 61
Email: petra@bergoint.de
www.bergoint.de

Sandra Brady
9608 Monclova Road,
Monclova, Ohio 43542, USA
Phone: + 1 - 419 - 866 - 04 35
Fax: +1 - 419 - 867 - 06 56
Email: sandyscrim@hotmail.com
www.knifeshows.com/brady

Philipp Branschi
Dammstr. 59, Postfach 225
CH-4502 Solothurn, Switzerland
Phone: +41 - 78 - 609 - 4072

Roberto Bruci
Mobile phone: +39 - 347 - 1 76 95 13
Fax: +39 - 05 86 - 63 27 89, Italy
Email: roberto.BRUCI@libero.it

Sharon Burger
Cluster Box 1625
Forest Hills / Kloof
3610 KZN, South Africa
Phone / fax: +27 - 31 - 762 - 1349
Email: scribble@iafrica.com
www.robbrownknives.com/sharonburger
www.kgsa.co.za/member/sharonburger

Jean Pierre Coudert
Le Mas
24800 Chalais, France

Stefan Dohnke
Wollmuths 51 b
D-87448 Waltenhofen, Germany
Mobile phone: + 49 -179 - 5 04 35 33

Andrey Dolenko
Krasnoznameny pereulok 9/ 11 ap. 11
690091 Vladivostok, Russia
Phone / fax: +7 - 42 32 - 43 38 64
Email: adinascrim@mail.ru / vladad@mail.ru

Maihkel Eklund
Stamvägen 9 Föne
SE-820 41 Färila, Sweden
Email: maihkel.eklund@swipnet.se
www.art-knives.com

Gary Fiedler
PO Box 53
Prairie Du Rocher, IL 62277, USA
Email : gary@scrimshawartist.com
www.scrimshawartist.com

Wolfgang Fubel
Menckenstr. 7
D-12169 Berlin, Germany
Phone / fax : +49 - 30 - 7 91 26 23
Mobile phone : +49 - 160 - 40 15 016
www.powderhorn-wolf.de
Email: powderhornwolf@web.de

Eva Halat
Obere Dorfstr. 30
D-71576 Burgstetten, Germany
Phone / fax: +49 - 7191 - 8 50 33
Email: info@evahalat.de
www.evahalat.de
www.evahalat-scrimshaw.com

Attila Harmat
H-7986 Kisdobsza, Fö ut 4, Hungary
Phone: +36 - 73 - 348 - 396
Fax: +36 - 73 - 348 - 117
Email: attilasc@mailbox.hu
www.attila-art.hu

Bob Hergert
12 Geer Circle
Port Orford, OR 97465, USA
Phone: +1 - 541 - 332 - 3010
Email: hergert@scrimshander.com
www.scrimshander.com

Dr. Hans Peter Jensen
Weinbergstr. 58
D- 69488 Birkenau, Germany
Phone: +49 - 62 01 - 3 25 76
Email: p.jensen@surfeu.de

Jan Jonsson
Lundbyvägen 5
SE-61073 Vagnhärad, Sweden
Phone: +46 - 156 - 1 09 58
Email: Jan.renhorn@passagen.se
www.hornart.se

Linda Karst Stone
903 Tanglewood Lane
Kerrville, Texas 78028-2945, USA
Phone: +1 - 830 896 4678
Email: karstone@ktc.com

Gary Kiracofe
P.O. Box 268
Ephraim, WI 54211, USA
Phone / fax: +1 - 920 845 5407
Email: gary@scrimshanders.com
www.scrimshanders.com

Richard Maier
Trompeter + Ritchi company
Schlesienstrasse 29
D-71069 Sindelfingen, Germany
Phone: +49 - 70 31 - 38 64 39
Fax +49 - 70 31 - 38 12 22
Email: rm@trompeter-ritchi.de
www.trompeter-ritchi.de

Faustina L. Mead
2550 E. Mercury Street
Inverness, Florida 34453-0514, USA
Phone / fax: +1 - 352 344 4751
Email: scrimsha@infionline.net
www.scrimshaw-by-faustina.com

Gerd Ohnesorge
Pyrastraße 2
D-06118 Halle / Saale, Germany
Phone / fax: +49 - 3 45 - 5 20 10 34

John van Opstal
Banda da Vila 17c
9900-088 Horta, Azores, Portugal
Phone: +351 292 392 720

Mirella Isnardi Pachi
Via Pometta, 1
I-17046 Sassello - Savona, Italy
Phone/ fax: +39 - 19 - 72 00 86
Email: info@pachi-knives.com
www.pachi-knives.com

Hilton Purvis
P.O. Box 371
Noordhoek, 7979, South Africa
Phone / fax: +27 - 21 - 7891114
EMail: hiltonp@telkomsa.net
www.kgsa.co.za/member/hiltonpurvis

Wayne und Karen Reno
2808 Stagestop Rd., Box SS-C 12
Jefferson, CO 80456, USA
Phone: +1 - 719 836 3452
Email: war@southparkco.com
www.artistsoftherockies.com

Lori Ristinen
14256 County Highway 45
Menahga, MN 56464, USA
Phone: + I - 218 538 6608
Email: Lori@LoriRistinen.com
www.LoriRistinen.com

Heidi Robichaud
Box 116
Gustavus, Alaska 99826, USA

Howard 'Howie' Rosenfeld
Friday Harbor Art Studio
30 Web St.
Friday Harbor, WA 98250, USA
Phone: +1 - 360 378 5788
Email: howie@howardrosenfeld.com
www.howardrosenfeld.com

Melida Sacher (Mori)
Via Olcia
Casa Pia
CH-6984 Pura, Switzerland
Phone: +41 - 91 - 6 06 52 86
Email: mataco@freesurf.ch

Viveca Sahlin
Konstvaktarevägen 9
SE-772 40 Grängesberg, Sweden
Email: viveca@scrimart.se
www.scrimart.se

Harald Schlott
Zingster Str. 26
D-13051 Berlin, Germany
Phone / fax: +49 - 30 - 9 29 33 46
Email: Harald.Schlott@t-online.de
www.gravur-kunst-atelier.de.vu

Toi Skellern
P.O. Box 323
Munster, 4278, South Africa
Phone: +27 - 39 31 92 537
Fax: +27 39 31 51 634
Email: skellern@venturenet.co.za

David Smith
Tiverton
Rhode Island 02878, USA
Phone: +1 - 401 624 2316
Email: DSmith2316@aol.com
www.scrimsmith.com

Kurt Sperry
Phone: +1 - 360 676 94 98
Email: kurt@fineartscrimshaw.com
www.fineartscrimshaw.com

John Stahl
2049 Windsor Road
Baldwin, NY 11510-2945, USA
Email: imivory@msn.com
www.imagesinivory.org

Stamm's Miniature Art
Dr.-Ehlen-Str. 44
D-91126 Schwabach, Germany
Phone / fax +49 - 91 22 - 7 21 95

Dorinel Stoica
Str. Slefuitorilor nr. 17
Medias 51137, Rumania
Phone: +40 - 2 69 82 45 47
Email: dorinels@gmx.net
www.sdorinel.home.ro

Matt Stothart
1155 N. State St. #600
Bellingham, WA 98225, USA
Phone: +1 - 360 671 9026
Email: mstothart@comcast.net
bellscrim@comcast.net
www.bellinghamscrimshaw.com
www.mstothart.com

Jane Tukarski
Crofton, Maryland, USA
Phone: +1 - 410 451 3101
Email: scrimshawJT@aol.com

David Warther
P.O. Box 6
Dover, Ohio 44622, USA
Phone: +1 - 330 343 1865
Email: ivorybuyer@adelphia.net
www.ivorybuyer.com

Robert Weiss
www.marinearts.com

Gary "Garbo" Williams
P.O. Box 210
Glendale, Kentucky 42740-0210, USA
Phone: + 1 - 270 369 6752; +1 - 270 369 6963
Email: garywilliam@alltel.net
www.scrimbygarbo.com

Melodie de Witt
P.O. Box 7363
Secunda 2302, South Africa
Phone: +27 - 17 6346194; +27 - 83 2327449
Email: amie@xsinet.co.za
www.kgsa.co.za/member/melodiedewitt

Richard Zirbes
Neustr. 15
D-54526 Landscheid-Niederkail, Germany
Phone + 49 - 65 75 - 13 71

Moundmaker and repair expert
ivory dealer, sanding and polishing
Ken Fredericks
2014 James St.
Bellingham, WA 98225
Phone: +1 - 360 731 8377
Email: tfgmm@msn.com

Blades and More

BLADES AND MORE

Antique and new blades, supplies for knife makers, Damascus steel, desert iron wood, and 120 species of wood. – Raw material: Ivory with CITES of elephant, walrus, narwhal, hippo. Oosik, Stellar seacow, warthog tusk, mother-of-pearl, vegetable ivory. – Horn of deer, ren, water buffalo, kudu, and oryx, ostrich eggs and bones. – Bone of zebu, elk, cow, camel, girafe, mammoth. Leather of sting ray, fish, buffalo, and more...

D.A.Olbricht
Schmiedebergstr. 13
D- 34593 Knüllwald, Germany

Phone: +49 - 56 86 - 93 01 08
Email: mail@bladesandmore.de
www.bladesandmore.de

DICK
FINE TOOLS

High quality tools for bowmaking,
Japanese tools, materials, courses. Free catalog.

Phone: +49 - 991 - 910 90
Fax: +49 - 991 - 910 950

Email: info@dick.biz
www.dick.biz

NORDELL knives

Supplies for knife makers
Nordell Knives

Box 207
827 24 Ljusdal
Sweden

Phone: +46 - 651 - 163 80
Fax: +46 - 651 - 76 73 70
Email: nordell.knives@telia.com
www.nordellknives.com

SCRIMSHANDERS
- two hundred years behind the times -

Men's and women's **scrimshaw jewellery**, Nantucket lightship baskets, custom knives, scrimshaw sperm whale teeth, **scrimshaw ancient** mammoth and old walrus ivory, nautical and ivory antiques, canes, ship models. Representing several award winning **scrimshaw artists**, custom orders, corporate gifts, repairs, supplies, and appraisals.

Newport Scrimshanders
14 Bowen's Wharf
Newport, RI 02840-3005
+1 - 401 849 5680
800 635 5234
Brian J. Kiracofe Owner/Artist

Mystic Scrimshanders
Olde Mistick Village
Building 8H
Mystic, CT 06355
+1 - 860 536 4827
Barbara Cullen Owner/Artist

Island Scrimshanders
P.O. Box 1277
Mackinac Island, MI 49757
+1 - 906 847 3792
Gary L. Kiracofe Owner/Artist

Door County Scrimshanders
10351 N. Water Street
Ephraim, WI 54211
+1 - 920 854 5407
Gary L. Kiracofe Owner/Artist

www.scrimshanders.com

Arthur Queue
Billiard Instruments

Custom made cues - made in Germany!
Billiard tables and equipment, set up and recovering

Arthur Queue, Marcus Dienst
Siemensstrasse 11
D- 67227 Frankenthal
Germany

Phone: +49 - 6233 - 73 72 69
Fax: +49 - 6233 - 73 71 66
Email: info@billard.cc
www.billard.cc

Here are some useful and interesting websites on scrimshaw and related subjects, like micro-carvings, used books, museums, materials, tools, and more.

Scrimshaw, etc.
www.petercafesport.com
www.coastalpeoples.com
www.inua.com
www.horn-net.com/ikd/specialta.shtml
www.thailandoutdoor.com
www.scrimshop.com
www.nantucketbaskets.com
www.scrimshanders.com/home.html
www.statelibrary.tas.gov.au/heritage/scrimshaw.htm
www.arctica.com
www.scrimshawartist.com
www.art-scrimshaw.com
www.scrimshaw-art.de
www.scrimshander.com
www.scrimshawcollector.com
www.scrimworks.com

Antique Scrimshaw
www.antiquescrimshaw.com
www.antiquesofthesea.com
www.westsea.com
www.angelfire.com/ca/antiquescrimshaw

Museums
www.hullcc.gov.uk/museums/maritime/index.php
(Hull Maritime Museum, also see Book and Source section)
www.mysticseaport.org (The Museum of America and the Sea)
www.civilization.ca
(Canadian Museum of Civilization, Inuit artifacts and much antique scrimshaw)
www.whalingmuseum.org {New Bedford Whaling Museum)
www.erbach.de/kultur/museum/Allgemein.htm (German ivory museum)
www.tmag.tas.gov.au/CollOnline/collections.html
(Many pieces from the whaling days and antique scrimshaw)

Galleries
www.mysticseaport.org/gallery
www.osofamoso.com
www.scrimshawgallery.com
www.mauigateway.com
www.scrimshawcollector.com

Material
www.coastivory.com (Exotic materials, USA)
www.ivoryworksltd.com (Ivory USA)
www.boonetrading.com (Very interesting, USA)
www.thesmithsshop.com (Hippopotamus teeth and more, USA)
www.boesner.com (Art supplies, Germany, Austria)
www.gerstaecker.de (Art supplies, Germany)

Tools
www.turbocarver.com (Compressed air engraving tools, USA)
www.handgravers.com (Hand and compressed air engraving tools, USA)

Guilds

www.kgsa.co.za (Knife Makers Guild -South Africa)
www.akg.org.a u (Knife Makers Guild -Australia)
www.ckg.org (Canadian Knife Makers Guild)
www.kmg.org (American Knife Makers Guild)
www.deutsche-messermacher-gilde.de (German Knife Makers Guild)

Links

www.members.lycos.nl/knifelinks (Many different worldwide knife-related links)
www.seagifts.com/seagifts/nautmus. html (Links to nautical subjects) www.webcom. com/maritime/links/links1.html www.webcom.com/maritime/links/centart.html (Much of interest. Maritime Museum) www.directory.google.com/Top/Shopping/ Crafts/Nature/Scrimshaw/ www.brisa.fi/links.html (Many knife links)
www.ajh-knives.com/links.html (Many knife links)

Other

www.dels-mfg.com (Nantucket Baskets and other interesting things)
www.eggzotica.com (Carved egg shells)
www.used.addall.com (For finding used scrimshaw books)
www.amazon.com
www.knifeworld.com (Knife site, books as well)
www.xs4all.nl/~ mobydick/whales. html (Books on the ocean, dolphins, and whaling)
www.beyars.com
(Very informative homepage of the Jewelry Branch. showing fine micro carvings of ivory)
www.knifedirectory.com (Everything about knives - worldwide)
www.spri.cam.ac.uk (Scott Polar Research Institute)
www.cutlerscove.com (Much about knives)
www.blackcues.com
www.messer-scrimshaw-leder.de (great scrimshaw needles)

The Maritime Gallery at Mystic Seaport
PO Box 6000,
47 Greenmanville Avenue,
Mystic, CT 06355, USA
Phone: +1 - 860 - 572- 5388,
Fax: +1- 860 - 572 - 5324
www.mysticseaport.org/gallery

Hull Maritime Museum
Queen Victoria Square,
Kingston upon Hull,
HU 1 3DX England
Phone.: +44 - 1482-613902,
Fax: +44 - 1482-613710
www.hullcc.gov.uk

Deutsches Elfenbeinmuseum Erbach
Otto-Glenz-Straße 1
D- 64711 Erbach, Germany
Phone: +49 - 60 62 - 9 19 99-0 and 94 33 13
Fax: +49 - 60 62 - 9 19 99 21 and 64 12
Email: elfenbeinmuseum@erbach.de

Whaleworld
Frenchman Bay Road
Albany, Western Australia 6330
Phone: + 61 (8) 9844 4021
Fax: + 61 (8) 9844 4621
Email: info@whaleworld.org
www.whaleworld.org

International Ivory Society
11109 Nicholas Drive
Wheaton, MD 20902-3532, USA
E-Mail: rweisblut@yahoo.com

Deutscher Elfenbeinverband e.V.
(German Ivory Association)
Otto-Straße 4
D- 84503 Altötting
Phone: +49 - 86 71 - 62 58
Fax: +49 - 86 71 - 54 84
Email:
info@deutscher-elfenbein-verband.de
www.deutscher-elfenbein-verband.de

Some books are also partly or only about scrimshaw technique itself, but most of the following books discuss traditional style scrimshaw or antique scrimshaw.

Azevedo, Jose. n.d. Peter Cafe Sport (English)
Quetzal Editores, E- 1200 Lisbon. 112 pages. Hardcover. ISBN 972-564-230-9
Covers scrimshaw in the Azores with many color illustrations of old and new scrimshaw on whale teeth.

Basseches, Joshua T.; Frank, Stuart M. 1997, Edward Burdett.
Americas First Master Scrimshaw Artist.
Mystic Seaport Museum Publications, USA. Paperback. ISBN 0-937854-29-8

Basseches, Joshua T. 1997.
Scrimshaw of Manuel Cunha: Late Work from Madeira Revealed.
Mystic Seaport Museum Publications, USA. Paperback. ISBN 0 937854-26-3

Burkhart, Dr.-Ing. Walter, 1991.
Handbuch fur das Schleifen und Polieren.
(Sanding and Polishing Handbook). 6th edition. Eugen G. Leuze Verlag, Saulgau, Germany. 384 pages. Hardcover. ISBN 3-87480-021-0
A very good technical book, for industrial use with many details on every aspect of polishing and sanding. Really only for readers who are professionals in the field. There are also some pages of interest to the scrimshander. A few pages are about ivory, horn, and mother-of-pearl. (German language)

Collins, Blackie, Michael Collins. 1978.
How to Scrimshaw and Carve Ivory. Knife World Publications.
Paperback. 45 pages. ISBN0940362015

Das Beizen, Schleifen und Polieren des Holzes, Elfenbeins, Horns, der Knochen und Perlmutter. (Etching, Sanding, and Polishing Wood, Ivory, Horn, Bone, and Mother-of-Pearl) Edition ,libri rari', im Verlag Th. Schafer, Hanover, Germany. 210 pages. Hardcover. ISBN 3-88746-360-9
Reprint of an old book from 1891 with many very interesting old formulae and techniques for treating the materials listed, with emphasis on wood. (German language)

Engnath, Bob. 1985.
The Second Scrimshaw Connection.
The House of Muzzle Loading. Glendale, CA 91206, USA. 242 pages. Paperback.
Everything about "new" scrimshaw. Many black-and-white illustrations. Working instructions, and much more. Unfortunately out of print.

Espinoza, Edgard O'Neill and Mary-Jacque Mann. 1991.
Identification Guide for Ivory and Ivory Substitutes.
Washington, D.C. World Wildlife Fund and the Conservation Foundation

Flayderman, E. Norman. 1972.
Scrimshaw and Scrimshanders, Whales and Whalemen.
New Milford, Conn. 06776, N. Flayderman & Co., ISBN 0-910598-09-6

Frank, Stuart M. 1991.
Dictionary of Scrimshaw Artists. Mystic, CT.
Mystic Seaport Museum Publications. Hardcover. ISBN 0-913372-58-7

Books and Sources

Frank, Stuart M. 1998.
More Scrimshaw Artists.
Mystic, CT. Mystic Seaport Museum Publications. Hardcover. ISBN 0-913372-82-X

Frank, Stuart M. 1988. (Third, expanded edition 2001).
Fakeshaw: A Checklist of Plastic ‚Scrimshaw', Machine-Manufactured Polymer Scrimshaw Fakes. Kendall Whaling Museum.

Gilkerson, William. 1975.
The Scrimshander. Troubadour Press, San Francisco, USA. 120 pages. ISBN 0-912300-53-1 (Paperback), ISBN 0-912300-54-X (Hardcover)
History and technique of traditional scrimshaw, many illustrations. (Out of print)

Hellman, Nina; and Norman Brouwer. 1992.
A Mariner's Fancy: The Whaleman's Art of Scrimshaw. New York. South Street Seaport and Balsam Press.

Lawrence, Martha. 1993.
Scrimshaw: the Whalers Legacy. Schiffer Publishing Ltd.
Hardcover ISBN 0-88740-455-3, 408 Color Photos.

Linsley, Leslie. 1992.
Scrimshaw: a Traditional Folk Tale. Penguin Books Ltd. Paperback. ISBN 0-525-48584-8

Malley, Richard C. 1983.
Graven by the Fishermen Themselves: Scrimshaw in Mystic Seaport Museum.
Mystic, CT. Mystic Seaport Museum.

McManus, Michael. 1997.
A Treasury of American Scrimshaw A Collection of the Useful and Decorative.
Penguin Books, Australia Ltd. Hardcover. ISBN 0-670-86234-7

Paszkiewicz, Steve / Roger Schroeder. 1998.
Scrimshaw, A Complete Illustrated Manual. Fox Chapel Publishing Co.,
Inc. East Petersburg, USA. 60 pages. Paperback. ISBN 1-56523-095-7
Introductory work for simple line scrimshaw with many color illustrations.

Rappahannock Design, Inc., **Whalebone**, Issues 1-6, 1988 and 1-3, 1989, bound as a book.

West, Janet / Arthur Credland. 1995. **Scrimshaw, the Art of the Whalers**.
Hull City Museums & Art Galleries and The Hutton Press Ltd. England. 96 pages. Paperback.
ISBN I 872167 72 1
Interesting book about the history of whaling and antique scrimshaw, many illustrations.

Zeitgenössische Kunst der Indianer und Eskimos in Kanada (Old and a lot of contemporary Indian and Eskimo art in Canada). 1988. Edition Cantz. Stuttgart, Germany. 642 pages. Hardcover. ISBN 3-89322-014-3
Many illustrations in both black-and-white and color. (German language)

Scrimshaw: Tools, Tips, and Techniques, instructional DVD or VHS tape. Available at www.scrimshander.com

Eva Halat, 2003
Modernes Scrimshaw, Geschichte, Arbeitsanleitung, Großer Galerieteil. German edition of "Contemporary Scrimshaw". Verlag Angelika Hörnig, Ludwigshafen, ISBN 3-9808743-1-1